4-99
SA/9

THE BATHERS' PAVILION

MENUS AND RECIPES

In memory of Len Evans

Other books by Serge Dansereau

Food & Friends
A chef's gastronomic journey through France & Italy
HarperCollins 1998

Serge, For the Love of Good Food
journey through the Australian food scene
ABC Books 2004

The Bathers' Pavilion Café Cookbook
ABC Books 2004

THE BATHERS' PAVILION

MENUS AND RECIPES

SERGE DANSEREAU

PHOTOGRAPHY BY WILLIAM MEPPEM

ABC
Books

CONTENTS

Introduction
{ 10 }

Chef's Notes
{ 12 }

Chapter One
Food for Friends
MENU
{ 14 }

Chapter Two
Amuse-bouche RECIPES
{ 34 }

Chapter Three
RECIPES from the garden
{ 58 }

Chapter Four
RECIPES from the shore
{ 82 }

Chapter Five
Summer Picnic
MENU
{ 106 }

Chapter Six
RECIPES from the sea
{ 136 }

Chapter Seven
RECIPES from the farm
{ 164 }

_____

Chapter Eight
Wine lovers'
MENU
{ 194 }

_____

Chapter Nine
RECIPES from the pastry kitchen
{ 214 }

Chapter Ten
Petits fours RECIPES
{ 252 }

_____

Chapter Eleven
Romantic Wedding
MENU
{ 262 }

_____

Chapter Twelve
RECIPES for celebrations
{ 280 }

Bathers' Basics
{ 296 }

Index
{ 312 }

Acknowledgements
{ 318 }

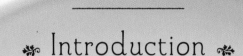

❖ Introduction ❖

I truly enjoyed putting this book together. The book illustrates the food I cook and serve at Bathers' Pavilion – food that shows respect for quality ingredients and highlights the full range of skills in my Bathers' kitchens.

The Bathers' Pavilion is an extraordinary place expressing history in a wonderful setting. Over the years I have created a place where people not only enjoy the food, but enjoy food in harmony with its environment – food that represents my personal style and beliefs.

The book will take you through a journey of beautiful produce prepared simply but with skill. It showcases many of the menus I create for the customers of the Bathers' Pavilion. These menus and recipes will take you from the complex world of haute cuisine to the casually elegant picnic as well as menus to enjoy with friends at home. There are dinner menus perfect for serious wine lovers and menus for special celebrations, like weddings.

Do not be daunted by the recipes – while they were created by talented chefs, with patience and dedication, all dishes are achievable at home. As we do at the restaurant, be flexible and adjust your recipes to the ingredients available. Consider cooking only part of a recipe, I do this at home and it is extremely rewarding. Imprint your own style on recipes by changing some of the key ingredients or retaining a cooking method but applying it to another recipe. There is a fantastic burnt anchovy butter recipe in these pages but, perhaps, instead of making the goat cheese capelletti just serve this butter with steamed asparagus or even artichoke. Select seasonal ingredients at your market and take them home to cook – choose a recipe to make the everyday extraordinary. Make the pheasant recipe with chestnuts but use a free-range chicken instead. Once you learn how to peel chestnuts, impress and stun your friends and family with the delicious chestnut soup.

Share your enthusiasm for cooking with your family and partner, as you will be rewarded for it. Great food derived from special menus and these recipes can live on in powerful memories of precious moments in your life.

At Bathers' Pavilion we are blessed with an amazing location in which to work and serve people. I believe the restaurant illustrates the best that Sydney can offer – the setting and the lifestyle paired with great food expressed in these menus and recipes. I believe this book is generous, approachable, skilful and personal – just like the Bathers' Pavilion. I hope you enjoy it.

Commissioned by the Mosman Municipal Council, the Bathers' Pavilion opened in February 1929, catering for locals and beachgoers that needed public facilites to change, shower and store their personal effects. The building, with its distinct and intriguing Moorish feel, became a much-loved icon for tourists and locals alike. It remained an essential part of beach life until the late '60s. Bathers' then began its life as a café and restaurant in the late '70s, and lunch at Balmoral became an institution. In 1998, Serge Dansereau became co-owner and chef, and Bathers' underwent a major restoration and rennovation of its facade and facilities. Re-opening a year later, with a new restaurant, café, function rooms and beach kiosk, Bathers' was ready for another century of service as the focal point of Balmoral Beach.

SERGE DANSEREAU is a recognised icon in the Australian food industry. An energetic native-born Québécois and now an Australian citizen, Serge grew up in Montréal and spent his formative years surrounded by his family whose love of cooking and appreciation of good produce were to leave a lasting impression.

Early in his career, Serge trained with Swiss and French chefs while studying at the Institut de Tourisme de d'Hotellerie du Québec. In 1983, at only 26, Serge accepted a position to help open the newly built Regent Hotel in Sydney. Soon after Serge was appointed Executive Chef. His brief was to make Kable's a defining Sydney restaurant. It was a success — Kable's became one of 'the' places to dine at. Serge became known for his relentless search of quality produce and the support he gave growers to achieve his aim.

After more than ten years with The Regent, Serge resigned to become co-owner and chef of The Bathers' Pavilion. He then oversaw the refurbishment and re-opening of one of Sydney's most iconic restaurants. In 2003 Serge became sole owner.

One of Australia's most applauded and awarded chefs. Serge has also long been associated with various charities including: The Starlight Foundation, The Humpty Dumpty Foundation and Opera Australia.

He lives at Clontarf Beach with his wife Yvette and his two children Céleste and Sasha.

Here are some general notes to keep in mind as you use this book:

- Olive oil, I use olive oil for sautéing and extra-virgin olive oil for dressings
- Vegetable oil, you can substitute with grape seed, canola, corn, vegetable or sunflower oils
- For frying, I prefer to use peanut oil, but any vegetable oil would do
- I like a special oil for dressings; it can be extra-virgin olive oil, walnut oil or hazelnut oil
- Butter for pastry is always unsalted, but I prefer salted butter for cooking and for using at the table. At Bathers', I offer both homemade salted butter and unsalted cultured butter at the table
- Eggs should be either free range or from ethically raised hens. The egg size is normally 55 grams
- Sugar is caster sugar
- Chocolate is couverture chocolate, a better quality chocolate used for cooking which contains at least 32% cocoa butter
- Salt for last-minute seasoning is sea salt; fine salt is used for dressing; and rock salt or fine salt is used for making stock
- There is an array of table salt in Australia from imported French Fleur de Sel to English Maldon and to Australian Pink Murray River salt, Horizon Crystal salt and so on, use your favourite
- Pepper in recipes is white freshly milled pepper unless specified. I prefer black for milling at the table
- The scallops I use in all my recipes are Saucer Scallops that come from the northern waters of Australia. They do not have roe and are mild in taste
- The potato I use for most dishes is the Désirée
- When I sauté any meat or fish to give colour, I use half oil and half butter
- Milk is always full fat
- Cream is 35% and can be table cream, thickened cream or pouring cream
- Balsamic vinegar will vary greatly in quality, generally the smaller the bottle the better the quality
- Veal bones are expensive and often quite hard to get, so for home if my local butcher doesn't not have veal bones I replace them with chicken wings
- Oven temperatures vary, the cooking times given are the ones that work in my oven. You need to get to know yours.

❧ Chef's Notes ❧

Most of the recipes in this book come from the Bathers' Pavilion Restaurant, but I have also included dishes that I enjoy preparing for friends and family, whether for a large gathering, a picnic or a casual meal. Some of the recipes may be quite challenging for the home cook, so I have given each dish a star rating to indicate its degree of difficulty, from simple to more complex. There are also chapters that provide menus for different occasions, but you need not follow these rigidly; I hope they will inspire you to plan your own menus for your special occasions. When preparing and cooking dishes, the rule is to be flexible: change or substitute some of the ingredients if you need to, and make only one part of a more complex recipe if it seems too difficult to attempt at first.

I use professional equipment to prepare many of these dishes and desserts, and for some of the recipes you may need to purchase some new kitchen equipment, such as a mould or a sugar thermometer from a specialty kitchenware store, to help you master the dish.

You will see that I use my master stock (recipe on page 298) in many of the recipes; it is worth making a large quantity and keeping it in the freezer to use whenever you need it, and its flavours will only improve with time.

WINE RATINGS

To guide you through the wine ratings I have devised a rating guide as follows:

✿ Under $20	
✿ ✿ Under $30	
✿ ✿ ✿ Under $50	
✿ ✿ ✿ ✿ Under $80	
✿ ✿ ✿ ✿ ✿ $80 +	

(prices are a guide only, subject to change)

STAR RATINGS

To guide you through the recipes, I've placed a ♣ at the start of each as an indication of the skill level required for each:

One	♣	easily crafted
Two	♣ ♣	some good skills required
Three	♣ ♣ ♣	a total commitment to prepare

❧ Conversion Tables ❧

DRY MEASURES

METRIC	IMPERIAL
15 gm	½ oz
25–30 gm	1 oz
40 gm	1 ½ oz
50–60 gm	2 oz
75 gm	2 ½ oz
100 gm	3 ½ oz
125 gm	4 oz (¼ lb)
150 gm	5 oz
200 gm	7 oz
225 gm	8 oz
250 gm	9 oz
300 gm	10 oz
350 gm	12 oz
400 gm	13 oz
450 gm	16 oz (1 lb)
500 gm	17 oz
900 gm	2 lb
1 kg	2 lb 2 oz

LIQUID MEASURES

METRIC	IMPERIAL	CUP AND SPOON
5 ml	⅙ fl oz	1 tsp
20 ml	½ fl oz	1 tbs
40 ml	1 fl oz	1 tbs + 2 tsp
60 ml	2 fl oz	¼ cup
85 ml	2 ½ fl oz	⅓ cup
100 ml	3 fl oz	
125 ml	4 fl oz	½ cup
150 ml	5 fl oz	
200 ml	7 fl oz	
250 ml	8 fl oz	1 cup
275 ml	10 fl oz (½ pt)	
300 ml	11 fl oz	
350 ml	12 fl oz	1 ½ cup
400 ml	14 fl oz	
450 ml	16 fl oz	
500 ml	18 fl oz	
575 ml	1 pt	
850 ml	1 ½ pt	
1 lt	1 ¾ pt	4 cups
2 lt	4 pt	

OVEN TEMPERATURES

°C (CELSIUS)	°F (FAHRENHEIT)		
100°C	210°F	Extremely slow	
125°C	250°F	Very slow	
150°C	300°F	Slow	Gas mark 2
180°C	350°F	Moderate	Gas mark 4
200°C	400°F	Moderately hot	Gas mark 6
225°C	440°F	Hot	Gas mark 7
250°C	480°F	Very hot	Gas mark 9

INGREDIENTS

capsicum	bell pepper
celeriac	celery root
coriander	cilantro
cream	heavy cream
green onion	scallion
guinea fowl	guinea hen
icing sugar	confectioner's sugar
mâche lettuce	lamb's lettuce
prawn	shrimp
stock	broth
witlof	Belgian endive
yabbies	crayfish

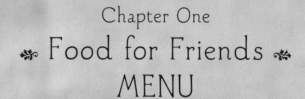

Chapter One
❧ Food for Friends ❧
MENU

Duck Salad on Betel Leaf
Anchovy Pillows and Paillettes aux Anchois
Pork Fritters with Cucumber Salad

Scallop Terrine with Saffron Cream Sauce
Baked Jewfish 'En Croute' with Mousseline Sauce
Fennel Risotto
Poussin 'En Cocotte'

Bombe Alaska
Chocolate Gâteau
Blood Orange Compote with Strawberries and Rhubarb
Cheese Platter

For lovers of anchovies, this is
a real treat. Look for the Spanish
brands of anchovies – they are
often the best quality. This recipe
shows how to make twists and
pillows. For a quick snack, try
serving your anchovies on toasted
focaccia bread fingers.

Anchovy Pillows and Paillettes
aux Anchois

There is no greater sign of friendship than to open your home to a group of friends and cook for them. I rarely get invited to friends' places unless they are chefs or experienced cooks. For some reason, people feel they will be judged on the food they cook and, in reality, like most people I am just happy to enjoy any food in the company of friends.

If you have more than six friends coming for dinner, the task can be quite daunting. To select a menu, purchase the food, do the preparation, organise the table setting, cook and serve the food is not an easy task — unless you are a whiz in the kitchen. It is a challenge and it is important to remember two things. First, be as prepared as possible so you are able to enjoy yourself and have time to spend with your friends. Second, it is a good idea to cook dishes that you have previously mastered.

If you have the luxury of time ahead of your meal, then it is worth doing a bit of planning and research — write a menu, print your recipes or photocopy them ready to use in the kitchen and for shopping. Dress your table appropriately and arrange fresh cut flowers in vases. Think of the sequence of the food preparation and have as much preparation and pre-cooking done as possible. Serve a limited number of courses at lunch, one hot dish is enough with a salad and maybe a hot vegetable, followed by one dessert or cheese.

Dinner is a more constructed meal and this is where one can stumble. I often find the difficult part is bringing all the elements of a meal together on a plate — one will go cold while another gets overcooked, or another goes unseasoned as you are rushing. At home, I find it easier to make platters of food for guests to serve themselves at the table rather than plate up. No matter what, try to have fun and stay near your friends during the cooking process — it is better for them to see you and help you if you wish than to have them sit down and hear cursing coming from the kitchen.

⁜ ⁜

DUCK SALAD
ON BETEL LEAF

SERVES 8

MAIN INGREDIENTS
4 cooked duck legs, confit (refer | Basics page 304)
1 garlic clove
1 teaspoon palm sugar
1 lime, juiced
1 teaspoon fish sauce
1 cup peanut oil
4 eschalot, cut in julienne
1 large red chilli, de-seeded and cut in julienne
1 cup picked bean sprouts
1 tablespoon chopped coriander
½ bunch betel leaves, washed and picked

PREPARATION AND PRESENTATION **Shred** the duck leg meat, discarding any skin, bone and gristle. Crush the garlic and palm sugar in a mortar and add the lime juice, fish sauce and 1 tablespoon of the peanut oil to make the dressing. Pour this over one-quarter of the eschalot and chilli in a bowl and marinate for 10 minutes. Add the duck, bean sprouts and coriander, mix well and spoon on the betel leaves. Heat the remaining peanut oil in a small pot and, when very hot, fry the balance of the eschalot then drain on paper towel. Sprinkle the fried eschalot on each mound of duck salad and serve.

I am not madly in love with coriander but it works well in this recipe with the lime juice. The crispy onion also adds a sweet and crunchy texture to this tasty salad.

ANCHOVY PILLOWS
AND PAILLETTES AUX ANCHOIS

30 PORTIONS

MAIN INGREDIENTS
250 gm (8 oz) puff pastry (refer | Basics page 311)
3 egg yolks, beaten, to use as glaze
200 gm (7 oz) anchovy fillets

PREPARATION AND PRESENTATION Preheat the oven to 200°C (400°F). On a lightly floured surface, roll out the pastry to about 3 mm (1/8 in) thick. Brush one half of the pastry with egg glaze. Arrange anchovy fillets lengthways 2.5 cm (1 in) apart on the glazed pastry. Cover with the other half of the pastry and gently roll over the pastry to press the two sheets together. To achieve a twisted effect, cut the pastry in strips about 15 cm (6 in) long and 5 cm (2 in) wide. Roll each strip with your hands, working in opposite directions to achieve a twisted effect. Place onto a lightly greased or baking paper-lined tray. Leave to rest for 20 minutes in a cool place. Cook in oven for 10–12 minutes until the pastry is crispy and golden.

To achieve a rectangle effect, cut the pastry into strips 5 cm (2 in) long and 2 cm (3/4 in) wide. Brush the tops with egg yolk and dry slightly. Score each rectangle with the edge of a sharp knife to create a lattice pattern. Place the rectangles onto a baking tray and place a piece of baking paper on top along with another baking tray. This will stop the puff rectangles from rising unevenly. Bake for 10–12 minutes until the pastry is crispy and golden. Serve warm or at room temperature.

PORK FRITTERS
WITH CUCUMBER SALAD

SERVES 8

FRITTERS
550 gm (18 ½ oz) pork mince
200 gm (7 oz) pork fat, finely minced
1 teaspoon ginger, finely chopped
4 cloves garlic, peeled and finely chopped
10 lime leaves, very thinly sliced
20 basil leaves, roughly chopped
2 tablespoons sesame oil
2 tablespoons roughly chopped coriander
1 teaspoon shrimp paste
fish sauce, to taste

CUCUMBER SALAD
80 ml (2 ½ fl oz) sugar syrup (equal parts of
    water and sugar)
120 ml (4 fl oz) white vinegar
4 mild red chillies, sliced
2 cucumbers, skin left on and diced

FRITTER PREPARATION Chill a blender bowl in the freezer then place all the ingredients (except the fish sauce) in the blender and blend into a fine paste. Season with the fish sauce. Shape small patties allowing three patties per person. Deep-fry until golden brown at 180°C (350°F) or pan-fry on moderate heat on both sides.

CUCUMBER SALAD PREPARATION Bring the sugar syrup and vinegar to the boil, add the chillies and cook for 5 minutes. Remove from the stove and cool. Strain and discard the chillies. When ready to serve the fritters, mix the cucumber and the chilli syrup together.

PRESENTATION Serve the fritters with the salad in a dish to the side.

SCALLOP TERRINE
WITH SAFFRON CREAM SAUCE

SERVES 8

SCALLOP TERRINE
550 gm (18 ½ oz) white scallops, cleaned
   and trimmed
200 gm (7 oz) salmon fillet, skin off, blood line
   and pin bones removed
8 egg whites
1 cup ice flakes
salt and white milled pepper
350 ml (12 fl oz) fresh cream

TERRINE PREPARATION Purée the scallop meat, roe and salmon with the egg whites, ice flakes and seasoning in a food processor until light and fluffy. Scrape down the sides and pulse in the cream quickly. Refrigerate. Preheat the oven to 170°C (330°F). Line a terrine mould 25 cm (10 in) long and 10 cm (4 in) tall, with non-stick baking paper. Spray non-stick oil onto the paper and, whilst avoiding air bubbles, spoon in the scallop terrine mixture. Use a plastic spatula to flatten the surface. Wrap excess baking paper over to enclose the mixture. Sit the terrine dish in a deep-sided baking tray with a tea towel laid on the base, or a wire rack. This stops the base of the terrine from browning. Fill the baking tray with boiling water half way up the side of the terrine and place in the middle shelf in the oven. Cooking time will depend upon the oven. At approximately 40 minutes, an internal temperature should be taken. When it reaches 38°C (100°F), remove the terrine from the water-filled baking dish and allow it to sit for 10 minutes.

SAUCE PREPARATION Reduce the white wine to two-thirds with the eschalots, bay leaf and peppercorns. Add the fish stock and reduce again down to two-thirds, skimming the surface regularly of any impurities. Add the cream and the saffron threads and reduce again by half. Refine the seasoning with lemon juice, salt and pepper to taste. Blend and pass through a muslin cloth.

An optional addition is to add a little hollandaise sauce just before serving the sauce; give it a frothy texture using a hand-held mixer or simply a whisk.

PRESENTATION Using a tray, turn the terrine over to drain the liquid. Be careful as the terrine will still be hot. With the help of a wide spatula, transfer the terrine to a warm serving plate and place on the table whole. Slice and serve onto individual plates. Pass the sauce around for your guests to pour.

✠ ✠

BAKED JEWFISH 'EN CROÛTE'
WITH MOUSSELINE SAUCE

One of Paul Bocusse's most celebrated dishes is the 'loup en croûte'. I have always admired it and has inspired this dish. The crunchy texture of the puff pastry is perfect served with a hollandaise sauce

SERVES 8

JEWFISH
1.8 kg (3 ½ lb) puff pastry rolled to 3 mm (⅛ in)
    thick (refer | Basics page 311)
3 medium zucchini, cut into julienne
3 medium carrots, peeled and cut into julienne
1.2 kg (2 ¾ lb) jewfish fillet, centre bone
    and skin removed
salt and milled pepper
5 egg yolks, beaten
1 large bowl mixed green leaves
¼ cup vinaigrette (refer | Basics page 302)

MOUSSELINE SAUCE
½ recipe of Hollandaise Sauce
    (refer | Basics page 305)
1 cup cream, whipped to soft peaks

JEWFISH PREPARATION Roll ¾ of the puff pastry into 3 mm (⅛ in) thickness. Lay some zucchini and carrot julienne on the pastry and then the fish fillet, cover with more julienne, season well and close the pastry tightly around the fish and the vegetables. With the remaining pastry, also 3 mm (⅛ in) thick and using a 3 cm (1 in) round cutter, stamp out the scales for the fillet wrapped in pastry. Place the scales in a shingled fashion over the fillet wrapped in pastry, using the egg yolks to stick them to the bottom layer of pastry, replicating the 'scales of a fish'. Return the completed fish to the refrigerator and rest it for 2–3 hours prior to baking.

Preheat oven to 170°C (330°F). Apply a little more egg yolk before placing in the oven and bake for 40 minutes depending upon the thickness of the fish fillet. Rest the fish prior to slicing for at least 15 minutes.

MOUSSELINE SAUCE PREPARATION To make the mousseline sauce, follow the instructions for the hollandaise sauce and, just prior to serving the fish, fold the semi-whipped cream into the hollandaise sauce.

PRESENTATION The whole fish 'en croute' will look stunning on the table. When ready to serve, slice into portions and arrange on plates with the mixed greens that have been dressed in the vinaigrette. Pass the sauce around separately for your guests to pour.

FENNEL RISOTTO

I find fennel a perfect vegetable to flavour risotto. You will often see mushroom and seafood risotto, but fennel risotto is ideal to serve with fish. When fennel is out of season, you could use eschalots. Slow cook them first and then add to your risotto.

SERVES 8

FENNEL
1 fennel bulb, trimmed
50 gm (2 oz) butter
1 teaspoon salt and white milled pepper

RISOTTO
500 ml (16 fl oz) vegetable stock
150 gm (5 oz) butter
6 eschalots, peeled and finely diced
1 cup dry white wine
250 gm (8 oz) arborio or carnaroli rice
90 gm (3 oz) Parmesan, shaved
salt and white milled pepper

FENNEL PREPARATION Trim the green stems from the fennel bulbs, peel one or two layers off the exterior layer to reach the softer interior layers. Keep the tough exterior layers for the stock later. Julienne the softer layers and gently cook in the butter until soft. Season with salt and pepper and reserve.

RISOTTO PREPARATION Before cooking the risotto, heat the vegetable stock and add the tough fennel leaves to the stock. Simmer for half an hour, then strain. Return the stock to the stove and keep the stock on a low simmer until it is needed.

In a new pot, melt half of the butter and sauté the diced eschalots without colouring them. Add the rice to the pan and heat the rice until warm. Increase the heat and add the wine then gradually add the hot stock while gently simmering the rice until cooked 'al dente' and almost dry. At this point, incorporate the fennel. Complete the risotto with the remaining butter and Parmesan and refine the seasoning.

PRESENTATION Spoon into individual serving bowls or into a large bowl for your friends to help themselves.

✤ ✤

POUSSIN 'EN COCOTTE'

SERVES 4

STUFFING (FOR 4 POUSSIN)
1 onion, peeled and diced
1 tablespoon butter
1 egg, beaten
½ cup milk or cream
4 slices sourdough loaf, crusts removed, soaked
   in milk and mashed
1 bunch of sage, chopped
250 gm (8 oz) pork mince
salt and milled pepper

POUSSIN
4 small poussin, approximately size 5
salt and pepper
12 small roasting potatoes, peeled
extra virgin olive oil
baking paper (to wrap the poussin) folded into
   long layers
1 punnet namenko or Swiss brown mushrooms,
   trimmed and rinsed
150 gm (5 oz) butter
1 cup chicken stock

STUFFING PREPARATION Fry the onion in the
butter. Add the beaten egg, milk, bread, sage and
the pork and mix well to combine all ingredients.
Season well.

POUSSIN PREPARATION Preheat oven to 200°C
(400°F). Clean and rinse the poussin and pat
dry. From each bird, remove all the bones and one
leg completely, leaving only the drumstick bone
in the remaining leg (reserve the removed leg
for another application). Sprinkle with salt and
pepper inside and out.

recipe continues over

An old favourite recipe, reinvented. Originally,
I roasted the baby chicken and when it was
cool drizzled it with cream, Madeira and
morel mushrooms. I then recooked it in a
small covered casserole dish, before revealing
it at the table. It produced amazing aromas.
This new version is just as good.

Poussin 'En Cocotte'

Baked Jewfish 'En Croûte'

Fennel Risotto

POUSSIN PREPARATION CONTINUED **Divide** the stuffing equally between the 4 poussin and place the stuffing inside the cavity wrapping the poussin meat around so it forms a tight bundle with the only leg on the top. Wrap the baking paper around the base of each bundled poussin and place it in a baking dish with a little butter on top.

Place the poussin and the potatoes with a little olive oil in the oven for 10 minutes. Remove from oven and baste with the pan juices, then return to the oven and cook for a further 20 minutes at 165°C (325°F). Sauté the mushrooms in the butter and add the mushrooms in the last 10 minutes of cooking so they absorb the pan juices and blend beautifully with the poussin flavours.

Remove the ingredients and place on warm plates and keep them warm in the oven while you finish the sauce. Heat up the baking dish on the stove top (with the remaining cooking juices and poussin bits), add the chicken stock and reduce the stock by half. Season, strain and skim off any fat before serving with the warm poussin.

PRESENTATION **Remove** the warm plates with the poussin, potatoes and mushrooms from the oven and pour the sauce over or serve sauce in a separate jug for your guests to pour.

One of Paul Bocusse's most celebrated dishes is the 'loup en croûte'. I have always admired it and it has inspired this dish. The crunchy texture of the puff pastry is perfect served with a hollandaise sauce.

Baked Jewfish 'En Croûte'

⚜ ⚜

BOMBE ALASKA

SERVES 14

VANILLA ICE-CREAM BASE
(you will need these quantities x 3)
400 ml (14 fl oz) milk
400 ml (14 fl oz) cream
1 vanilla bean, split
12 egg yolks
150 gm (5 oz) caster sugar

STRAWBERRY ICE-CREAM
1 quantity of Vanilla Ice-Cream Base (see recipe
   below)
280 gm (9 fl oz) strawberry purée
60 gm (2 oz) caster sugar

APRICOT ICE-CREAM
1 quantity of Vanilla Ice-Cream Base
   (see recipe below)
10 well-ripened apricots
4 tablespoons apricot brandy

SWISS ROLL SHEET
4 eggs, separated
120 gm (4 oz) caster sugar
120 gm (4 oz) plain flour

MERINGUE
6 egg whites
400 gm (14 oz) caster sugar

VANILLA ICE-CREAM PREPARATION For the whole recipe, you will need to make three separate quantities of the vanilla ice-cream base. One will remain vanilla, one will be strawberry and one will be apricot.

Put the milk and cream in a heavy-based saucepan. Scrape the seeds from the vanilla pod into the pan and also add the pod and slowly bring to the boil over a gentle heat. Meanwhile, beat the egg yolks and sugar together in a bowl until pale and thick. Pour onto the milk whisking until well blended. Cook over a low heat stirring constantly until it forms a custard consistency, enough to coat the back of the spoon. Do not allow to boil or it will curdle. Remove from the heat and pass through a fine sieve. Allow to cool then churn the mixture in an ice-cream machine.

STRAWBERRY ICE-CREAM PREPARATION Prepare the vanilla ice-cream base. Mix the strawberry purée and sugar and pass through a strainer. Add to the vanilla ice-cream base. Churn the mixture in an ice-cream machine.

APRICOT ICE-CREAM PREPARATION Prepare the vanilla ice-cream base. Blanch 10 well-ripened apricots. Peel, stone and then purée the apricots mixed with 4 tablespoons of apricot brandy. Add to the vanilla ice-cream base and churn the mixture in an ice-cream machine.

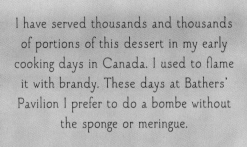

I have served thousands and thousands of portions of this dessert in my early cooking days in Canada. I used to flame it with brandy. These days at Bathers' Pavilion I prefer to do a bombe without the sponge or meringue.

Bombe Alaska

SWISS ROLL SHEET PREPARATION Preheat the oven to 220°C (425°F). Whisk the egg yolks and 40 gm (1 ½ oz) of the caster sugar until pale and creamy. Whisk the egg whites in a separate bowl until they form stiff peaks. Gradually whisk in the remaining sugar until you have a stiff and glossy meringue. Fold the meringue into the egg yolk mixture then sift the flour over the mixture and carefully fold in. Spread the Swiss roll batter into a rectangular tray (25 cm x 35 cm) (10 in x 14 in) lined with baking paper. Bake in the oven for 14 minutes until risen and just firm to the touch. Allow to cool before use.

MERINGUE PREPARATION Whisk the egg whites in a bowl until they form stiff peaks. Gradually add in the sugar a spoonful at a time to make a firm glossy meringue. Put the meringue into a piping bag with a plain nozzle tube (5 mm (¼ in), wide.

ASSEMBLING THE BOMBE ALASKA Spread layers of the softened ice-cream in the middle of the well-cooled sponge. Roll it up at once tightly from one of the short sides. Wrap the roll in aluminium foil and leave to set firm in the freezer for 1 hour. Remove the foil and place on a 12 cm x 35 cm (5 in x 14 in) board. Pipe the meringue onto the roll in strips set closely together and spread the rest of the meringue on the ends.

PRESENTATION Keep frozen until required, then brown using a blow torch. Slice and place on serving plates.

WINE NOTES

CANAPES

❀❀ **NINTH ISLAND SPARKLING NV, TAS**
A quality sparkling wine or Champagne always gets a good mood going at the start of a gathering. Made from a blend of Chardonnay and Pinot Noir, this sparkling has some lovely fruit drive on the palate and fine creamy mousse.

FENNEL RISOTTO

❀❀❀ **KELLEREI KALTERN SÖLL PINOT GRIGIO , Alto Adige, Italy** A single site wine made under the Kaltern co-operative facility. This wine has a lovely intensity of pear fruit, spice and quince aroma. With a minerality and dry lingering acidity, it works very well with the anise character of the fennel. Italian whites work really well with fennel — try some of the light aromatic styles of Northern Italy such as Arneis, Pinot Grigio or Vernaccia di San Gimignano.

JEWFISH

❀❀ **PHILLIP SHAW NO. 11 Chardonnay, Orange, NSW** A Chardonnay that is not too heavily oaked would go well with the Jewfish. The is a good example of a cool climate style. The ex-Rosemount winemaker has long hailed the potential of this region. Light melon, stonefruit and gently creamy mouth feel. This wine should change the mind of those who think all Chardonnay comes under one full bodied heavily oaked banner.

POUSSIN

❀❀ **PIZZINI NEBBIOLO, King Valley, VIC**
Nebbiolo is a grape variety with great structure and ageability which is best expressed in those grown in Piedmonte. It is characteristically not big in colour, which can deceive you as to its power; however it has an array of rose petal, violet, cherry, red fruits, earth, tar and truffle flavours and notable tannin structure which needs food.

❀❀❀ **BEAURENARD, Côtes du Rhône Villages, Rasteau** This wine is Grenache dominant and has a lovely fruit driven palate, supported by some spice, liquorice root and earthiness. A wine which is softer in tannin and full of flavour.

BOMBE ALASKA

❀❀❀ **DOMAINE DE DURBAN MUSCAT Beaumes de Venise, RhôneValley, France** Muscat Beaumes de Venise has a beautiful bouquet of grape juice, rose petal, Turkish delight and spice. The wines are well matched with fruit based desserts, their fresh grapey flavour is very appealing.

CHOCOLATE

❀❀❀ Try something different such as: Sparkling Shiraz, a fortified style such as Vintage Port, Rutherglen Muscat, Pédro Ximenez or Banyuls. There are even fruit beers which can be matched well with chocolate and offer an interesting alternative. Look for the Belle Vue Lambic Kriek (Cherry) or Framboise (Raspberry) from Belgium.

CHEESE PLATTER

It is interesting that most of us think that cheese should go with red wine; in fact most cheese is paired better with white wine. That advice should not stop you enjoying a few great cheeses at the end of a meal.

CHOCOLATE GÂTEAU

SERVES 4

PLAIN SPONGE
8 eggs, separated
240 gm (8 oz) caster sugar
240 gm (8 oz) plain flour
100 gm (3 ½ oz) cooking chocolate, melted (for
coating the sponge)

SUGAR SYRUP
500 grams (1 lb) caster sugar
1 litre (32 fl oz) water
3 tablespoons lemon juice

BUTTER GANACHE
300 ml (10 fl oz) cream
360 gm (12 oz) dark chocolate
100 gm (3 ½ oz) softened butter

PLAIN SPONGE PREPARATION Preheat oven to 220°C (425°F). Draw four 16 cm (6½ in) squares onto baking paper then place paper onto a baking tray. Whisk the egg yolks with 60 gm (2 oz) of the sugar until pale and creamy. Whisk the egg whites in a separate bowl until they form soft peaks. Gradually whisk in the remaining sugar to make a stiff, glossy meringue. Fold the meringue into the egg yolk mixture. Sift the flour over the mixture and carefully fold in.

Spread the sponge mixture evenly over the marked squares. Bake in the oven for 14 minutes until risen and just firm to the touch. Allow to cool. Cut each sheet in half. Spread a thin layer of cooking chocolate on one of the strips of sponge sheet sets and cool to set. Turn it over and moisten with sugar syrup. Spread each layer thinly with ganache and set the layers on top of each other as you go. Top with smooth layer of ganache. Place in the freezer for about 1 hour to make the ganache firm.

SUGAR SYRUP PREPARATION Put the sugar and water in a saucepan and dissolve over a low heat. Add the lemon juice and bring to the boil. Boil for 1 minute then allow to cool. Strain and use as required. The syrup will keep in the refrigerator for 1–2 weeks.

GANACHE PREPARATION Heat the cream and chocolate in a double boiler over gentle heat until the chocolate has melted and the two are combined. Whisk in the butter until smooth and well incorporated. Remove from heat and reserve in the refrigerator, allowing to firm a little before spreading on the cakes.

PRESENTATION Trim the side of the gâteau with a knife dipped in hot water. Cut individual portions about 8 cm x 4 cm (3 in x 1 ½ in). Serve with poached fruit or with soft whipped cream.

This is one of my favourite chocolate recipes. It takes a little bit more time than just a straight chocolate gateau but the effort will be well appreciated and it looks great.

Chocolate Gâteau

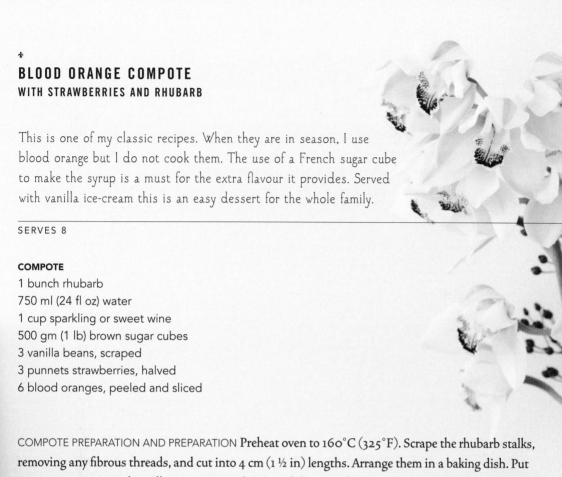

BLOOD ORANGE COMPOTE
WITH STRAWBERRIES AND RHUBARB

This is one of my classic recipes. When they are in season, I use
blood orange but I do not cook them. The use of a French sugar cube
to make the syrup is a must for the extra flavour it provides. Served
with vanilla ice-cream this is an easy dessert for the whole family.

SERVES 8

COMPOTE
1 bunch rhubarb
750 ml (24 fl oz) water
1 cup sparkling or sweet wine
500 gm (1 lb) brown sugar cubes
3 vanilla beans, scraped
3 punnets strawberries, halved
6 blood oranges, peeled and sliced

COMPOTE PREPARATION AND PREPARATION Preheat oven to 160°C (325°F). Scrape the rhubarb stalks,
removing any fibrous threads, and cut into 4 cm (1 ½ in) lengths. Arrange them in a baking dish. Put
water, wine, sugar and vanilla into a pan and stir until the sugar has dissolved. Boil the syrup, without
stirring, for 3 minutes over gentle heat. Remove from the heat. Pour the hot liquid over the prepared
rhubarb. Cover the dish with a lid or foil and bake for 25 minutes or until the rhubarb is tender. While
the sauce is still warm, add the strawberries and allow to cool. When cool, add the orange slices. Serve
in a glass bowl for best visual effect.

Chapter Two
❧ Amuse-Bouche ❧
RECIPES

One of the most creative courses in a restaurant is often the little amuse-bouche or bite teasers served after you have ordered your food. This is a course where we can be really creative and people love the presentation and taste. It is always a good start to a meal as people are surprised by an unexpected offering.

These recipes express the generosity of the restaurant and showcase the skills of the kitchen. A preview of things to come, amuse-bouche herald the arrival of exciting dishes and I know the guests never tire of these little samplings.

In its simplest form, an amuse-bouche can be a small cup of chestnut soup, a steamed anchovy custard or fried little whitebait. They are based on daily fresh produce and are only served on that night. The next day is a fresh start and a fresh preview of the best from that day's markets.

Sometimes I like to offer a menu based on a series of small dishes – either totally new dishes or deconstructed from the larger dishes on the menu. Such a menu gives a clearer and cleaner taste sensation and many guests are happy to leave the composition of the menu to me and my chefs. Make the time to spoil yourself with these fantastic tasty little food morsels.

Despite the fact that these little offerings feel like a modern custom it is in fact a very traditional way of starting either lunch or dinner. These days in France, Italy and indeed Russia, where the custom started, you would still see a buffet-table set with a wide range of small dishes on offer to start your meal.

Rabbit Terrine **I** page 49

⚜

SILKY TOFU
WITH SHIITAKE AND ENOKITAKE MUSHROOMS

SERVES 6

MAIN INGREDIENTS

300 gm (10 oz) fresh bean curd, semi-firm,
   cut into 6 cubes
4 tablespoons vegetable oil
1 tablespoon ginger, peeled and cut into very fine strips
1 spring onion, peeled and cut into small dice
80 gm (3 oz) shiitake mushrooms, trimmed and sliced
80 gm (3 oz) enokitake mushrooms, trimmed
2 tablespoons light soy sauce
3 tablespoons vegetarian oyster sauce
2 tablespoons sesame oil
200 ml (7 fl oz) water
1 tablespoon corn starch (mixed with 1 tablespoon
   water)
salt and pepper to taste

PREPARATION Steam the bean curd until hot. Drain
the excess water by patting dry with a paper towel.
Keep warm, covered, in the oven.

Heat a wok to a high temperature and add the
vegetable oil and lightly sauté the ginger and spring
onion for about 1 minute until fragrant. Add the
mushrooms and stir-fry for another minute. Add the
soy, oyster sauce and sesame oil and sauté for another
30 seconds. Add the water, bring to the boil and lightly
thicken with the corn starch mixture. Season to taste.

Place the bean curd pieces in small dishes and cover
with mushroom ragôut in an aesthetic manner and
serve hot with the juices.

⚜

SCALLOPS
WITH PICKLED DAIKON

SERVES 8

MAIN INGREDIENTS

8 sea scallops, cleaned and trimmed

SALAD

½ daikon, peeled and cut into fine julienne
½ English cucumber, peeled, de-seeded and cut
   into fine julienne

MARINADE

100 ml (3 ½ fl oz) sugar syrup (refer | Basics page 309)
100 ml (3 ½ fl oz) rice vinegar
4 limes, juiced
1 garlic clove, cut into brunoise (tiny dice)
1 large chilli, de-seeded and cut into brunoise

GARNISH

1 teaspoon pickled ginger, cut into a fine julienne
¼ bunch small coriander leaves

PREPARATION Mix together sugar syrup, rice vinegar,
lime juice, garlic and chilli. Pour half of this liquid over
the scallops and cure them until they turn opaque,
about 20 minutes. Add the other half to the daikon
and marinate for 10 minutes. When the daikon is soft,
add the cucumber. Drain off the liquids and pat
scallops dry keeping some of the dressing to one side.

PRESENTATION Place the pickled daikon and
cucumber in the middle of small plates, place the
scallops over it and spoon the dressing over the
scallops. Garnish the top with the fine julienne of
pickled ginger and the picked tiny coriander leaves.

⚜ ⚜
BOCCONCINI
WITH TOMATO QUENELLE

SERVES 8

MAIN INGREDIENTS

2 balls of bocconcini (similar to buffalo milk mozzarella)
extra virgin olive oil, for garnish and flavour
white milled pepper, for garnish
baby oregano leaves, for garnish

TOMATO QUENELLE

8 large very ripe vine tomatoes, peeled, partly
   de-seeded
2 tablespoons virgin olive oil
2 tablespoons sherry vinegar
1 teaspoon fine salt
freshly milled black pepper

TOMATO QUENELLE PREPARATION In a blender put
the tomato flesh with the olive oil, vinegar and
seasoning and process until you have a smooth paste,
about 2 minutes. Wet some muslin cloth then squeeze
out the excess moisture. Set the muslin over a strainer,
put the strainer over a pot and leave for a few hours to
drain the juice. Put the tomato mixture in a clean bowl,
check the seasoning and reserve to shape the quenelle.

PRESENTATION Pour a pool of olive oil in the bottom
of each serving dish. Slice the bocconcini in even slices
(save the extremities for another use). Dry the slices
on absorbent paper if required and place in the centre
of the pool of olive oil. Make a small quenelle or scoop
of the tomato mixture and place in the centre of the
bocconcini. Sprinkle some pepper and a few leaves of
oregano on top. Serve at room temperature.

⚜
SALMON CARPACCIO

SERVES 8

MAIN INGREDIENTS

150 gm (5 oz) celeriac, peeled and cut into fine
   brunoise (tiny dice)
½ side of Atlantic salmon, skinned, boned using
   boning tweezers, blood removed and sliced thinly
1 teaspoon baby capers, washed
½ cup shaved or grated Parmigiano-Reggiano
3 eschalot, peeled and cut into brunoise
a few chives, cut into little sticks
100 ml (3 ½ fl oz) extra virgin olive oil

PREPARATION Blanch the celeriac in boiling salted
water for 20 seconds, remove and refresh in iced water
briefly to cool.

PRESENTATION Place the salmon on small plates.
Place the baby capers, Parmigiano-Reggiano, celeriac,
eschalot and chives on top.

Decorate the plate by pouring the olive oil around the
salmon at the table for your guests.

✦ ✦

BATHERS' BRIOCHE
WITH MUSHROOM DUXELLE

MAKES APPROXIMATLY 30

BRIOCHE

300 gm (10 oz) baker's flour

1 teaspoon salt

35 gm (1 ¼ oz) sugar

2 eggs

75 ml (2 ½ fl oz) milk

15 gm (½ oz) fresh yeast or 30 gm (1 oz) dried yeast

110 gm (3 ½ oz) butter, softened

1 egg, lightly beaten, for egg wash

SPINACH PURÉE

1.5 kg (3 lb) baby spinach

5 cloves roasted garlic

100 gm (3 ½ oz) unsalted butter

salt and white milled pepper

MUSHROOM DUXELLE

6 field mushrooms peeled,
 stems removed, diced

3 cloves garlic, crushed

50 ml (1 ½ fl oz) cream

2 tablespoons chopped parsley

1 bunch chives, finely cut

TO SERVE

3 cm (1 in) square of speck per brioche, sautéed

BRIOCHE PREPARATION Mix the flour, salt, sugar, eggs, milk and yeast together to form a smooth dough. Knead the butter in until smooth. Place in a bowl, cover with plastic wrap and rest in the refrigerator overnight. The next day, cut a portion of dough approximately 150 gm (5 oz) and set aside. Divide the remaining mixture into 15 gm (½ oz) portions. Roll each portion out to form a circle. Place 1 teaspoon of the mushroom duxelle mixture into the centre of each circle. Fold the dough into the middle covering the duxelle mixture. Turn the ball over. Divide the 150 gm (5 oz) portion of dough into 30 small balls. Place each small ball on top of the larger balls. Place on a baking tray then brush with egg wash. Rest brioche in a warm place to prove for 20 minutes. Preheat the oven to 180°C (350°F). Bake in the oven for 20 minutes.

MUSHROOM DUXELLE PREPARATION Preheat oven to 180°C (350°F). Place field mushrooms and garlic in a roasting tray with a splash of olive oil and cover with foil. Bake for 30 minutes. Remove from oven and drain the liquid, reduce the liquid and pour back into the mushrooms. Purée the mushrooms, transfer to a pot and simmer until the liquid has evaporated. Add cream and reduce by half, season well. When cool, add parsley and chives and reserve.

SPINACH PURÉE PREPARATION Blanch 1 kg (2 lb) of baby spinach, and while still hot, purée with the unsalted butter and the roast garlic, season. Blanch the remaining spinach, refresh in iced water and squeeze dry. Finely chop and add to the puréed spinach.

PRESENTATION Warm the spinach purée and place a spoonful on each serving plate. Top with the sautéed speck and hot mushroom brioche.

✦ ✦
BATHERS' YABBY TAIL
WITH SQUID INK CANNELLONI

SERVES 6

YABBY

6 yabby tails, cooked, shelled and cleaned

1 lime, juiced

50 ml (1 ½ fl oz) extra virgin olive oil

sea salt

¼ bunch bush basil

COD BRANDADE FILLING

4 désirée or sebago potatoes, medium sized

4 garlic cloves, peeled

200 ml (7 fl oz) olive oil

200 gm (7 oz) fresh cod, salted overnight in
    20 gm (¾ oz) salt

salt and freshly ground white pepper

300 ml (10 fl oz) fish stock (refer | Basics page 301)

PASTA DOUGH

225 gm (7 oz) plain flour

2 eggs (65 gm/2 oz or large egg)

50 ml (1 ½ oz) squid ink

table salt

BRANDADE FILLING PREPARATION Cook the potatoes with the garlic cloves, starting in cold salted water and bringing to the boil. Reduce heat and simmer for approximately 20 minutes. When fully cooked, drain and peel, using kitchen gloves to handle the hot potatoes. Mash the potato and the garlic with the olive oil to achieve the right consistency (which must be fairly soft and light). Season with salt and pepper and put aside. Rinse the salted cod with fresh cold water and poach in the fish stock for a maximum of 5 minutes. Cool to a warm temperature and drain (save the poaching stock). Clean the cod, remove the skin and bones and all fatty parts. Shred into small pieces and add to the mashed potatoes. When ready to fill the cannelloni, warm up the mash and adjust the consistency with a touch of the poaching stock. Refine the seasoning.

PASTA PREPARATION Blend together all the pasta dough ingredients in a food processor. Remove and knead on a floured bench. The pasta dough should be black in colour. Roll out the pasta dough on the lowest setting of a pasta machine or very thin with a rolling pin. Cut into sheets of 20 cm (8 in) squares. Place the sheets on a floured tray to prevent sticking while you roll and cut the remainder. Poach the sheets in salted boiling water for about 4 minutes then refresh them in iced water. Once cooled, place them on towels to dry and cut them into six 8 cm (3 ¼ in) squares. Fill a piping bag with the brandade and spread a nice even amount the size of your thumb on the edge of each pasta square. Roll to form a cannelloni. Just before serving, steam for 30 seconds to warm them through.

PRESENTATION Place the warm cannelloni in small serving dishes. Place a yabby over each cannelloni. Mix the lime juice with the extra virgin olive oil and salt. Drizzle the dressing over both components of this amuse-bouche. Garnish with the bush basil and serve.

⚜ ⚜

PRAWN TOAST
WITH SESAME SEEDS

SERVES 6

PRAWN TOAST

200 gm (7 oz) scallops, cleaned and trimmed

1 onion, finely grated

¼ teaspoon garlic powder

1 egg white

sea salt and white milled pepper

2 slices white bread, crusts removed

green prawn tails, shelled and de-veined

1 cup sesame seeds

1 litre (32 fl oz) peanut oil for frying

PRAWN AND CHILLI OIL

200 gm (7 oz) prawn shells, fresh and cleaned

200 ml (7 fl oz) olive oil

2 cloves garlic, peeled and crushed

4 red chillies, de-seeded and thinly sliced

sea salt

TOAST PREPARATION Place the scallops with the onion, garlic powder and egg white in a food processor. Blend into a smooth paste and season with salt and pepper.

Spread a thin layer on the bread slices and place the prawns evenly spaced across the mousse. Fill the gaps in between the prawns with the mousse and cover them completely making a square shaped pillow with the mousse. Dip the mousse side of the prawn toast in the sesame seeds to coat the entire surface; turn over and cover the other side.

Deep-fry in the peanut oil on moderate heat (150°C/300°F) until the toast is golden brown. If it is not sufficiently cooked in the centre, place the toasts in the oven on 180°C (350°F) until they feel firm. When ready, cool toast for 10 minutes and slice into 1 cm (½ inch) slices, cutting across the prawn tails so that a nice pattern can be seen.

PRAWN AND CHILLI OIL PREPARATION Sweat off the prawn shells in a quarter (50 ml /1 ½ fl oz) of the olive oil until they turn bright red. Add the crushed garlic and chilli and continue to cook slowly for 15 minutes. Add the rest of the olive oil, increase the heat for 3 minutes to extract the flavours. Cool down and cover with foil. Let the oil sit in a warm place for 24 hours. The following day, strain through a fine cheesecloth and season with salt.

PRESENTATION Place a slice of prawn toast in each small dish. Drizzle the oil around it and sprinkle a little sea salt over the toast.

✢ ✢ ✢

BLUE CHEESE TORTELLINI
WITH CAULIFLOWER AND BROCCOLI JUS

SERVES 6

PASTA

2 whole eggs

3 egg yolks

300 gm (11 oz) pasta (durum wheat) flour

pinch salt

1 teaspoon vegetable oil

extra egg and a little milk, for egg wash

BLUE CHEESE FILLING

100 gm (3 ½ ounces) mild blue cheese

200 gm (7 oz) dry ricotta cheese

1 whole egg

1 tablespoon marjoram leaves, picked and chopped

1 pinch nutmeg

salt and pepper

CAULIFLOWER PURÉE

20 gm (¾ oz) butter

½ head cauliflower, trimmed and grated

salt and fine white pepper

100 ml (3 ½ fl oz) cream

30 ml (1 fl oz) milk

BROCCOLI JUS

1 head broccoli, blanched

40 ml (1 ½ fl oz) extra virgin olive oil

salt and fine white pepper

PASTA PREPARATION Beat the eggs together and combine all of the ingredients (except the egg wash) in a mixer with a hook. Once completely combined, remove from the bowl and knead on a floured bench until the dough is smooth. Cover and rest for 30 minutes.

BLUE CHEESE FILLING PREPARATION Soften the blue cheese in a bowl and break it up with a fork, keeping it slightly chunky. Incorporate the ricotta then add the egg, marjoram, nutmeg and salt and pepper.

TORTELLINI ASSEMBLY Using a pasta machine, roll the pasta out into thin sheets. The sheets should be thin enough that you can just see your hand through them. Cut the pasta into 8 cm (3 ¼ in) squares using a pasta cutter. Place the blue cheese filling onto the centre of each pasta square. Brush the exposed pasta with egg wash. Fold the pasta in half sealing the edges well with your fingers. Repeat this process with all the squares. Reserve in the refrigerator. When ready to serve, cook the tortellini in plenty of salted water until they float (3–4 minutes). Remove and drain on a towel.

CAULIFLOWER PURÉE PREPARATION Melt the butter in a saucepan and add the grated cauliflower. Sweat gently for about 10 minutes. Season slightly, add the cream and simmer gently until the cauliflower is cooked, blend into a fine paste (add the milk to adjust the consistency) and pass through a fine sieve. Refine seasoning before serving.

BROCCOLI JUS PREPARATION Simply juice the broccoli in a juice extractor and pass though a fine sieve. Just before serving, pour into a small saucepan to heat. Emulsify with the olive oil using a hand blender. Refine the seasoning and reserve. Do not worry if the oil separates before serving.

PRESENTATION Place the warm cauliflower purée in the middle of a small dish. Delicately present the tortellini on top of the purée and pour the broccoli jus around the purée.

✢ ✢

ANCHOVY CUSTARD
WITH FOCACCIA GRISSINI

SERVES 8

ANCHOVY CUSTARD
200 ml (7 fl oz) cream
125 ml (4 fl oz) milk
5 anchovy fillets, finely chopped
3 eggs
2 egg yolks
salt and white milled pepper
60 ml (2 fl oz) olive oil

FOCACCIA GRISSINI
¼ focaccia loaf, thinly sliced 3 mm (¹/₁₀ inch) thick,
    cut into long slivers

ANCHOVY CUSTARD PREPARATION Preheat oven to 130°C (260°F). Spray 8 dariole mould or demi tasse cups lightly with non-stick spray and place in a deep baking tray.

In a small pan, heat the cream and milk to 38°C (98°F) or barely a simmer. Add the anchovy fillets and allow the flavours to infuse for 15 minutes off the heat. Beat in the eggs. Season with salt and pepper. Strain the mixture through a fine sieve into a jug then pour the mixture into the cups filling each cup to two-thirds. Allow to rest for 20 minutes.

Pour boiling water into the baking tray up to the level of the filling in the cups and cover the tray with greased foil pressing firmly onto the tops of the cups. Stand for 5 minutes. Place the tray into the oven and check every 10 minutes for firmness (the firmness should resemble a set jelly). Remove and rest for 1 hour. Reheat lightly when needed (in the baking dish with water) in the oven at 130°C (260°F).

FOCACCIA GRISSINI PREPARATION Lightly toast the grissini on a griller until golden. Rest on a rack to dry completely prior to serving.

PRESENTATION When ready to serve, gently reheat the custards in the oven. When heated, remove from baking dish, wipe the bottom of the mould and turn onto the plate (best done if the plate is inverted over the cup first). Drizzle a little oil over the custard and place a golden focaccia sliver on the top.

SWEET ONION AND SPINACH RAVIOLI
WITH GOAT'S CURD CHEESE

SERVES 8

CARAMELISED ONION FILLING

50 gm (1 ½ oz) butter

4 onions, peeled and sliced lengthwise

50 gm (1 ½ oz) palm or brown sugar

2 cloves garlic, chopped

250 ml (8 fl oz) port

350 ml (12 fl oz) red wine

salt and milled white pepper

RAVIOLI DOUGH

225 gm (7 oz) plain flour

2 eggs (65 gm/2 oz or large egg)

2 tablespoons chlorophyll (refer | Basics page 309)

table salt

TOPPING AND GARNISH

100 gm (3 ½ oz) salted butter

1 bunch thyme, leaves picked

140 gm (5 oz) fresh ricotta or goat's curd cheese

CARAMELISED ONION FILLING PREPARATION Melt the butter and sweat the onions in a wide-bottomed pot until soft. Add the palm sugar and garlic and cook on a medium heat to caramelise them. Increase the heat and deglaze the pan with the port and red wine in small equal quantities a little at a time. Cook gently until all the liquid has evaporated. The resulting marmalade should be thick and nearly dry. Season, cool and refrigerate until needed.

RAVIOLI PREPARATION Blend all the ingredients together in a food processor. Remove dough and knead on a flat, lightly floured bench. The pasta dough should be a dark green colour. Roll pasta dough to the lowest setting with a pasta making machine or to a thickness of 2 mm (⅛ in). Cut eight 4 cm (1 ¾ in) diameter rounds and eight 6 cm (2 ½ in) diameter rounds.

Place a teaspoon of the onion mix in the centre of each of the smaller circles. Brush egg wash around the edge and place the larger rounds of pasta on top, making sure that the parcel is sealed properly. Cut to a perfect round using a crinkled cutter. When ready to serve, simmer ravioli in salted water until the ravioli start floating to the top (3–4 minutes).

PRESENTATION Place each hot ravioli in a small dish. Melt the butter in a hot pan until it turns golden brown and foamy, add the picked thyme and spoon over the ravioli. Garnish with the fresh ricotta or goat's curd cheese.

Salmon Carpaccio | page 37

Scallops with Pickled Daikon | page 36

Sweet Onion and Spinach Ravioli | page 45

Bathers' Brioche | page 38

Anchovy Custard | page 44

Yellowfin Tuna | page 50

Gazpacho Sorbet | page 54

Squid Ink Pasta Stack | page 48

Steamed John Dory on Toast | page 50

Prawn Toast | page 42

Silky Tofu | page 36

Grilled Scampi Tail | page 51

Blue Cheese Tortellini | page 43

Tuna Niçoise | page 55

Bocconcini | page 37

Beef Carpaccio | page 56

Bathers' Yabby Tail | page 39

Caviar Brioche | page 51

✢ ✢

SQUID INK PASTA STACK
WITH AVOCADO, CRAB AND GOAT'S CURD

SERVES 8

AVOCADO SALAD

2 avocados, peeled, cored, cut into small dice and
   sprinkled with lime juice to prevent discolouration
½ lime, juiced (for the avocado)
200 gm (7 oz) cooked, picked crab meat
200 gm (7 oz) fresh goat's curd
¼ bunch mint, picked and sliced into fine strips
   (chiffonnade)
1 punnet baby mizuna or other little leaves,
   picked and washed
olive oil, to garnish

PASTA DOUGH

225 gm (7 oz) plain flour
2 eggs (65 gm/2 oz or large egg)
50 ml (1 ½ oz) squid ink
table salt

PASTA DOUGH PREPARATION Blend together all the ingredients in a food processor. Remove and knead on a floured bench. The pasta dough should be black in colour. Roll out the pasta dough to the lowest setting on a pasta machine and cut into approximate 5 cm x 4 cm x 2.5 cm (2 in x 1 ¾ in x 1 in) triangles. Place the triangles on a floured tray. The pasta is then deep-fried. Heat oil to 180°C (350°F) in a deep pan. Test that the oil is hot enough by dropping just one pasta triangle in. If it sizzles immediately, the oil is hot enough. When the triangles are crispy, remove from the pan and drain on absorbent paper.

PRESENTATION Place the diced avocado sprinkled with the lime juice on the bottom of the plate. Place a few pieces of crab next to it and sit the first crisp sheet of squid ink pasta over it. Repeat this arrangement. When placing the second sheet of pasta on top, add a spoon of goat's curd, the little leaves and finally a fine julienne of mint over it as garnish. Drizzle a little olive oil and serve at room temperature.

⚜ ⚜

RABBIT TERRINE
WITH PICKLED ONION SALAD

SERVES 16

TERRINE

100 ml (3 ½ fl oz) vegetable oil

1 rabbit, quartered, trimmed and seasoned

1 carrot, peeled and finely diced

1 onion, peeled and finely diced

1 stick celery, string removed, finely diced

1 head garlic, peeled and crushed

1 spice bag (bayleaf, thyme (stems reserved), white
   peppercorns)

½ bunch flat leaf parsley, picked and roughly chopped
   (stems reserved)

400 ml (14 fl oz) white wine

1 litres (2 pints) chicken stock or beef bouillon

200 gm (7 oz) pork fat, rendered

table salt

ONION RELISH

3 Spanish onions, peeled and thinly sliced

2 teaspoons sugar

50 ml (1 ½ fl oz) red wine vinegar

SALAD AND GARNISH

1 punnet baby cress

1 tablespoon extra virgin olive oil

RABBIT TERRINE PREPARATION Preheat oven to
160°C (325°F). Heat the oil in a braising pan, add the
seasoned rabbit and cook until lightly coloured. When
evenly coloured, remove the rabbit from the pan and
add the mirepoix (carrot, onion and celery) and garlic
to the pan and sweat until aromatic and soft. Add the
spice bag, thyme and parsley stems, white wine and
bring to the simmer. Add the stock. Once the stock
simmers, skim the surface and place the rabbit in the
braising pan making sure it is covered by the liquid.

RABBIT TERRINE PREPARATION CONTINUED Reheat to
a boil and then quickly turn the heat down to a simmer.
Cover and braise in the oven for 2–3 hours until the
meat is tender and falls away from the bone. Pick the
meat off the bone and set aside. Pass the stock through
a fine strainer and cover the rabbit momentarily to
avoid it from drying.

Soften the pork fat in a pan so that it is a creamy
consistency. In another pan, pour 300 ml (10 fl oz) of
the stock and reduce it to a glaze. Cut the rabbit into
small dice and coat with the glaze while both are still
warm. Add the chopped parsley and finally the soft
rendered pork fat. Season well with salt and pepper.

Pour into a terrine mould lined with plastic wrap and
pack the mixture tightly. Set overnight in the
refrigerator with a weight over the top.

ONION RELISH PREPARATION Preheat the oven to
200° C (400°F) place the sliced onions in a bowl and
mix with the sugar and the vinegar, place between two
sheets of grease-proof paper, securing the top sheet with
a wire rack and cook for 10 minutes until the sliced
onions are soft and bright red, reserve for plating.

PRESENTATION Disperse the pickled red onions in the
middle of small dishes. Carefully remove the terrine
from the mould, remove the plastic wrap and cut slices
approximately ¾ cm (¼ in) thick. Place the terrine
slices on top of the onion. Garnish the top of the
terrine with picked baby cress and a drizzle of virgin
olive oil. Serve at room temperature.

✢

YELLOWFIN TUNA
WITH SEA URCHIN DRESSING

SERVES 8

MAIN INGREDIENTS

8 x 45 gm (1 ½ oz each) very fresh yellowfin tuna cubes
    (approximately 3 square cm/1 ¼ in)
black and white sesame seeds, for garnish

BRAISED DAIKON

1 litre (3 ½ fl oz) chicken stock, clear
100 ml white wine vinegar
1 pinch saffron threads
1 pinch saffron powder
1 pinch salt
1 daikon radish, trimmed and peeled

SEA URCHIN DRESSING

120 gm (4 oz) sea urchin roe
50 ml (2 fl oz) millet vinegar or verjuice
25 ml (1 fl oz) mirin
25 ml (1 fl oz) peanut oil
1 teaspoon sesame oil
sea salt and white milled pepper

DAIKON PREPARATION To cook the daikon radish, heat
the chicken stock and vinegar with the saffron and salt,
and simmer for 15 minutes. Meanwhile, cut the daikon
radish into 3 cm (1 ¼ in) squares and ½ cm (¼ in) thick.
Gently poach the daikon in the saffron stock until
tender, remove from stock. Cool stock over ice then
replace daikon into the chilled and strained stock —
this intensifies the colour and flavour of the daikon.

SEA URCHIN DRESSING PREPARATION Place the sea
urchin roe, millet vinegar and mirin in a blender and
blend until combined. Slowly add peanut and sesame
oils as if making a mayonnaise. Season to taste with
sea salt and pepper. Make this dressing as close to
serving the dish as possible.

PRESENTATION Put the daikon squares in the middle
of the serving plates and the tuna cube on top of the
radish. There is no need to season the tuna — its
natural flavour and contrast with the intense dressing
will be distinct enough in flavour and colour. Spoon the
dressing around the tuna. Garnish with sesame seeds.

✢

STEAMED JOHN DORY ON TOAST

SERVES 6

MAIN INGREDIENTS

6 x 50 gm (1 ½ oz) John Dory, boned, trimmed (whiting
    or sole are also suitable for this recipe)
sea salt and white milled pepper
6 pieces of brioche, sliced into fingers approximately
    7 cm x 2.5 cm, crust removed and toasted
½ bunch oregano, small leaves
1 tablespoon olive oil

JOHN DORY PREPARATION The sliced portions should
be cut into finger shapes. Season with sea salt and
pepper. Steam gently until the fish is cooked to opaque.

PRESENTATION Place the toasted brioche rectangles in
the middle of small serving plates. Place the steamed
Dory on top. Garnish with the oregano leaves around
the toast and drizzle with a little olive oil. Serve warm.

✠ ✠

GRILLED SCAMPI TAIL
WITH FRISÉE SALAD

SERVES 6

GARNISH

2 very thin slices prosciutto ham

1 small parsnip, peeled and very thinly sliced

700 ml (24 fl oz) peanut oil

2 slices of brioche, thinly sliced and cut into small dices

30 gm (1 oz) butter

SCAMPI AND SALAD

3 scampi tails, raw, cleaned

80 ml (2 ¾ fl oz) standard vinaigrette
   (refer | Basics page 302)

sea salt

¼ head frisée lettuce, picked and washed

GARNISH PREPARATION The garnishes for this amuse-bouche need to be prepared prior to grilling the scampi.

FOR THE PROSCIUTTO LARDONS, preheat oven to 120°C (240°F). Place the slices in between two sheets of baking paper on a baking tray with a wire rack securing the top sheet. Place in oven and bake them until they are gold and crisp. Once baked and still warm from the oven, cut them into small strips and set aside.

FOR THE PARSNIP CHIPS, simply deep-fry them at 150°C (300°F) in the peanut oil in a pot on the stove over low heat. Once they are gold and crisp, drain them on absorbent paper and season.

FOR THE BRIOCHE CROUTONS, sauté them in a frying pan with hot butter until gold and crisp, then drain on absorbent paper.

SCAMPI PREPARATION Butterfly the scampi by laying them flat on their belly and splitting with a large knife. Season and quickly grill the scampi tails over high heat on a char grill or barbecue; alternatively, they can also be pan-fried in hot butter.

PRESENTATION Separate the two half tails using a knife and place each one in a small dish, drizzle with the vinaigrette and a little sea salt. Toss the picked frisée lettuce in the vinaigrette as well and place next to the scampi, garnish with the lardons, croutons and the fried parsnip.

✠ ✠

CAVIAR BRIOCHE

SERVES 8

20 gm (¾ oz) butter

4 whole eggs, half beaten

30 ml (1 fl oz) pouring cream

salt and white milled pepper

4 slices brioche bread

8 teaspoons farmed caviar

a few chives, finely snipped

PREPARATION Place a stainless steel frying pan or non-stick pan on the stove on low heat. Melt the butter, add the eggs and slowly cook them while stirring with a spatula. When a creamy consistency is reached, incorporate the cream. Lastly, season and set aside for a couple of minutes in a warm spot.

Toast the brioche slices until golden, then cut them using a round cutter (5 cm (2 in) diameter). Place the round brioche in small dishes and spoon the warm scrambled eggs on top. Place the caviar over the eggs and garnish with the snipped chives.

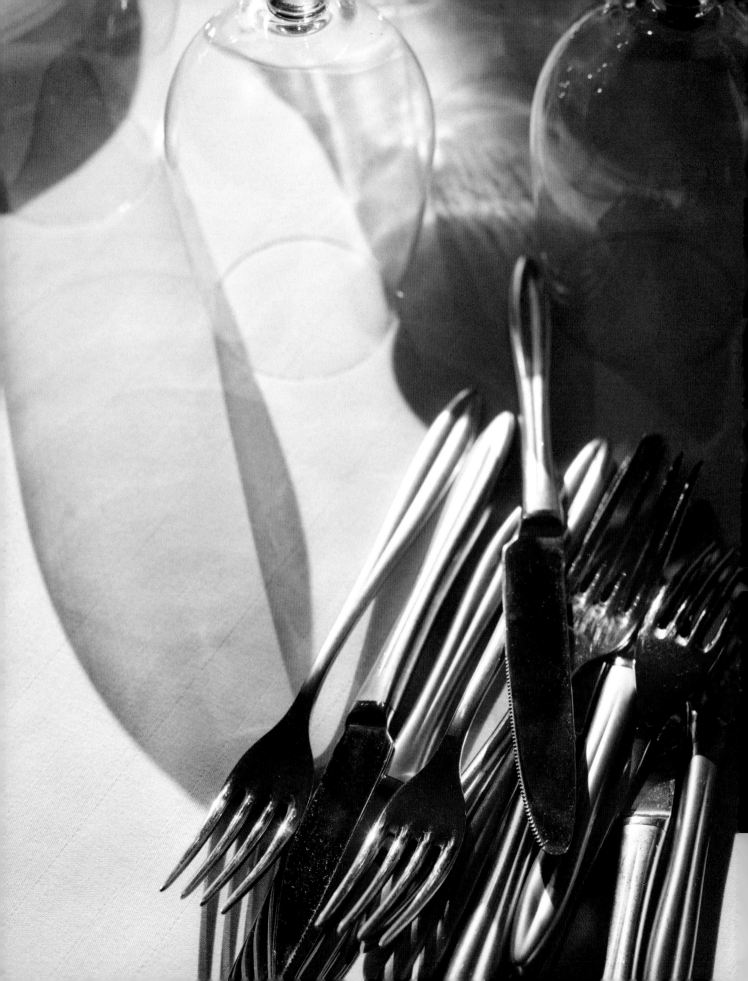

✠ ✠

GAZPACHO SORBET
WITH BASIL OIL

SERVES 8

GAZPACHO

350 gm (12 oz) vine tomatoes, very ripe

3 red capsicum, de-seeded and chopped

¼ English cucumber, peeled and de-seeded

¼ red onion, peeled and sliced

2 garlic cloves, peeled and finely chopped

40 ml (1 ½ fl oz) sherry vinegar

1 teaspoon Tabasco Sauce

50 ml (2 fl oz) verjuice

2 pinches sea salt

white milled pepper

SUGAR SYRUP

20 gm (¾ oz) caster sugar

20 ml (¾ fl oz) water

40 ml (1 ½ fl oz) glucose

BASIL OIL

1 bunch basil, picked

1 cup extra virgin olive oil

GARNISH

2 whole tomatoes, blanched, peeled, cut into
    quarters and de-seeded

2 sprigs bush basil, picked, for garnish

GAZPACHO PREPARATION Blanch, peel and de-seed the tomatoes. Place tomatoes, capsicum, cucumber, onion and garlic in the sherry vinegar, Tabasco, verjuice, salt and pepper and marinate at room temperature for 1 hour. Blend until smooth, strain through a fine sieve discarding the pulp and reserving the liquid.

SUGAR SYRUP PREPARATION To make the sugar syrup, bring water, sugar and glucose to the boil. Reduce heat to medium and simmer until sugar is dissolved.

In a large bowl, combine the gazpacho and sugar syrup. Place in an ice-cream machine and churn until it reaches a solid consistency. Remove from the machine and place in the freezer for 1 hour or until firm.

BASIL OIL PREPARATION Lightly blanch the leaves for 2 seconds in rapidly boiling salted water, refresh in iced water briefly and remove, pat dry. Place the leaves in a food processor and blend, slowly adding the olive oil, strain through a fine sieve lined with muslin cloth and reserve.

PRESENTATION Prior to serving, chill serving dishes in the refrigerator. Quenelle or scoop the frozen gazpacho and place onto peeled and de-seeded tomato quarters. Drizzle with a little basil oil and some picked bush basil leaves. Serve immediately.

✤ ✤

TUNA NIÇOISE
ON POTATO FONDANTE

SERVES 8

MAIN INGREDIENTS

8 pommes fondantes (refer | Basics page 307)

NIÇOISE

50 ml (1 ½ fl oz) extra virgin olive oil

1 lemon, juiced

½ garlic clove, peeled and finely chopped

4 anchovy fillets, finely diced

sea salt and white milled pepper

1 red capsicum, roasted, de-seeded, peeled
    and finely diced

2 tomatoes, peeled, pitted and finely diced

½ fennel bulb, trimmed, diced and cooked in
    a little stock

1 eschalot, peeled, and finely chopped

8 Ligurian olives, pitted and diced

2 cups water or fish stock

200 gm (7 oz) bluefin tuna steak, trimmed whole

¼ bunch parsley, picked and chopped

¼ bunch chervil, picked

SAFFRON BOUILLON

100 ml (3 fl oz) chicken stock

1 pinch saffron

2 tablespoons white wine vinegar

salt and pepper

NIÇOISE SALAD PREPARATION First make a dressing by mixing the oil, lemon juice, garlic, anchovy, salt and pepper. Add the capsicum, tomato, fennel, eschalot and olives and allow this mixture to marinate for 1 hour.

Heat 2 cups of water or fish stock, season and bring to a simmer. Remove from the heat and place the tuna in the liquid. The tuna will cook slowly to the rare stage. This will take approximately 10 minutes. Remove the tuna from the hot liquid, drain and cool. Once at room temperature, cut the tuna into small even dices and add to the niçoise ingredients. Fold in carefully and refine the seasoning.

SAFFRON BOUILLON PREPARATION Prepare the saffron boullion by cooking all ingredients in a saucepan for 5 minutes. Allow to cool.

PRESENTATION Place the cutter you used to shape the pommes fondante on a preparation plate. Put a fondante in the bottom, sprinkle a layer of chopped parsley, then push the tuna mixture inside. Spoon the saffron bouillon into the base of a small serving dish and carefully place the potato topped with niçoise over the bouillon. Garnish with the picked chervil.

✦ ✦ ✦

BEEF CARPACCIO
WITH OXTAIL JELLY & PORCINI PANNACOTTA

SERVES 8

BEEF CARPACCIO

1 teaspoon white peppercorns

1 teaspoon celery seeds

1 teaspoon black peppercorns

1 teaspoon porcini powder

salt

500 gm (1 lb) beef tenderloin from the centre,
    to make 2 nice rounds, trimmed

OXTAIL CONSOMMÉ JELLY

1 ½ litres (50 fl oz) veal stock (refer | Basics page 301)
    or chicken stock, cold

200 gm (7 oz) raw oxtail meat, minced

200 gm (7 oz) veal mince, lean

3 egg whites, slightly beaten

1 tomato, de-seeded and diced

1 medium carrot, peeled and diced

1 medium onion, peeled and diced

7 gelatine leaves

BEEF CARPACCIO PREPARATION Toast the whole spices in a dry pan just until the aroma is evident. Cool slightly and grind to a fine powder using a mortar and pestle or an electric grinder dedicated to spices. Mix the freshly ground spices with the porcini powder and salt (to taste).

Trim the beef tenderloin to a consistent and even cylinder. Lay on a sheet of plastic wrap and sprinkle the spices over the tenderloin and the plastic wrap. Roll the tenderloin over the plastic wrap and roll the plastic wrap tightly to form a tight cylinder. Freeze the tenderloin on a tray overnight ready for plating. Reserve a little of the spice mix for the plating.

OXTAIL CONSOMMÉ PREPARATION Combine all ingredients except the gelatine leaves in a saucepan over medium heat. Stir in the same direction with a wooden spoon. Bring to the boil, removing the spoon at the first sign of steam. Simmer this mixture very gently for 1 hour or until the full potential of the flavour has been reached. Cool a little and strain the clarified amber liquid into another pot, season with salt and remove any fat from the top with non-lint forming paper towel until the surface is completely free of any fat particles.

Soak the gelatine leaves in cold water until soft, squeeze completely free of excess water and add to the pure consommé. Completely dissolve the gelatine into the consommé, stirring with a very clean spoon. Pour into a 5 cm (2 in) deep container with a volume capacity of 2 litres (4 pints) and refrigerate. This is best done 3–4 hours before making the pannacotta to allow plenty of time to set, but not so far ahead that the two mixtures won't stick together.

WHITE ASPARAGUS AND PORCINI PANNACOTTA

2 spring onions, peeled and trimmed, cut into thick
    slices (white part only)
1 tablespoon butter
2 bunches white asparagus, trimmed, peeled and diced
4 medium porcini mushrooms, cleaned, fresh is
    preferred (dried porcini are also a good choice when
    fresh is not available, use half of the fresh quantity)
500 ml (16 fl oz) milk
250 ml (8 fl oz) cream
salt and fine white pepper
8 gelatine leaves

PANNACOTTA PREPARATION In a medium pot, sauté the spring onions in the butter until translucent, add the white asparagus and the porcini mushrooms and gently sauté until aromatic. Add the milk and the cream and very slowly and gently bring to a slight simmer (the first sign of a bubble) then remove from the heat. Allow this mixture to infuse for a further 15 minutes while it cools a little, then strain. Season with salt and pepper.

Soak the gelatine leaves in cold water until soft, squeeze completely free of excess water and add to the strained liquid. Completely dissolve the gelatine into the warm pannacotta liquid stirring with a very clean spoon. Cool over ice until it becomes slightly thicker and cooler than body temperature. Test the oxtail consommé to make sure it is at a 'just set' stage. Pour pannacotta slowly over the 'just set' consommé to the same depth in the container. Refrigerate overnight.

PRESENTATION Slice finger-sized portions of the oxtail consommé jelly and the pannacotta and lay in small dishes. Very thinly slice 3 slices of the tenderloin for each dish and overlap the slices on the bottom of the plate. Sprinkle with some of the reserved spice mix and serve immediately.

Chapter Three
❧ RECIPES ❧
from the garden

My parents used to have a huge vegetable garden. Preparing and eating vegetables at home in their most simple form, it taught me to respect their natural integrity. Now as a chef, I love working with fresh vegetables. For my customers, my role as chef is to challenge their taste buds and to transform vegetables – showcasing their natural beauty and exploring the possiblities of their unqiue flavours. Any chef relishes the challenges of working with the perfect simplicity of sweet carrots, as well as the more complex flavours of white asparagus or plump artichoke.

The essence of cooking is often about restricting yourself to the simplest methods to prepare and dress vegetables and salads. The goal should be to enhance and improve their already perfect or unique flavours – either serving them on their own, or as a complement to a complex meat or fish dish. While vegetarians know it, we often forget that vegetables can, and should, be served as their own meal. There is nothing better than serving steamed asparagus with melted butter, or a tomato and basil salad, or eating a salad, perfectly dressed with hazelnut oil, red wine vinegar, or a touch of mustard.

Over the years, I have also enjoyed working with many boutique and small growers to support the development and release of new varities. Now, each new vegetable I see on the market or in our restaurant, such as salsify, yellow sweet beetroot, a new type of potato or a different salad green, it makes me proud to have been a small part of this exciting part of our industry and broadening the range of vegetables for us to enjoy.

This is one of my customer's favourite
dishes from the menu. In season, I would use
artichokes or sometimes roasted fennel instead
of the asparagus. The trick here is to serve the
cappelletti with plenty of burnt butter. You
could use thyme without the anchovies but
a little of the magic disappears.

Goat's Cheese Cappelletti

✢ ✢

GOAT'S CHEESE CAPPELLETTI
WITH ASPARAGUS AND THYME BUTTER

SERVES 8

CAPPELLETTI

1 kg (2 ¼ lb) désirée potatoes, making about
    700 gm (1 ½ lb) of potato purée
few pinches fine salt
300 gm (10 oz) baker's flour
250 gm (8 oz) fresh goat's cheese
1 tablespoon thyme leaves (reserve half)
100 gm (3 ½ oz) butter, diced
2 tablespoons anchovy paste (made from Spanish
    anchovies in oil pounded to a paste)
1 lemon

VEGETABLES

8 spears green asparagus, trimmed, peeled
    and blanched
8 spears white asparagus, trimmed, peeled
    and blanched
24 kalamata olives, pitted and gently roasted
few pinches fine salt

CAPPELLETTI PREPARATION Preheat oven to 180°C (350°F). Bake the potatoes in their skins for 1 ½ hours to remove as much moisture as possible. While still warm, cut the potatoes in half, scoop the flesh out and pass through a Mouli or potato ricer. Add the salt and flour and combine using a wooden spoon. While the dough is still warm roll onto a floured bench and fold a few times to create smooth dough like a gnocchi dough.

Using a pasta machine will ensure the best result for the sheets of pasta needed to create the cappelletti. Reduce the setting gradually until you have a sheet 3 or 4 mm (⅛ in) thick, brush off the excess flour and cut into circles of about 8 cm (3 ¼ inch) diameter. (You could use a rolling pin.)

Roll the goat's cheese into mini log shapes to fit inside the disc. Set a piece of goat's cheese on each circle and sprinkle with thyme leaves. Brush one edge with water and close over to form a half circle, fold the two ends in and close, with a little water on one end only to form cappelletti. Set on a towel on a tray and cover with another towel until all completed. Refrigerate for half an hour to firm before cooking.

VEGETABLE PREPARATION Blanch the asparagus in salted boiling water, drain and season with fine salt. Reserve in a warm place with the olives.

PRESENTATION These next steps need to happen simultaneously to bring the dish together. Poach 3 cappelletti per serve in salted boiling water with a little olive oil added. When they float to the top, remove and drain immediately. Heat a frying pan until it begins to smoke lightly. Add the diced butter and heat the butter until it turns light brown and foamy. Add the anchovy paste and, with a small whisk, integrate the paste and cook until it stops foaming. Remove from heat, add a squeeze of lemon juice and the remaining thyme leaves. Plate the cappelletti, asparagus, olives and drizzle the thyme anchovy butter over.

WINE NOTES

❀ **PRIMO ESTATE JOSEPH D'ELENA PINOT GRIGIO**
Adelaide Plains, SA Capturing the Italian style with pear,
honeysuckle and spice. Lightly herbaceous with savoury finish.

❀ ❀ **LUCIEN ALBRECHT PINOT GRIS Alsace, France** Shows
stonefruit and honeysuckle with lovely mid-palate richness and
slight mushroom savouryness.

❀ ❀ ❀ **SHAW & SMITH M3 CHARDONNAY Adelaide Hills,
SA** A wine that gets better each vintage. Taut and focused
with subtle layers and a long finish.

❀ **ANTINORI CAMPOGRANDE ORVIETO CLASSICO Umbria, Italy**
A light, fresh wine with a subtle fruit and fresh herb palate from the picturesque hilltop town of Orvieto.

❀❀ **GEMBROOK HILL SAUVIGNON BLANC Yarra Valley, VIC** From the northern Yarra Valley, a delicious citrus, minerally wine.

❀❀❀ **FREYCINET RIESLING East Coast, TAS** More-ish riesling with lime blossom, spice, hint of passionfruit and refreshing finish.

If you have the chance, use mini chabichou cheese made by Gabrielle Kervella from Kervella Cheeses. Her goat's cheese comes from her own herd raised on organic feed, and respects the true tradition of French cheese making, where Gabrielle trained. Her farm in Gidgegannup in Western Australia is a model for a sustainable organic operation.

Provençale Vegetable Plate

✳ **TAMAR RIDGE PINOT NOIR** Tamar, **TAS** Lovely juicy floral fruit-driven pinot from Northern Tasmania.

✳✳ **BOROLI MADONNA DI COMO DOLCETTO D'ALBA** Piedmont, Italy Dolcetto, known as the 'little sweet one' is at home with a dish containing truffles.

✳✳✳ **MARTINBOROUGH VINEYARDS PINOT NOIR** Martinborough, NZ Classy pinot with fragrant, sweet fruit palate, depth and velvety texture.

Is this a decadent or indulgent dish or is it a beautiful way to use this unique fungus? I guess my natural restraint goes out the door when the truffle comes into season. Whether they are from Tasmania, Western Australia, France or Italy this is a perfect dish to illustrate their aura.

Truffle and Eschalot Flan

PROVENÇALE VEGETABLE PLATE
WITH CHABICHOU

SERVES 8

METHOD À LA GRECQUE
100 ml (3 ½ fl oz) chardonnay vinegar
1 cup water, chicken stock or vegetable stock
150 ml (5 fl oz) extra virgin olive oil
juice of 1 lemon
1 sprig each of rosemary and thyme
1 bay leaf
4 cloves garlic, crushed
½ teaspoon white peppercorns
½ teaspoon coriander seeds
1 teaspoon sea salt

BASIL OIL
2 large bunches basil
200 ml (7 fl oz) extra virgin olive oil
1 clove garlic
salt and milled pepper

VEGETABLES, CHEESE AND GARNISH
40 champignons à la grecque (see method)
24 long green asparagus tips, blanched
24 long white asparagus tips, peeled and blanched
24 baby turned carrots, blanched
24 pods of peas, blanched whole, one half-shell
   removed with peas intact
24 confit radishes (refer to Basics page 304)
8 x 50 gm (1 ½ oz) chabichou farmhouse
   natural-rind cheese at room temperature
200 ml (7 fl oz) basil oil
8 golf ball tomatoes, blanched and peeled
sprigs of bush basil

À LA GRECQUE PREPARATION Place all the ingredients in a heavy-based pot and simmer gently for
20 minutes. Strain and cool. Divide mixture in half in two separate saucepans and simmer mushrooms
until slightly soft but still with an element of firmness. Cool at room temperature. You can make this
ahead of time and store in an air tight jar in the refrigerator.

VEGETABLE PREPARATION Blanch the asparagus, carrots and peas in salted water, then refresh in salted
iced water briefly until cool. Drain and reserve for plating.

BASIL OIL PREPARATION In a large pot of boiling salted water, blanch the basil briefly for 5 seconds. Refresh
in iced water and remove and dry with absorbent paper. When cool, squeeze all the water from the basil
and roughly chop it. Place in a blender with the oil and garlic, add a little seasoning and blend until you
have a bright green mixture. Pour the blended basil oil through a strainer over a bowl with a double sheet of
muslin cloth and drain for a few hours. Place the oil in a glass jar and keep in the refrigerator.

PRESENTATION Place the chabichou in the centre of serving plates. Gently toss all the vegetables in a little
extra virgin olive oil and season. Place the vegetables around the plate and then drizzle with basil oil.
Place the golf ball tomato on the top of each piece of chabichou and scatter a few sprigs of bush basil
around the plate.

TRUFFLE AND ESCHALOT FLAN
WITH MÂCHE

SERVES 4

FLAN

2 winter truffles (40 gm/1 ½ oz each)

4 x baked puff pastry discs, 3 mm (⅛ in) thick
  and 8 cm (3 ¼ in) in diameter

2 thin slices bacon, trimmed of fat and
  cut into very tiny cubes

16 eschalots, peeled and sliced as
  thinly as possible

1 medium onion, peeled and sliced as
  thinly as possible

2 tablespoons goose fat or duck fat (or
  vegetable oil)

½ cup cream

freshly milled black pepper

50 ml (1 ½ fl oz) veal jus

1 handful mâche lettuce

VINAIGRETTE

4 tablespoons hazelnut oil

1 tablespoon white wine vinegar

1 teaspoon chopped black truffle

salt and freshly milled pepper

PREPARATION Trim the truffles slightly to give them a cylindrical shape. Save the trimmings and chop them finely for the vinaigrette. Slice the truffle cylinders very thinly on a sharp Japanese mandolin or truffle slicer.

Preheat oven to 180°C (350°F). Bake puff pastry circles on a baking sheet until golden brown. Bring a small saucepan of water to the boil. Place the bacon into a sieve and submerge in the boiling water for 20 seconds, remove and reserve.

In a large frying pan, combine the finely sliced eschalots, onions and goose fat over high heat. Season and cook for 10 minutes stirring constantly without colouring them. Add the blanched diced bacon and cook for a further 2 minutes. Add the cream and cook until it is boiled down while stirring constantly. Season with plenty of pepper.

VINAIGRETTE PREPARATION Combine all vinaigrette ingredients at least 20 minutes prior to serving to allow the flavours to combine. Season just prior to serving.

PRESENTATION Place puff pastry onto serving plates, spoon onion mixture on top, then place finely sliced truffles, overlapping their arrangement. Spoon vinaigrette and warm veal jus around the tart and decorate with a few mâche leaves in an aesthetic manner.

RECIPES FROM THE GARDEN

This has been an all-time favourite on my menus. The secret of the flavour and colour of my pea soup is the light cooking it receives. Be careful not to boil this soup as the stunning colour will degrade quickly and part of the enjoyment will be lost.

Silky Spring Pea Soup

Tomato and Basil Terrine

Sautéed Beans

SILKY SPRING PEA SOUP

SERVES 12

INGREDIENTS

200 gm (7 oz) unsalted butter
5 eschalots, roughly chopped
2 leeks, white part only, washed and roughly
   sliced
2 cloves garlic, peeled and sliced
1 large sebago potato, peeled and diced
3 litres (5 ¼ pints) vegetable stock
2 kg (4 ½ lb) blanched fresh peas (frozen may also
   be used)

½ bunch mint, chopped
sea salt and milled white pepper
200 ml (7 fl oz) cream, whipped
sorrel leaves, free of stems and finely sliced

PREPARATION In a medium pot melt the butter and sweat the eschalots, leek and garlic. Add the diced potato and warmed vegetable stock and simmer for 20 minutes or until the potato is tender. Remove from heat and allow to cool. Drain and reserve the excess cooking liquid. Add the peas and the mint.

Purée in a food processor as soon as the peas have been added, correcting the consistency of the vegetables with the reserved cooking liquid. Pass through a fine sieve and adjust the seasoning with a little sea salt and milled white pepper. Return the soup to the saucepan and warm gently.

PRESENTATION Serve 2 cups per bowl. Garnish with a quenelle of lightly whipped cream. To achieve this, dip a tablespoon into hot water and scrape the spoon against the cream's surface; a roll of cream will develop (this is a quenelle). Set the quenelle in the bowl and sprinkle with sorrel. Enjoy hot.

WINE NOTES

❋ **TELMO RODRIGUEZ BASA VERDEJO**
Reuda, Spain Verdejo is little known outside of Spain. It is a soft, fruity, slightly herbal and minerally white wine.

❋ ❋ **FERMOY ESTATE SAUVIGNON BLANC** **Margaret River, WA** Citrus and herbal tone with pleasant mid-weight palate.

❋ ❋ ❋ **MÜLLER-CATOIR HAARDTER BURGER GARTEN RIESLING KABINETT TROCKEN Pfalz, Germany** Floral, pretty wine with lovely white stone fruit weight and lingering finish.

CARAMELISED TOMATO, ESCHALOT AND FETTA TART

SERVES 4

INGREDIENTS

8 whole tomatoes
sea salt and freshly milled black pepper
12 basil stalks
2 sprigs thyme
30 ml (1 fl oz) or a good drizzle of olive oil
4 garlic cloves, roasted
12 eschalots, roasted
½ cup sugar
¼ cup water

¼ cup sherry vinegar
12 Niçoise olives, pitted
2 sheets puff pastry (defrosted if frozen)
150 gm (5 oz) fetta cheese
sage leaves, to garnish

PREPARATION Preheat oven to 250°C (480°F). Cut the tomatoes in half, toss them with sea salt, pepper, basil stalks and sprigs of thyme and add a good drizzle of olive oil. Cook skin side up in oven until the skin blisters. Turn the tomatoes over, reduce the heat to 120°C (250°F) and cook for 3–4 hours. Remove skin and reserve for assembly.

Apply this same technique to the garlic and eschalots except that they should be left whole at this stage. Their roasting time will be significantly less, approximately 20–30 minutes. Reserve for assembly.

Combine the sugar with the water in a small saucepan over medium heat swirling the pan until the sugar completely dissolves. Bring to the boil. When the caramel becomes nut brown, remove the saucepan from the heat and add the sherry vinegar to the caramel carefully continuing to swirl the pan until thoroughly combined.

Pour the caramel into four 8 cm–10 cm (3 in–4 in) tart tins. Allow the caramel to cool for a minute or so; it will set hard. Cut the garlic and eschalots in half and place in the bottom of the tart tin with the olives. Add 4 tomato halves to each tart tin. Add salt and pepper and press gently. Preheat the oven to 180°C (350°F). Cut the puff pastry into circles slightly larger than the opening of the tart tins (these will become the tart crusts). Place the pastry circles over the roasted tomatoes and transfer the tart tins to a baking sheet. Bake until the pastry is puffed and golden, about 20 minutes.

PRESENTATION Allow the tarts to cool for 1–2 minutes and then carefully turn them onto a plate, serving warm or at room temperature, with sliced fetta cheese and sage leaves to complement.

✦ ✦

TOMATO AND BASIL TERRINE
WITH YELLOW CAPSICUM SALAD AND BASIL OIL

You will need plenty of crusty Italian unsalted bread to go with this dish. I love the contrasting colours and well harmonised flavours in this recipe. One of the best ways to extract a great flavour from capsicum is to gently peel them when raw and confit them in olive oil.

SERVES 8

TERRINE

2 tablespoons extra virgin olive oil
2 garlic cloves, peeled and finely grated
½ bunch basil, thinly cut (save half of the amount
     for garnish)
sea salt and milled white pepper
12 ripe tomatoes, cut in half (across the grain)
9 leaves of gelatine, soaked in cold water

*Start the preparation of the terrine the day
     before serving.*

GAZPACHO BASE

1 garlic clove, peeled and crushed
½ small Spanish onion, peeled and sliced
½ small red capsicum, peeled and de-seeded
1 small English cucumber, peeled and de-seeded
1 slice white bread, crust removed and cut into
     four pieces
50 ml (1 ½ fl oz) extra virgin olive oil
50 ml (1 ½ fl oz) red wine vinegar
200 ml (7 fl oz) tomato juice
sea salt and milled white pepper

GAZPACHO BASE PREPARATION Place all the ingredients into a stainless steel container and cover with plastic wrap. Stir occasionally, while allowing the flavours to develop for 4 hours in the refrigerator.

TERRINE PREPARATION Preheat the oven to 120°C (250°F). Drizzle 2 tablespoons of extra virgin olive oil on a stainless steel tray with the garlic, basil, sea salt and milled white pepper. Place the halved tomatoes (cut side down) on the tray over these ingredients. Bake in the oven for 45 minutes then, while still warm, remove the skins. While the tomatoes bake, soak the gelatine leaves in cold water.

Blend the Gazpacho base until smooth and adjust the seasoning to your taste. Squeeze excess water from the gelatine and slowly melt in a pan on the stove. Add melted gelatine to the Gazpacho base and blend completely. Strain this liquid through a fine sieve and set aside.

Line a rectangular terrine mould approximately 20 cm (8 in) long x 8 cm (3 ¼ in) wide with plastic wrap and place a layer of the peeled, slow roasted tomatoes on the bottom of the mould. Pour the gelatinous but still liquid Gazpacho over the tomatoes. Continue making layers until all the ingredients are used. Set the terrine in the refrigerator overnight.

❀❀ **CAMPAGNOLA LE BINE SOAVE CLASSICO Veneto, Italy** Regional wine of Northern Italy. It is subtle in nature with dried herbs, almond and light lemony fruit.

❀❀ **BROKENWOOD SEMILLON Hunter Valley, NSW** Classic wine for this region. Straw coloured with citrus, lemongrass and fresh herbs, flinty, long and refreshing.

❀❀❀ **HENRI BOURGEOIS LES BARONNES SANCERRE Loire Valley, France** Sauvignon blanc with quite a fruit drive for sancerre, still showing characteristic minerality and racy acidity.

SALAD
8 medium yellow capsicums, ripe and
    full of flavour
½ bunch bush basil, leaves picked
100 ml (3 ½ fl oz) extra virgin olive oil

BASIL OIL
1 clove garlic, peeled and blanched in
    salted boiling water
¼ bunch basil leaves, picked and blanched
½ cup extra virgin olive oil
sea salt and black milled pepper
1 wedge lemon

CAPSICUM SALAD PREPARATION Firstly, bring a pot of salted water to the boil. Cut the flesh of each capsicum into four flat and square pieces. With the help of a peeler or a very sharp knife delicately separate the outer skin from the flesh keeping the pieces whole. Using a round cutter of 3 ½ cm diameter (1 ½ in) cut even round pieces, make as many pieces as possible. Plunge the capsicum rounds in the boiling salted water for 20 seconds then refresh in salted ice water to keep them bright yellow and still crunchy.

BASIL OIL PREPARATION Simply blend the blanched garlic, basil and olive oil into a smooth paste. Allow paste to infuse for a few hours then strain and discard the solids. Adjust the seasoning, add a drop of lemon juice prior to serving.

PRESENTATION Place the round yellow capsicum slices in the centre of each chilled plate. Drizzle the pesto oil over the capsicum and season with the sea salt, lemon juice and black milled pepper. Slice the terrine and place over the capsicum pieces displaying the contrasting shapes and colours on the plate. Pour a little olive oil around the edge of the plate, garnish the terrine with a couple of bush basil leaves, sprinkle a little sea salt and serve.

SAUTÉED BEANS
WITH BEETROOT

This is all about eating vegetables in an interesting way. I love beetroot, but roasted mushrooms could be a good substitute. The most important thing is to select the freshest vegetables available without worrying about replicating this dish – just use what you have on hand that is fresh.

SERVES 4

INGREDIENTS

16 baby golden beetroots
2 large beetroots
100 ml (3 ½ fl oz) cabernet vinegar
100 gm (3 ½ oz) brown sugar
300 gm (10 oz) green beans
300 gm (10 oz) yellow beans
2 large roma tomatoes
½ bunch tarragon
¼ bunch parsley
2 eschalots cut into brunoise (fine dice)
1 ½ tablespoons baby capers, washed
micro leaves of parsley, celery, shiso (perilla)
    and chard (spinach)

CONFIT OIL FOR BEETROOT

2 cups (500 ml/16 fl oz) extra virgin olive oil
1 cinnamon quill
4 star anise
zest of 1 orange
1 teaspoon fennel seeds
2 cloves garlic, crushed
2 sprigs thyme
2 sprigs rosemary

CONFIT OIL PREPARATION Add all ingredients to the oil in a medium sized pot. Bring oil to a very slow simmer to bubble slightly without frying the aromatic ingredients. Allow the oil to gently bubble for 20 minutes. Remove from the heat and cool. Strain the oil once it is cold and reserve in a bottle with a tight fitting lid.

VEGETABLE PREPARATION Wash the golden beets scrubbing gently with a light brush to remove any dirt. Trim stems leaving 2.5 cm (1 in) of stem. Place into the aromatic confit oil in a small to medium pot. On very low heat (and to one side of the element) cook the beets until soft. Peel the skin and tops when tender and cool enough to handle.

For the larger red beetroots, place in a pot, add cabernet vinegar and brown sugar and cover with water. Bring to the boil then simmer until a knife just eases into and out of the beetroots. Remove from the heat and let the beetroots sit in the liquid to cool. The beetroots will reabsorb any colour lost during cooking. Once cool, use a mandolin to cut 1 cm (½ in) thick slices.

✽ **STONELEIGH PINOT NOIR**
Marlborough, NZ A bright fruit-
driven style loaded with cherry and
red berry fruits.

✽ ✽ **LOST VALLEY CORTESE** Upper
Goulburn, VIC Cortese is best known
as the grape in Gavi, Piedmont. This
version has apple and pear fruit aroma
and a slight earthy palate.

✽ ✽ ✽ **CASCABEL TEMPRANILLO,**
GRACIANO McLaren Vale, SA
A Spanish-styled blend with fruit, spice
and earthy components mingling.

VEGETABLE PREPARATION CONTINUED Then, using a 6 cm (2 ½ in) round cutter, cut 12 pieces from the beetroot slices. Warm half of the beetroot confit oil and marinate the round beetroot pieces for at least 3 hours.

Top and string the beans, trim a 2.5 cm (1 in) tip from the bottom of each bean, and continue to cut the remainder of the beans into ½ cm (¼ in) long pieces. Blanch the bean cubes and the bean tips separately for 1 minute. Refresh both in salted iced water for 1 minute.

Blanch the tomatoes in boiling salted water (10 seconds) until the skins peel. Remove the skin, quarter and de-seed by cutting the inner flesh from the outer flesh. Square up the edges of each quarter's outer flesh and cut into little dice the same size as the beans. Cut the picked tarragon leaves into little squares being careful not to bruise them. Finally, finely cut the parsley (at the last possible moment), and trim and wash the micro leaves in iced water spinning them dry in a salad spinner or colander.

Warm the baby golden beets in a little oil on the stove. Place the capers, beans, tomatoes, cut herbs and eschalots together in a small pan, add the bean tips and gently warm.

Heat a small frying pan, add the beetroot discs and gently fry in a little of the confit oil. Season with sea salt and fresh white pepper. Drain the beetroots on absorbent paper ready for plating.

PRESENTATION Place one beetroot disk on the plate adding a little of the sautéed beans then another beetroot disc and so on with the remainder of the beans and finish with a beetroot disc. Scatter a little of the sautéed beans and the tips around the plate and place four golden beetroot bulbs around the plate. Garnish with micro leaves dressed in a little lemon juice and confit oil.

WINE NOTES

❋ ❋ **SYMPHONIA PINOT GRIGIO King Valley, VIC** Delicious dry wine with subtle apple and pear fruit, spice and minerality. Captures the feel of Italy.

❋ ❋ **LA QUERCE SORRETTOLE CHIANTI CLASSICO Tuscany, Italy** Medium bodied with cherry, raspberry bouquet, characteristic mid-weight savoury palate with drying tannins.

❋ ❋ ❋ **TRIMBACH CUVÉE FRÉDÉRIC EMILE RIESLING Alsace, France** Leading producer of the region, this wine is refined and balances fruit richness with subtle blossoms and spice.

You could nearly mistake this dish for a dessert. Guy Martin, the chef from Grand Véfour in Paris, specialises in desserts made of vegetables like artichoke or fennel. I am not quite brave enough to serve this dish as a dessert, but with a salty fetta I find this tart walks the line perfectly.

Caramelised Tomato, Eschalot and Fetta Tart

WINE NOTES

❀ **NEBBIOLO PIZZINI King Valley, VIC** This nebbiolo is a very good example of this variety; perfumed, floral with cherry scents and long fire tannins.

❀ ❀ **BERNARD MÉTRAT FLEURIE 'LA ROILETTE' VIEILLES VIGNES Beaujolais, France** Gamay with characteristic cherry fruit, however more complex and structured than what you may expect from beaujolais.

❀ ❀ ❀ **MOUNT LANGI GHIRAN SHIRAZ Grampians, VIC** An elegant spicy shiraz which is versatile with food and ages gracefully.

This is an ideal dish for a vegetarian main course and the recipe uses miniature vegetables.

Confit Vegetable Parmentier

This salad contrasts flavours and textures and would go very well with a bowl of pasta. The bitterness of the radicchio is well balanced with the sweetness of the pear. Roquefort, gorgonzola or an Australian blue goat's cheese would also work perfectly with this salad.

Pear and Rocket Salad

WINE NOTES

❀ **TORRESVIÑ ESMARELDA MUSCAT, GEWÜRZTRAMINER, Spain** A fresh grapey wine with floral scents and spice intermingling.

❀ ❀ **FROGMORE CREEK RIESLING, TAS** An organic wine from just outside of Hobart. Fruit driven with gentle lingering acidity in a Germanic style.

❀ ❀ ❀ **KELLEREI KALTERN SÖLL PINOT GRIGIO, Italy** Excellent Northern Italian example with lovely pear and spice texture which plays nicely with the palate with its long acidity.

CONFIT VEGETABLE PARMENTIER

SERVES 4

CONFIT VEGETABLES

12 baby turnips, trimmed and scrubbed
12 baby parsnips, trimmed and peeled
12 baby carrots, trimmed and peeled
12 garlic cloves, peeled
400 ml (14 fl oz) extra virgin olive oil
4 thyme stalks
sea salt
12 cherry tomatoes, from the vine
12 baby zucchini, trimmed, blanched in salted
    water and drained
12 baby leeks, trimmed, blanched in salted
    water and drained
Other Vegetables (Optional): Baby green beans,
    baby beetroot, fresh peas, broad beans,
    sugar snap peas, baby fennel, small radishes,
    eschalots and any other delicate vegetables

FIELD MUSHROOMS

4 jumbo flat field mushrooms
2 garlic cloves, peeled and crushed
2 pinches dried thyme
150 ml (5 oz) olive oil

MOREL MUSHROOMS

12 fresh or soaked dried morels
50 gm (1 ½ oz) butter

POTATO

400 gm (14 oz) of quite firm pomme purée
    (refer | Basics page 307)

FIELD MUSHROOM PREPARATION Preheat oven to 140°C (280°F). Peel and core field mushrooms, place in ovenproof dish and sprinkle with the crushed garlic and thyme. Set aside 2 tablespoons of the olive oil, then drizzle the rest over the mushrooms, crushed garlic and thyme. Roast mushrooms for 30 minutes, then remove from oven and cool.

CONFIT VEGETABLES PREPARATION In a small pot put all the root vegetables that will fit snugly. Add the garlic and the extra virgin olive oil to cover with a few pinches of sea salt and the thyme. Cook on low heat until all the vegetables are tender. This could take 1 hour; it is better to cook them at the lowest heat possible for a long time to develop the flavours and still retain their colour. Add the cherry tomatoes, and the blanched leek and zucchini just before serving to warm them up.

MUSHROOM PREPARATION Sauté the morels and roasted field mushrooms in butter and oil, season with salt and pepper.

PRESENTATION Using an 8 cm (3 ¼ in) diameter ring, fill to about 3 cm (1 in) high with the pommes purée and top with a warm field mushroom. Drain the confit vegetables and morels from the oil and butter and arrange around the plate. Sprinkle with sea salt and serve.

PEAR AND ROCKET SALAD
WITH RADICCHIO AND BLEU DE BRESSE

SERVES 4

SALAD

12 red radicchio leaves, washed, drained
    and ripped
2 handfuls rocket lettuce, picked, washed
    and drained
300 gm (10 oz) Bleu de Bresse cheese, slices
1 Nashi pear, thinly sliced
1 bunch seedless red grapes, washed

TOASTED WALNUTS

80 gm (2 ½ oz) peeled walnuts (see method)

DRESSING

65 ml (2 ¼ fl oz) tarragon vinegar
½ small onion, peeled and grated
1 teaspoon Dijon mustard
1 tablespoon honey
100 ml (3 ½ fl oz) grape seed oil
salt and white milled pepper

TOASTED WALNUT PREPARATION Preheat oven to 150°C (300°F). Blanch the walnuts in a touch of water or milk to soften the skin. Drain and, with a small knife, remove as much as possible of the skin. Dry well, place on a baking tray and toast in the oven until crunchy and golden brown.

DRESSING PREPARATION Place the vinegar, onion, Dijon mustard and honey in a bowl, mix well and slowly incorporate the grape seed oil. Refine the seasoning, chill and reserve.

PRESENTATION Lightly toss the radicchio leaves together with the rocket, then the sliced pear and grapes into the dressing. Build a pile of salad components on four plates, or a flat platter, starting with the radicchio leaves at the base, then the cheese slices, the pear and rocket. Drizzle a fine thread of extra honey over the salad, place a few walnut pieces on top and garnish by sprinkling with the grapes.

In winter there is no better soup than Bathers'
chestnut soup. It is a labour of love and best
prepared on a cold rainy night at home. If you
have a fireplace, it is wonderful to roast the
chestnuts in a heavy cast iron pot.

Bathers' Chestnut Soup

BATHERS' CHESTNUT SOUP
WITH LENTILS, GARLIC AND ESCHALOTS

SERVES 8

INGREDIENTS

750 gm (1 ½ lb) chestnuts
2 tablespoons olive oil
5 eschalots, peeled
3 cloves garlic, peeled
50 gm (1 ½ oz) butter
8 cups chicken stock
sea salt and white milled pepper
100 gm (3 ½ oz) cold diced butter (optional)
1 cup cooked lentils, for garnish

PREPARATION Preheat oven to 200°C (400°F). Score the chestnuts with a paring knife. Start at the base and continue all the way around (be very careful!). Lightly rub with olive oil and place on a baking tray. Roast in oven until the chestnuts start to split open, approximately 5–7 minutes.

Peel the chestnuts while still hot they are much easier to peel while hot. Gloves might also be needed. Roughly slice the roasted chestnuts, eschalots and garlic cloves. In a medium sized pot, melt the butter and gently sweat the eschalots, garlic and chestnuts without colouring. This should take about 8–10 minutes. Add the chicken stock and bring to the simmer. Cook until all ingredients are soft, about 1 hour.

Drain the soup and reserve the cooking liquid. Purée the solids in a blender, adding some cooking liquid a little at a time to achieve a nice smooth consistency. Pass through a coarse strainer to remove any remaining solids. Finally, adjust the seasoning with a little sea salt and white milled pepper.

PRESENTATION When it is time to serve, heat the soup and use a hand blender to froth the soup lightly. I also like to add a little cold butter when I blend the soup but I normally never admit this to my wife and guests! It does make it a richer and more beautiful flavour, albeit with a few more calories.

⚹ ⚹

TOMATO ASPIC
WITH RADISH SALAD

SERVES 8

TOMATO ASPIC

(Allow two days)
550 gm (18 ½ oz) fresh ripe tomatoes, chopped
2 cloves garlic, peeled and finely chopped
½ celery stick
¼ bunch basil, washed and picked
¼ bunch parsley, washed and picked
1 tablespoon chardonnay vinegar
2 cups (500 ml/16 fl oz) tomato juice
1 cup (250 ml/8 fl oz) vegetable stock
12 gelatine leaves, soaked in cold water
salt and milled pepper

RADISH SALAD

16 red radishes, peeled and thinly sliced
   (save the small leaves)
1 daikon, peeled and thinly sliced
8 small whole radishes with the leafy tail left on
30 ml (1 fl oz) Vinaigrette (refer | Basics page 302)

TOMATO ASPIC PREPARATION Combine all of the ingredients (except gelatine) in a blender and pulse for 30 seconds. *Leave this mixture to marinate overnight.*

The following day, strain through a sieve and then through cheesecloth. Measure out the liquid and use 8 gelatine leaves per litre of drained liquid. Soak leaves in water separately to soften, squeeze out excess liquid. Heat 1 cup of tomato liquid and melt the gelatine leaves in the hot liquid. Once the gelatine has completely melted, strain through cheesecloth and pour into the remaining tomato water. Pour the tomato and gelatine mixture into the moulds. Fill to half way and allow to set in the refrigerator. *A minimum of 1 hour is required to set each layer before pouring the next.*

Place the pulp left in the cheesecloth in a blender and process until it is very smooth. Pass through a fine sieve. Measure out 2 cups of this smooth tomato purée, bring it to a simmer and add 4 gelatine leaves (previously soaked in cold water). Strain again and cool to room temperature. Pour a thin layer of this mixture over the first half of the 'just set' jelly and allow this layer to 'just set' also. Add the remaining jelly and fill to the top of the moulds (you might need to warm this slightly if the jelly has set). Set in the refrigerator until ready to serve, 3–4 hours. *The 'just set' principle allows each of the three jelly layers to stick to the other without mixing or separating upon the removal of the mould.*

PRESENTATION Delicately remove the tomato aspic from the moulds (by putting a warm cloth around the mould to slightly melt the aspic) and arrange on plates. Place the whole dressed radishes next to the aspic. Season the radishes and daikon with the vinaigrette and arrange.

My mother used to regularly serve tomato
aspic at home. She added blanched celery
and occasionally some baby prawns which
you could also introduce to this aspic.
Serve this aspic set in a glass or moulded
in ring. A watercress salad with marinated
red onion sliced thinly would work
perfectly as an accompaniment.

Tomato Aspic

WINE NOTES

❊ ❊ **MITCHELL WATERVALE RIESLING**
Clare Valley, SA Try a young release of
this wine with this dish; it has classic lime
and mandarin peel fruits and a long
minerally palate.

❊ ❊ **STAETE LANDT SAUVIGNON**
BLANC Marlborough, NZ A more citrussy
flavoured sauvignon, with some mid-palate
creaminess. A wine often released with
a couple of years bottle age.

❊ ❊ ❊ **EGON MÜLLER**
SCHARZHOFBERGER Riesling Kabinett,
Germany A wine with beautiful fruit
purity and clarity, tasting of floral apples,
blossom and spice.

Chapter Four
❧ RECIPES ❧
from the shore

In Australia, we are fortunate to have one of the best ranges of shellfish in the world – from the humble and sweet blue swimmer; to the spanner, sand and fleshy mud crab; to the mighty, giant king crab. In addition, there are many lobsters, oysters, clams, bugs, scallops, prawns, scampi, mussels, abalone and yabbies.

I especially like to create dishes with marron. This indigenous crustacean, originally from the rivers of West Australia, is now farmed in many places. Try my Poached Tail of West Australian Marron with Parsnip Brandade on page 200 and Bathers' Veal Fillet with Marron Tail and Hollandaise on page 174.

There is something very special about cooking with, and adding shellfish to your menus. While it can sometimes expensive to buy, labour-intensive to work with, and demands a well-developed sense of timing in its cooking, to achieve perfect results – but with a little courage and a precise touch you will develop your skills. It is worth all the effort, for it is the perfect food for our Australian summers and ideal for special occasions.

We are blessed with an abundance of wild seafood, my recommendation would be to enjoy them now, as with time, their supply will diminish and they may become a rare delicacy. I would encourage you to be adventurous with the recipes in this chapter – I hope they give you some news ways with your old favourites, as well as inspire you discover and master some new ingredients and dishes.

Tuna Sashimi

TUNA SASHIMI
WITH STEAMED SCALLOP

This is a very yin and yang dish. The rawness of the tuna balancing the warm steamed scallops is perfect. The black millet vinegar dressing has two elements that, while separating, are still perfect together. Hirimashi kingfish could be a good substitute for the tuna.

SERVES 4

INGREDIENTS
800 gm (1 ½ lb) blue fin tuna loin
2 eschalots, peeled and julienned
1 tablespoon olive oil
sea salt and milled white pepper

FUN-GOR DOUGH
2 ½ cups wheat starch (found in Asian grocery stores)
1 ½ cups tapioca flour
1 ½ teaspoons peanut oil
2 cups boiling water

FUN-GOR FILLING
125 gm (4 oz) scallops, chopped
125 gm (4 oz) mud crab meat, cooked and picked
1 green onion, thinly sliced
a few chives, thinly shaved
8 snow peas, picked, blanched and cut brunoise (fine dice)
salt and white pepper

FUN-GOR FILLING PREPARATION Gently mix the prepared ingredients in a small bowl adding 1 tablespoon of the dressing to this mix. Allow the flavours of the filling components and dressing to develop for at least 20 minutes before steaming the dumplings.

FUN-GOR DOUGH PREPARATION Mix the flours with the oil in a stainless steel bowl. Add the boiling water and incorporate all ingredients well. Turn the bowl over onto a clean bench for 3 minutes, allowing the dough to 'steam' itself and reach the desired consistency.

Knead the dough until it is smooth and then rest it prior to rolling through a pasta roller or with a rolling pin to form thin sheets.

Dust the bench surface with cornflour and cut the pastry into circles 7 cm (2 ¾ in) in diameter. Place a small amount of the filling into the centre of the pastry circles. Join the edges of the pastry together and crimp the edges with a Chinese ravioli (Fun-Gor) maker or by pinching the pastry with the tips of your fingers to enclose the filling. When ready to serve, simply steam the dumplings until they become translucent and are cooked in the centre (firm). Refresh in salted iced water but do not chill completely. Reserve.

❀ **HIDALGO LA GITANA MANZANILLA,** **Spain** Dry sherry either fino or manzanilla is delicious with sashimi. This one has a fresh almond and slightly sea spray character.

❀ ❀ **FRANKLAND ESTATE ISOLATION RIDGE RIESLING Frankland River,** **WA** Leading producer of riesling in this region; in their youth they have a pear, floral and lime freshness.

❀ ❀ ❀ **BILLECART-SALMON ROSÉ** **NV CHAMPAGNE, France** A favourite rosé champagne. Delicate rose coloured, with red berry fruits and rose petals.

DRESSING
2 tablespoons Chinese millet vinegar
1 teaspoon Dijon mustard
1 teaspoon light soy sauce
3 tablespoons virgin olive oil
1 tablespoon sesame oil
salt and milled white pepper

SALAD
2 cups mustard cress or baby cress
½ daikon radish, peeled and cut
   into a fine julienne

DRESSING PREPARATION Mix the vinegar, mustard and soy sauce in a bowl. Using a hand blender or whisk, slowly add the two oils, as you would do for an emulsified vinaigrette. Refine the seasoning with salt and milled white pepper and reserve.

SALAD PREPARATION Mix the julienned radish with the cress and reserve ready to be dressed. Keep salad in the refrigerator until needed.

TUNA PREPARATION Prepare the tuna at the last minute for optimum freshness. Trim any dark flesh and remove the sinew. Cut into ½ cm (¼ in) slices. You will need 5 or so slices per portion. Reserve for plating.

PRESENTATION Steam the Fun-Gor parcels until they become translucent. While steaming the dumplings, deep-fry the eschalots in hot oil until gold and crisp, drain and season, reserve. Place tuna slices aesthetically on the plate and place the steamed Fun-Gor next to the tuna. Dress the salad lightly, and place it near the tuna and serve the remaining dressing over or next to the Fun-Gor. Garnish with the fried eschalots.

WINE NOTES

❀❀ **CHÂTEAU THIEULEY BORDEAUX BLANC, France** A semillon, sauvignon bland blend, lemon and melon aromas, a slight hay character and hint of toasty oak.

❀❀❀ **PETALUMA VIOGNIER Adelaide Hills, SA** A newer wine in the line-up of this great Australian producer, white peach, quince, spice and intense fruit drive.

❀❀❀ **MCWILLIAMS MOUNT PLEASANT SEMILLON Hunter Valley, NSW** Another classic name in the Australian wine industry. Beautiful long living semillon.

This is a classic dish and the simplicity of the presentation makes it a picture of refinement.
This dish is not about big bold flavours; it is about subtlety and harmony.
For an extra edge, cut the lobster raw and let the boiling consommé cook the flesh gently.

Bathers' Lobster Ravioli

✠ ✠ ✠

BATHERS' LOBSTER RAVIOLI
WITH TOMATO AND SHELLFISH CONSOMMÉ

SERVES 8

RAVIOLI

400 gm (14 oz) blue eye cod, de-boned and
  trimmed of all blood and tough skin

1 egg white

½ pinch cayenne pepper and salt

100 ml (3 ½ fl oz) cream

150 ml (5 fl oz) cream, extra, to be whipped

1 cooked lobster tail, cleaned

1 tablespoon shao hsing wine

5 litres (9 pints) water, boiling with a pinch of salt
  and a splash of oil

TOMATO AND LOBSTER BOUILLON

50 ml (1 ½ fl oz) olive oil

1 kg (2 lb) rock lobster bodies, crushed

2 cloves garlic, peeled and diced

1 carrot, peeled and diced

4 eschalots, peeled and diced

2 tablespoons tomato paste

200 ml (7 fl oz) white wine

80 ml (2 ¾ fl oz) brandy

8 cups water

500 gm (1 lb) fresh tomatoes

12 stalks parsley

6 stems thyme

1 bay leaf

10 white peppercorns and fine salt

TOMATO AND LOBSTER BOUILLON PREPARATION Heat the olive oil in a large saucepan and sauté the crushed lobster bodies. When the shells turn red, add all of the vegetables except the tomatoes and sweat them on a low heat for a further 10 minutes. Add the tomato paste and cook stirring rapidly for 5 minutes. Add the white wine and brandy and reduce this liquid by half. Add the water at this stage, and the tomatoes, herbs and peppercorns. Simmer for 2 ½ hours. Strain through a fine sieve or cheesecloth, season with salt and cool. Reserve this mixture in the refrigerator ready to be a part of the consommé recipe.

CONSOMMÉ CLARIFICATION PREPARATION Mix the chicken mince together with the vegetables, herbs and egg whites. Whisk this mixture into the chilled bouillon in a saucepan and heat stirring in the same direction until coagulation has started. Cease stirring at this stage. A raft will form raising the impurities to the surface. Once the raft has formed, slowly simmer for 1 hour. Pass the liquid through a fine cheesecloth and refine the seasoning.

RAVIOLI FILLING PREPARATION Dice the blue eye cod and place in the food processor bowl. Place the bowl in the refrigerator for 20 minutes. Once cold, mince the fish with the egg white and the seasoning until very fine. Then gradually add the 100 ml (3 ½ fl oz) cream while the blade is still moving. Pass this mousse through a fine sieve and refrigerate. In the meantime whip the 150 ml (5 fl oz) cream and keep it cool.

CONSOMMÉ CLARIFICATION

500 gm (1 lb) minced chicken breast
1 medium carrot, peeled and cut into strips
1 medium onion, peeled and cut into strips
1 stick celery, cut into strips
3 tomatoes, roughly chopped
¼ bunch dill
2 egg whites

PASTA DOUGH

550 gm (18 ½ oz) plain flour
5 eggs
20 ml (¾ fl oz) beetroot juice
salt

GARNISH

1 cooked lobster tail,
    cleaned and sliced into medallions
3 tomatoes, peeled, de-seeded
    and finely diced
½ bunch bush basil

RAVIOLI FILLING PREPARATION CONTINUED Cut the lobster tail into small dice and fold through the mousse. Season with the shao hsing wine and extra salt if needed. Fold in the whipped cream and refine seasoning if necessary. Refrigerate.

PASTA DOUGH PREPARATION Blend all the ingredients in a food processor. Remove dough and knead on a flat bench. The pasta dough should be light red in colour and smooth to the touch.

Roll the pasta dough on the lowest setting through a pasta machine or very thin with a rolling pin. Lay the pasta flat on the bench. Cut the dough in half. Place a large tablespoon of the lobster ravioli filling on one sheet of ravioli dough every 5 cm (2 in) with 3 cm (1 in) between. Brush egg wash around the outside of each spoon of filling. Lay the other pasta sheet over and seal well around each filling bundle to ensure no air bubbles. To do this, press the top pasta layer using your palms rather than your fingers. Cut ravioli to a triangular shape using a plain pasta wheel and rest it in the refrigerator for at least 20 minutes before cooking and serving.

PRESENTATION Plunge the ravioli into the boiling salted and lightly oiled water until they float to the top. Drain and place in hot soup bowls with 1 lobster medallion, the diced tomato garnish and the bush basil. Pour the hot consommé in the bowl at the table.

Bathers' Oxtail Gow-Gee

Casserole of Seafood

✤ ✤ ✤

BATHERS' OXTAIL GOW-GEE
WITH SEARED SCALLOPS, SOY AND GINGER SAUCE

There are probably no bolder flavours than this classic dish of the Bathers' Pavilion. It is all about sweetness, richness and contrasting texture. I have always made an oxtail ravioli – when I opened Bathers' I paired it with scallop and it became a defining dish of my menu.

SERVES 8

MAIN INGREDIENTS
3 kg (7 lb) oxtail, cut in pieces
½ cup vegetable oil
6 cups beef stock
48 gow-gee wrappers
   (round Chinese steaming ravioli skin)
egg for egg wash
2 large Idaho potatoes, for deep-fried
   allumettes or matchstick potatoes
1 litres (2 pints) deep-frying oil
salt and milled white pepper
24 scallops, cleaned and trimmed
2 tablespoons butter, for sautéing the scallops

OXTAIL GOW-GEE PREPARATION *The day before serving this recipe the oxtail and sauce preparation begins.* Preheat oven to 180°C (350°F). Sear the oxtail using ½ cup vegetable oil in a very hot cast iron pan; colour all sides. Remove the oxtail and place in a braising tray. In the same pan, sauté ⅔ of the chopped aromatics from the 'Aromatics for Braising and Sauce' until golden. Add these to the oxtail. Pour the beef stock over so that it is just covering the ingredients and cover with a lid or baking paper and cook in a moderate oven until the meat falls off the bone (approximately 2 ½ hours). Drain and cool. When cool enough to handle, shred the meat from the bone, removing any fat and gristle, and place in a bowl.

Reduce the liquid until the flavours are strong and rich and skim frequently to remove any surface fat. Pour enough of this reduction over the shredded meat to moisten and crush the mix between your hands rather than your fingers to refine the texture, cool to room temperature and roll tablespoons of mixture into small balls.

The next day, place into the centre of a gow-gee wrapper, brush around the wrapper with egg wash, place a second wrapper on top and press around to seal tightly. Ensure no air pockets are left. Cut to size with a round pastry cutter to eliminate excess dough.

❊ MAS DE BRESSADES CUVÉE TRADITION, Costièris De
Nîmes, France Grenache blanc and roussane blend, designed
to be drunk young and fresh, enjoying its floral bouquet and
soft texture.

AROMATICS FOR BRAISING AND SAUCE

Note: Utilise ⅔ of the following ingredients for the
    braising and ⅓ for the sauce reduction.

100 gm (3 ½ oz) galangal, peeled
    and roughly sliced

75 gm (2 ½ oz) ginger, peeled
    and roughly sliced

1 large onion, peeled and roughly sliced

1 large head garlic, cloves peeled and chopped

2 red chillies, de-seeded and sliced

2 sticks lemongrass, thinly sliced

SOY AND GINGER SAUCE

75 ml (2 ½ fl oz) red wine vinegar

40 ml (1 ½ fl oz) soy sauce

40 ml (1 ½ oz) kecap manis

75 ml (2 ½ fl oz) braising stock of the oxtail

40 ml (1 ½ oz) chicken stock

150 gm (5 oz) unsalted butter

1 lime, juiced, to finish the sauce

+ ⅓ of the aromatic ingredients from
    the 'Aromatics for Braising and Sauce'
    ingredients list left.

SAUCE PREPARATION Bring all the ingredients to the boil (except the butter), including the ⅓ of
aromatics ingredients. Cover with a tight lid or foil *and leave to infuse overnight.*

The next day, strain, then do the following steps. Place 100 ml (3 ½ fl oz) of the liquid in a saucepan,
heat until it boils. Gradually whisk in diced cold butter, a little at a time, until it thickens and looks
creamy. Refine the seasoning with a little lime juice. Place in a warm area while you prepare the rest
of the dish for serving.

PRESENTATION Cut potatoes into matchstick sized pieces and reserve in cold water. Strain and pat dry
to deep-fry. Deep-fry matchstick potatoes until golden and crisp, 3–5 minutes. Drain on kitchen paper
and season. Drop gow-gees into a pot of boiling water. Place scallops into a hot pan with the butter,
season and turn when golden 1–2 minutes. Drain on kitchen paper when ready.

Scoop the floating gow-gees (when they float they are ready) out and place onto serving plates with the
scallops and matchstick potatoes. Finish the dish with the reserved soy ginger sauce by frothing with a
hand blender for a light texture and beautiful finish. Serve hot.

✦ ✦

CASSEROLE OF SEAFOOD
WITH TURMERIC AND CHILLI

This is such an easy dish to cook once you have selected a good range of seafood. The secret is in the sauce, which most people adore. It is a swanky version of steamed mussels and would work equally well with mussels alone if you prefer them to a selection of seafood.

SERVES 4

SEAFOOD

8 x large fresh green prawns or Yamba prawns if in season, peeled, shells reserved

8 live yabbies, iced and cut in half, washed and cleaned

500 gm (1 lb) mussels, scrubbed, beard removed

500 gm (1 lb) pippies, washed

250 gm (8 oz) fresh calamari or squid cut into squares

8 scallops, cleaned and trimmed

2 cups Turmeric Soup (see recipe over)

PASTE FOR THE TURMERIC SOUP

1 teaspoon shrimp paste

2 fresh turmeric roots

1 tablespoon turmeric powder

1 knob ginger

1 knob galangal

3 cloves garlic

1 stalk lemongrass

4 lime leaves

2 small chillies

2 coriander roots

(you could substitute coriander leaves for the green onion in the pot)

vegetable oil to assist the purée process

TUMERIC SOUP PASTE PREPARATION Place all ingredients in a food processor and purée until a smooth consistency is reached.

TURMERIC SOUP PREPARATION Preheat oven to 190°C (375°F). Roast lobster and prawn shells in a roasting tray until nice and red. Heat a heavy-based pot and add Turmeric Soup Paste, cook until it caramelises (scraping it off the bottom with a spoon if necessary). Deglaze the pot with shao hsing wine, add tamarind paste, palm sugar, fish sauce, coconut cream, saffron threads and stock. Add shells and simmer for 45 minutes or until you achieve a creamy soup consistency. Take off the heat, strain and skim. Check the seasoning and add the lime juice to achieve a sweet and sour flavour. Reserve and keep warm.

❋ ❋ CAVE DE TURCKHEIM RÉSERVE PINOT GRIS Alsace, France A rich pinot gris with honeyed, spiced fruits and a generous mouth feel.

❋ ❋ SCORPO PINOT GRIS Mornington Peninsular, VIC One of the newer producers to the region producing some excellent wine. This wine is modelled on the style of Alsace.

❋ ❋ ❋ DOMAINE COURBIS ST JOSEPH Rhône Valley, France Marsanne, Coussanne blend. Pale lemon in colour with a stone fruit palate and inner ginger and cinnamon spice core.

TURMERIC SOUP

2 lobster bodies (crushed shells)
prawn shells from Seafood ingredients list
all of the 'Paste for the Turmeric Soup'
½ cup shao hsing wine
½ cup tamarind paste
2 tablespoons palm sugar
2 tablespoons fish sauce
1 tin (or 2 cups) of coconut cream
1 teaspoon saffron threads
1 litre (32 fl oz) chicken or vegetable stock
2 limes, juiced

VEGETABLES

clarified butter
2 garlic cloves, cut into brunoise (fine dice)
3 eschalots, cut into brunoise
1 cup shao hsing wine
2 cups bean sprouts, tips picked
1 red chilli, cut julienne
4 green onions (green part), cut julienne

VEGETABLE AND SEAFOOD PREPARATION This is best made in cast iron pot that can be served at the table. Heat the pot or pots so they are extremely hot. Add a touch of clarified butter and sauté your prawn and yabbies to give them colour without fully cooking them, remove and add the brunoise of garlic and eschalots. Sauté briefly and then add the mussels, pippies and shao hsing wine. Place a lid on top and cook for one minute or until the mussels open. Add the soup to the pot, bring to the simmer and add the seasoned calamari, scallops, prawns and yabbies. Cover and cook for one minute on high heat to steam the seafood.

PRESENTATION Top with the bean sprouts, chilli and green onion or coriander tossed with lime juice and olive oil. Serve in the covered pot to the table then remove the lid to reveal the beautiful flavours to your guests.

Pan Seared Rouget

Bathers' Moreton Bay Bug

✦ ✦ ✦

PAN SEARED ROUGET
WITH SQUID INK LASAGNE

Rouget is revered in Europe. We are blessed with a good supply in Australia and should rightly take advantage of this delicate but versatile fish.

SERVES 8

8 x 80 gm (3 oz) rouget fillets, cleaned,
   trimmed and pin boned

SHELLFISH BISQUE

BISQUE PASTE INGREDIENTS

2 dry chillies, de-seeded and tops removed
1 stick lemongrass, bruised and roughly chopped
1 teaspoon fresh grated turmeric
3 eschalots, peeled and finely chopped
3 cloves garlic, peeled and finely chopped
½ teaspoon white peppercorns, cracked
1 tablespoon gapi (roasted shrimp paste,
   re-cooked in a baking paper packet for
   5 minutes in the oven)

BISQUE INGREDIENTS

1 tablespoon peanut oil
2 lobster bodies, cleaned
6 prawn heads, cleaned and washed
100 ml (3 ½ fl oz) tamarind paste, diluted
   in ¼ cup water
1 tablespoon fish sauce
1 tablespoon palm sugar
200 ml (7 fl oz) fish stock
100 ml (3 ½ fl oz) coconut milk

SHELLFISH BISQUE PREPARATION Grind all of the paste ingredients using a mortar and pestle. Fry the paste in the peanut oil, add the lobster bodies, prawn heads and moisten with the tamarind water, fish sauce, palm sugar and fish stock. Cook for 20 minutes on low simmer then add the coconut milk and cook for another 10 minutes. Blend and pass through a fine sieve. Dilute with a little fish stock if necessary if it becomes too thick.

LASAGNE PASTA PREPARATION Place the flour on a clean surface and make a well in the centre, pour the broken egg and the yolks in the middle, add the squid ink and the seasoning. Bring all of the flour into the centre of the well to form a ball of pasta and knead for 10 minutes until the dough is perfectly smooth, wrap the pasta in plastic wrap and allow the dough to rest for at least 1 hour. Divide the pasta into four pieces. Using a pasta machine, roll the pasta into sheets that will fit into the pot you use, then place them onto a floured tray to dry for about 15 minutes. When dried, blanch them in plenty of boiling, salted water. Place the pasta sheets into ice water to quickly refresh them, lay the pasta sheets on a board and pat them dry with absorbent paper.

❀ **MAS CARLOT ROSÉ** Languedoc, **France** Juicy Grenache shiraz blend. Red berry fruits, rose petals and slight butter finish.

❀ ❀ **PALA CRABILIS VERMENTINO** **Sardinia, Italy** Delicious Mediterranean wine with tropical fruit flavour. Enjoy as a young wine.

❀ ❀ ❀ **BANNOCKBURN SAIGNÉE** **Geelong, VIC** This savoury rosé made with pinot noir has a cherry and Provence herb palate. Excellent food wine.

SQUID INK LASAGNE
200 gm (7 oz) plain flour, sifted
1 egg
3 egg yolks
40 gm (1 ½ oz) squid ink, purchased in tube
1 teaspoon fine salt

EGGPLANT
2 tablespoons peanut oil
1 eschalot, peeled, finely diced
1 medium eggplant, diced
1 tomato, peeled, de-seeded and diced
½ lime, juiced
1 tablespoon chopped coriander leaves

SQUID SALAD AND ZUCCHINI
40 gm (1 ½ oz) poached squid, julienne
40 gm (1 ½ oz) tomato, peeled and
    cut into large dice
1 tablespoon chopped basil
lemon juice
olive oil
40 gm (1 ½ oz) zucchini, julienne

CHILLI JAM
(refer | Basics page 304)

LASAGNE PASTA PREPARATION CONTINUED Cut the pasta so that you have two squares per portion, spread the chilli jam onto eight squares and place another square on top to form the lasagne, set aside to be steamed later.

EGGPLANT PREPARATION In a frying pan heat the peanut oil and fry the eschalot and eggplant until golden. Add the tomato and lime juice, finish with the coriander leaves and some chilli jam.

SQUID SALAD PREPARATION Mix the julienne of squid, tomato dice and basil into a salad, adding a little lemon juice and olive oil.

PRESENTATION Heat a pan with a little oil. Season the rouget and pan fry skin side down first, holding the fish with a spatula to prevent it curling. Turn over and cook for a few seconds. Remove from the heat and allow the fish to 'carry over cook' in a warm area while you prepare the other components of the dish. Place the lasagne squares in the steamer with the squid and the zucchini julienne to the side, steam briefly. Place a spoonful of the eggplant mixture in the centre of the warm plates and sandwich some eggplant between the pasta sheet and zucchini. Set the fish on top. Finish with the squid salad and pour bisque over generously.

✤ ✤

BATHERS' MORETON BAY BUG
WITH CARAMELISED PORK AND ASIAN MUSHROOMS

What is not to like about these ingredients? It is an easy match tied together with a delicious master stock and with textures that complement each other perfectly. There is serious work in preparing the pork, but make more than you need and keep it for a meal on its own.

SERVES 4

PORK BELLY

1 kg pork belly
2 litres (4 pints) Asian Master Stock
 (refer | Basics page 298)

PORK CONSOMMÉ

1 carrot, cut into brunoise (fine dice)
1 stick of celery, cut into brunoise
½ leek, whites only, cut into brunoise
1 clove garlic, cut into brunoise
3 eschalots, cut into brunoise
5 egg whites
125 gm (4 oz) chicken mince
sea salt and milled pepper
liquid from braising the pork belly

BRAISED PORK BELLY PREPARATION Preheat oven to 150°C (300°F). You will need a braising pan big enough to fit the pork belly in as a whole or you may need to break the pork belly down a little. When you have made the Asian Master Stock, pour it over the pork belly, cover with a lid and braise the belly in the oven for 2–3 hours checking it regularly and checking for tenderness. Once the belly has achieved a level of tenderness similar to braised lamb shanks, cool.

Loosely line a tray with plastic and lay the belly skin side down covering with more plastic on top. Place another tray which fits inside the pork belly tray on top and, with a friend to help you, press the top tray down on the belly pushing as hard as you can then wrap with masking tape 3–4 times across the tray. Weights are also a good idea if you can't get a good enough grip. When the belly is cold, cut four, 3 cm x 5 cm (1 in x 2 in) rectangles, and keep to one side.

PORK CONSOMMÉ PREPARATION Combine all the vegetables, egg whites and mince. Season with sea salt and milled pepper. (This is called a clarification and will clear the impurities from the stock.) Place the braising liquid from the pork belly into a pot and vigorously stir in the mince mixture. Bring it slowly to the boil then simmer for 20 minutes. Once clear liquid appears, let it settle for 30 minutes to the side of the stove. Then, scoop a little hole in the raft, remove the consommé with a ladle and strain it through muslin cloth. Keep warm.

❀ ❀ **SPRING VALE PINOT MEUNIER**
East Coast, TAS A light simple juice wine, oozing with
red cherries and plums.

❀ ❀ **CLOS DES PAULILLES COLLIOURE**
ROSÉ Roussillon, France A rosé that packs a punch. Flavours of dark berries and spice, melon and concentrated Grenache, shiraz blend.

❀ ❀ ❀ **JOSMEYER 'LE FOLASTRIES'**
GEWÜRZTRAMINER Alsace, France
Intense, richly perfumed nose, concentrated Turkish delight, spice and lychee palate, spicy long finish.

MUSHROOMS AND VEGETABLE
1 punnet shiitake
1 punnet shimeji
1 punnet white fungus
1 punnet black fungus
1 punnet enoki
2 bunches broccolini, trimmed at the base
salt and pepper

MORETON BAY BUG
2 bug tails trimmed and de-veined
100 gm (3 ½ oz) soft butter
2 limes

MUSHROOM AND VEGETABLE PREPARATION Trim tails of all mushrooms except enoki and cut into quarters or similar size. For the enoki, just pull them apart loosening the top of the bunch a little and showing the nice looking 'trumpets' on the end. Keep the tails intact as this will keep them neat during cooking. Cut broccolini into lengths that will fit on the plate. Remove the little leaves as they are bitter and will overcook. You will need two pieces per serve.

FINAL COOKING Preheat oven to 100°C (200°F). Heat up a cast iron pan with a little olive oil and cook the pork belly rectangles until they are golden brown. Keep warm in the oven. Heat another pan until hot, add olive oil and place the bug tails (brushed with soft butter) in the pan, cooking until they are golden brown. Season with salt and keep warm.

In another saucepan and at the same time as cooking the bugs, cook the broccolini and the enoki mushrooms (separately) in boiling salted water for 1 minute. Sauté all the mushrooms in a hot pan with a little olive oil finishing with 1 tablespoon of soft butter and fresh pepper and salt.

PRESENTATION Place the pork belly in the centre of warm serving plates. Place the mushrooms and broccolini around. Trim the tail of the enoki, place them on the plate. Carve the bug tails down the middle removing the insides, season with fresh lime juice and salt. Place the bug tails on top, pour over some pork consommé and serve.

CRAB AND PICKED MUSHROOM SALAD
WITH ASIAN NOODLES

Freshly picked crab is a treat so share the work of cracking and cleaning the crab with friends before a meal. However, if you're not a fan of cracking the shell and wearing a bib then you can purchase some beautiful picked crab. The slippery texture of the mushrooms with the noodles combines perfectly with the crab in this recipe.

SERVES 8

CRAB AND GARNISH
500 gm (1 lb) crab meat
1 English cucumber, peeled, de-seeded and
   cut into julienne
¼ cup mint, cut in julienne

THE ASIAN MUSHROOMS
1 punnet black fungus, sliced
1 punnet oyster mushrooms, picked
1 punnet shiitake mushrooms, cut into quarters
1 punnet shimeji mushrooms (or chestnut
   mushrooms), cut into halves
800 ml (28 fl oz) Asian Master Stock (refer | Basics
   page 298)

NOODLE DRESSING
2 limes, juiced
80 ml (2 ¾ fl oz) peanut oil
salt and pepper

NOODLES
250 gm (8 oz) dried Chinese yellow
   (or thin Japanese) noodles
1 tablespoon peanut oil
1 pinch salt

MUSHROOM PREPARATION Bring the Master Stock to the boil, drop all the mushrooms in the stock and simmer for 2–3 minutes. Cool in the liquid, drain the mushrooms, strain the stock through a fine sieve and reserve.

NOODLE PREPARATION Bring a large pot of salted water to the boil with the peanut oil. Drop the noodles into the boiling water and simmer for 2 minutes. Refresh in salted iced water, drain. Toss noodles in the Dressing before serving.

PRESENTATION Pour a small ladle of mushroom Master Stock in the bottom of each serving bowl. Next, scatter the drained mushrooms in the bottom of each bowl. Mix the noodles, crab meat and half the cucumber and place on top of the mushrooms. Top this with a fine julienne of any remaining cucumber and mint to garnish.

WINE NOTES

❀ **DE IULIIS VERDELHO Hunter Valley, NSW** A fruity wine to be enjoyed in the summer months, with tropical fruit and citrus freshness.

❀ ❀ **HUIA GEWÜRZTRAMINER Marlborough, NZ** Perfumed wine showing lychee and rosewater character, fruit driven, spicy palate.

❀ ❀ ❀ **POL ROGER NV, France** More-ish champagne with its blend of white stone fruit, citrus and lightly creamy mousse.

Chapter Five
❧ Summer Picnic ❧
MENU

Bathers' Oysters with Cucumber Shots
Lemongrass Thai Style Pork Sticks
Marinated Saffron Chicken Brochettes
Marinated Goat's Cheese with Summer Vegetables
Bathers' Leek Tartlet
Glass Noodle Salad in Asian Box
Bathers' Lamb Rissoles with Couscous and Stone Fruit Salad
Barbecue Trout Bundles with Prosciutto and Button Mushrooms
Barbecue Prawns with Lime Butter
Homemade Lemonade
Bathers' Duck Confit and Potato Terrine
Blueberry Vanilla Tart

WE ALL LOVE A BARBECUE — it is probably one of the favourite ways of eating in Australia. The barbecue is a great leveller — a way to share food and cooking with friends and strangers alike. In a world of near gender equality, the barbecue seems to stand as the last male bastion, defended and preserved by all true-blue males. I actually shy away from wrestling the tongs from any so-called experts for fear of getting shoved aside not so gently. People always seem happy for me to step in and help prepare a dinner or provide guidance but I am never asked my culinary opinion when it comes to a barbecue. There is a great difference between a barbecue and a picnic. In most cases the level of grilling at a picnic is limited if non-existent. The picnic is a portable gourmet meal and it is all about enjoying the environment one finds oneself in — from picnics in the mountains to a relaxed meal in a park or near the beach.

To me, a picnic is all about celebrating the produce of the season — fresh fruit, tasty salads, fresh seafood, flavoursome terrines, exotic spiced dishes, great bread and yummy desserts. You can dress a picnic up or down; you can have a great range of dishes or you could focus on very few. You can serve only cold food or you can fire up that barbecue and challenge an expert!

WINE NOTES

❋❋❋ **JACQUESSON CUVÉE NV, Champagne, France** One of the smaller champagne houses which is located in Dizy. Their non-vintage has a cuvée number each year making it easier to determine how old the bottle is. A classy drink with citrus and berry flavours, fine creamy mousse.

❋ **KAESLER OLD VINE SEMILLON, Barossa Valley, SA** From a vineyard established over 100 years ago, this wine is great for a picnic. Light, fresh with lemony beeswax and honeysuckle palate. Lovely texture and length.

❋❋ **WELLINGTON PINOT GRIGIO, Cambridge, TAS** This wine reminds me of the style of the Veneto in Northern Italy. Crisp with pear and whole stonefruit, honeysuckle and almond. Great for seafood and vegetable dishes.

❋❋ **BETHANY GRENACHE, Barossa Valley, SA** Delicious Grenache made from old vines in the Barossa Valley. Black fruits and spice, juicy without being overly sweet. Keep in the esky to enjoy at 'cellar' temperature.

❋ **DIAMOND VALLEY Blue Label Pinot Noir, Yarra Valley, VIC** Diamond Valley is one of the best producers of pinot noir in the Yarra Valley. This entry level wine in their portfolio is reliably good with black cherry, pinot fragrance and spice. Perfect for a picnic and can handle chilling on a hot day.

❋❋ **BOROLI MOSCATO D'ASTI, Piedmonte, Italy** A light, refreshing sweet wine which can be just as delightful as an aperitif as it can with dessert. Is slightly spritzy and tastes of blossom, passionfruit, apricots and tropical fruits. Try with fresh summer fruit.

BATHERS' OYSTERS
WITH CUCUMBER SHOTS

Little shooters are always a fun addition to a light meal. Combined with oysters, this shooter offers more substance and certainly a more punchy taste. These could be made with a tomato and celery jelly or with lime and cucumber or just serve your oyster plain with lime and cracked pepper.

SERVES 8

INGREDIENTS
16 Sydney rock oysters, freshly shucked
2 limes, cut in wedges

CUCUMBER SHOTS
8 shot glasses
1 English cucumber peeled (¼ diced in a brunoise (fine dice), the rest juiced
60 ml (2 fl oz) vodka
zest of 1 lime
20 ml (½ fl oz) sugar syrup (refer | Basics page 309)
2 sheets gelatine, soaked in cold water and squeezed of excess water
160 ml (5 ½ fl oz) cucumber juice (from the cucumber above)

PREPARATION Put a small quantity of diced cucumber in each shot glass and set aside. Heat up the vodka, lime zest and the sugar syrup and dissolve the gelatine sheets in this warm syrup. Cool this to room temperature, add the cucumber juice and strain into a clean bowl. Set the bowl on an ice bath and gently mix until the cucumber jelly starts to set. Fill each shot glass, the jelly should still be liquid enough to let the cucumber float to the top. If you do not chill this the mixture on the ice bath, the vodka and cucumber juice will separate. Set in the refrigerator, covered, for 4 hours.

PRESENTATION Set the cucumber shot on a tray out of the cooler just before serving. Have the shots near the oysters and ensure you have plenty of lime wedges available and a pepper mill. Present with a small spoon so your guests can refresh themselves with their cucumber vodka jelly.

Bathers' Oysters

Try to use local oysters if you are at the beach or near a river mouth where most oysters are grown. The name of these can be so evocative, Nambucca Heads, Wallis Lake, Hawkesbury River, Port Stephens, Streaky Bay, Moreton Island, Coffin Bay or many others. Their freshness will certainly be ensured and you will support their local oyster farmers.

Lemongrass Thai Style Pork Sticks
Marinated Saffron Chicken Brochettes

LEMONGRASS THAI STYLE PORK STICKS

This is a pretty and flavoursome way of serving mince patties. There are so many herb and spice flavours interplaying here that it makes for a very different offering at a picnic. The ginger overlays the turmeric and then the coriander kicks in balancing the pungent cumin.

SERVES 4

PORK STICKS
250 gm (8 oz) pork fillet (tenderloin)
8 sticks lemongrass
½ teaspoon ground turmeric
½ teaspoon ground coriander
½ teaspoon ground cumin
2 tablespoons dry chillies, de-seeded and soaked
1 tablespoon dried shrimps, soaked
1 tablespoon peeled and chopped garlic
1 tablespoon peeled and chopped ginger
¼ bunch coriander, picked and chopped
½ teaspoon sugar
salt and white milled pepper

SAUCE FOR DIPPING
2 tablespoons palm sugar
¼ pineapple, peeled and cut into small dice
1 tablespoon tamarind concentrate
1 lime leaf, shredded
1 stick lemongrass, peeled and finely diced
3 limes, juiced
1 tablespoon fish sauce
100 ml (3 ½ fl oz) water

PORK STICK PREPARATION Mince the pork and refrigerate. Peel the first layers of lemongrass and cut a slant at one end. Soak in water for 20 minutes only.

In a mortar and pestle, pound the remaining ingredients into a paste and add to the minced pork. Mould portions of the mince mixture around the end of each piece of lemongrass. Refrigerate until required.

Cook the pork sticks in a non-stick pan in a little oil or cook them on the barbecue.

DIPPING SAUCE PREPARATION Heat a shallow pot, add the palm sugar and a few drops of water when the sugar starts to caramelise lightly. Add the pineapple and allow it to cook for 30 seconds to 1 minute.

Add the tamarind, lime leaf and chopped lemongrass and then the lime juice, fish sauce and water. Simmer for 5 minutes until the flavours combine and the mixture is aromatic. Cool and strain. Best to serve the sauce at room temperature.

PRESENTATION Serve the pork sticks on a platter or on banana leaves with the dipping sauce close by.

MARINATED SAFFRON CHICKEN BROCHETTES

These days you are able to purchase chicken tenderloin fillets, which are ideal for this dish, otherwise you can easily cut some chicken from a breast. The saffron in this recipe is quite distinct but it is balanced superbly with the cucumber and yoghurt.

SERVES 4

INGREDIENTS

4 chicken tenderloins or 1 chicken breast
   cut in slices
4 small bamboo skewers (soaked in water)
1 teaspoon saffron threads
½ teaspoon saffron powder
½ teaspoon ground cumin
½ teaspoon peeled and finely chopped ginger
½ cup grated onion
1 cup yoghurt

CUCUMBER RAITA

½ English cucumber, peeled, de-seeded
   and grated
1 teaspoon cumin seeds, roasted in a dry pan
1 teaspoon sugar
1 tablespoon chopped coriander
1 tablespoon chopped mint
1 cup yoghurt

CHICKEN PREPARATION Remove any membrane from the tenderloins, slice lengthways in half and thread onto the soaked skewers. Trim the chicken 'square' on the skewers, it will allow for even cooking.

Mix the saffron, cumin, ginger and onion with the yoghurt and dip the chicken in it. Marinate the chicken for 2 to 3 hours before grilling over a low flame, don't forget to season. Cooking on the barbecue is amazing for that smoky flavour!

CUCUMBER RAITA PREPARATION Simply combine all of the ingredients and allow them to mature for 1 hour before serving. You could serve these brochettes with the pork sticks on the same platter with their respective dressings separate.

Goat's cheese is unlike any other cheese due to its low fat content. It is an ideal cheese for a picnic as it retains its texture even if not chilled. You could grill a slice of sourdough bread, spread it with goat's cheese and serve a few roasted vegetables and it becomes a great tartine.

Marinated Goat's Cheese

Bathers' Leek Tartlet

✤

MARINATED GOAT'S CHEESE
WITH SUMMER VEGETABLES

SERVES 8

INGREDIENTS
approximately 400 gm (13 oz)
marinated goat's cheese
1 sourdough loaf, freshly baked, thickly sliced.

VEGETABLE SALAD
8 cherry tomatoes, roasted
8 baby carrots, peeled and cooked
8 baby peas, blanched and partly husked
8 baby zucchini, blanched
8 baby field mushrooms, roasted
8 baby fennel, washed, trimmed and confit
100 ml (3 ½ fl oz) extra virgin olive oil
1 lemon, zested and juiced
¼ garlic clove, peeled and finely grated
3 sprigs thyme, picked
sea salt and freshly ground black pepper

PREPARATION Marinate all of the vegetables with the olive oil, lemon zest and juice, garlic, half of the thyme leaves the salt and pepper. Allow to sit at room temperature for 10 minutes. Toast the sourdough bread slices and place them in the centre of a plate. Top the sourdough with the prepared vegetables and goat's cheese. Drizzle a little of the marinade over and around the toast, season the top with the black milled pepper, sea salt and garnish with the rest of the picked thyme leaves. Serve at room temperature.

✠ ✠
BATHERS' LEEK TARTLET

SERVES 8

SHORT CRUST PASTRY AND FILLING
250 gm (8 oz) butter, diced
550 gm (18 ½ oz) flour
1 teaspoon salt
110 ml (3 ⅓ fl/oz) water
2 leeks, washed and sliced, white and light green
    part only, sautéed in clarified butter
100 gm (4 oz) Gruyère or Gouda cheese, cut
    into tiny cubes

QUICHE MIXTURE
3 eggs
200 ml (7 fl oz) milk
120 ml (4 fl oz) cream
2–3 pinches salt
1 pinch paprika
3 tablespoons roughly chopped Italian parsley
½ cup Parmesan, finely grated
2 tablespoons picked thyme
1 pinch ground white pepper

PASTRY PREPARATION Preheat the oven to 170°C (330°F). Place the butter, flour and salt into a food processor and pulse until the mixture resembles breadcrumbs. Add the water and pulse further until the pastry has become a ball. Remove the pastry and knead the mixture on a floured bench until it is smooth. Wrap in plastic wrap and rest in the refrigerator for 1 hour.

After chilling, roll the pastry to 3 mm (⅛ in) thick and fill eight quiche shells or one large quiche form with pastry, avoid cutting the pastry and allow a little excess to overhang. Fill the pastry shells with baking weights and blind bake the short crust pastry until almost fully cooked, approximately 15 minutes.

FILLING PREPARATION Whisk the quiche mixture together, season well and allow to sit for 10 minutes.

Add the leek and cheese to the base of each pastry shell and pour the quiche mixture over the top. Bake until set and golden, approximately 20 minutes, still at the same oven temperature as used for the shell.

The beauty of these little boxes is the content
can be changed at will or you could add
a topping like a grilled piece of beef thinly sliced
or chicken seasoned with a touch of chilli, salt
and lime juice. I love this salad also with cashew
nuts instead of meat or with some prepared
kimchi, the Korean pickled spiced cabbage.

Glass Noodle Salad in Asian box

To me, these are the flavours of a picnic – lamb, mint and garlic. These little rissoles can be cooked ahead of time or just done on the barbecue plate. Use whatever fruit is in season but I like to use yellow nectarines, plums, tomato or, simply, cut pomegranate.

Bathers' Lamb Rissoles

✢ ✢
GLASS NOODLE SALAD
IN ASIAN BOX

SERVES 8

SALAD

500 gm (1 lb) vermicelli noodles pre-soaked in hot
    water until they are just translucent
½ cup bean sprouts, picked
½ cup shredded Chinese cabbage
½ carrot, peeled and shredded
½ bunch coriander leaves, picked
¼ bunch basil (Thai or Italian) leaves, picked
¼ bunch mint leaves, picked
1 chilli, chopped
1 English cucumber, peeled and sliced lengthways
½ bunch Chinese chives or garlic chives

DRESSING

2 limes, juiced
1 teaspoon sugar
2 tablespoons fish sauce
1 teaspoon sesame oil
1 small clove garlic, peeled and bruised
3 tablespoons peanut oil
1 teaspoon black sesame seeds
milled black pepper

DRESSING PREPARATION Combine all of the ingredients, allowing the flavours to infuse overnight, then remove the garlic the following day and season well.

SALAD PREPARATION Ideally you should have all the salad ingredients prepared but stored in separate, sealed containers and kept cold. Toss the salad ingredients (except the chives and cucumber) with the dressing.

PRESENTATION Curl a piece of sliced cucumber in a corner of the box, add the salad loosely, spike the chives behind the cucumber and dress with any remaining dressing.

BARBECUE TROUT BUNDLES
WITH PROSCIUTTO AND BUTTON MUSHROOMS

SERVES 6

INGREDIENTS
12 fillets fresh water trout
sea salt and milled white pepper
12 thin slices prosciutto, trimmed of rind
500 gm (1 lb) medium button mushrooms,
    thinly sliced
twine, for tying
baking paper
2 tablespoons butter
2 tablespoons oil

PREPARATION Rinse the fillets in water, and trim any excess from the fillet edges. Lay each fillet skin-side down on a cutting board. Season each fillet with the sea salt and milled white pepper. Lay one slice of prosciutto onto each fillet. Shingle the sliced mushrooms over each fillet and press 2 fillets together. Wrap in plastic wrap tightly and refrigerate for at least 1 hour.

Tie the fillets together with the baking paper and twine. The baking paper stops the string from burning and breaking during the cooking process. Pan sear the trout bundles in a pan on top of the barbecue in the oil and butter .

BATHERS' LAMB RISSOLES
WITH COUSCOUS AND STONE FRUIT SALAD

SERVES 8

LAMB RISSOLES

1 cup couscous
500 gm (1 lb) lamb mince
½ bunch mint, rinsed, picked and chopped
1 white onion, grated
½ cup roughly chopped raw almonds
2 eggs
salt and black milled pepper
oil

MINT AND COUSCOUS TOPPING

1 cup rehydrated couscous remaining from
  the rissoles
2 tablespoons chopped mint
1 tablespoon dried oregano
1 tablespoon dried thyme
1 tablespoon dried mixed herbs
milled black pepper

STONE FRUIT SALAD

3 pieces of stone fruit, such as nectarines
  or peaches
½ cup sugar syrup (refer | Basics page 309)
2 limes, juiced
1 bunch mint

LAMB RISSOLE PREPARATION Soak 1 cup of dried couscous and this will yield the 2 cups you need altogether for the crumble topping and for the lamb rissoles. Combine 1 cup of the couscous with all the other rissole ingredients and mix with a wooden spoon until it becomes a homogenous mass. Pinch off portions of the mixture and mould into small rissoles with wet hands. Preheat oven to 180°C (350°F).

In an oiled baking tray at home, place the rissoles well spaced apart and top with mint and the couscous topping. Drizzle a lit bit of oil on top and bake in the oven until brown, about 20 minutes. Cool and pack in a container.

MINT AND COUSCOUS TOPPING PREPARATION In a bowl, combine the remaining 1 cup couscous and all other ingredients and mix well into a loose crumble topping, as you would for an apple crumble. Reserve for use during the rissole cooking process.

STONE FRUIT SALAD PREPARATION AND PRESENTATION Just before serving the rissoles, cut the stone fruit into wedges. Mix the sugar syrup with the lime juice. Drizzle the syrup over the stone fruit and serve with loose fresh mint. Serve the rissoles with the stone fruit salad and mint to the side.

This recipe is a good alternative to smoked
salmon if you'd like something more substantial.
You could pre-cook this or cook it on a wood
fire if you are able to light one. The prosciutto
could be substituted with spinach. Fennel is
a nice side vegetable to serve with the trout.

Barbecue Trout Bundles

✤

BARBECUE PRAWNS
WITH LIME BUTTER

I cannot think of a better marriage of flavours than prawns and lime. Once, at Le Bernadin in New York, I was served superb prawns with a light chive cream sauce – a dish I always remember. For a picnic or barbeque, I prefer to use my classic lime butter, the tang is perfect for the prawns.

SERVES 8

PRAWNS
16 medium sized raw/green Banana prawns
2 tablespoons vegetable oil

LIME BUTTER
250 gm (8 oz) unsalted butter, softened
4 limes, rinsed, zested and juiced
sea salt
milled white pepper

PRAWN PREPARATION Preheat the barbecue to medium heat or flame. Remove the head of each prawn. With a sharp pair of scissors snip the legs off all the prawns. Lay the prawns on one side and with a very sharp serrated knife cut the prawn into a butter-flied fashion by cutting the back of the prawn open towards the belly, without cutting through. Remove the vein and rinse quickly in a bowl of lightly salted water. Press them down so they are flat and remain fairly flat for the grilling.

LIME BUTTER PREPARATION Place all ingredients, except the lime juice, in a small bowl and crush with the back of a wooden spoon, add the lime juice and leave at room temperature covered with plastic wrap.

TO COOK AND FLAVOUR THE PRAWNS Brush each prawn, back and front, with the oil and place flesh side down onto the hot grill of the barbecue for 1–2 minutes. Turn the prawn so the shell has contact with the hot grill and brush the meat sufficiently with the lime butter so it soaks into the meat while it is cooking. Cook on the shell side for 1 minute or until the meat is cooked.

Barbecue Prawns

Homemade Lemonade

HOMEMADE LEMONADE

What better than homemade lemonade for a picnic? Everyone enjoys it and it is a real thirst quencher. I find offering either lemonade or sparkling mineral water gives guests a choice and the added advantage is you can use the sparkling water to mix with your lemonade concentrate.

MAKES APPROXIMATELY 20 GLASSES

1.7 kg (3 ½ lb) sugar
4 cups lemon juice
2 whole lemons, sliced
a few lime leaves

To make the lemonade, boil the juice and sugar together. Pour the boiled syrup over the sliced lemons and lime leaves and allow it to steep until it is cool. Chill in the refrigerator until you are ready to make the lemonade. This mix will keep for a week. When ready to use, just mix one part of syrup to 3 parts of flat or sparkling mineral water. Plain tap water could certainly be used. Fill a glass with ice and top with the lemonade.

Bathers' Duck Confit

✢ ✢

BATHERS' DUCK CONFIT
AND POTATO TERRINE

I remember when I worked in Montréal I would often go out with a few colleagues for lunch. My favourite place was a little shop that only served crispy baguettes with your choice of cut terrine or pâté, maybe 30 types – for me it was just heaven.

SERVES 8

TERRINE INGREDIENTS

5 duck legs, confit bones with skin removed and
    meat shredded (see instructions below)
½ apple, chopped
½ onion, chopped
½ bunch rosemary
½ bunch thyme
1 litre (32 fl oz) standard olive oil
4 eggs
300 gm (10 oz) chicken mince
200 gm (7 oz) fresh pork belly or sliced bacon,
    thinly sliced to layer the terrine
1 teaspoon juniper berries

duck juices (these will accumulate at the bottom
    of the confit duck legs when the cooking of
    the legs is finished — also known as cooking
    juices), strained and reserved
2 tablespoons picked and chopped thyme,
    rosemary, Italian parsley
1 cup cream (35% fat)
5 medium sized potatoes, peeled, trimmed into
    a rectangle and thinly sliced
100 gm (3 ½ oz) sliced speck, rind off
salt

TERRINE PREPARATION Preheat oven to 120°C (250°F). To make the confit duck legs, place the 5 duck legs in a wide pot, add the apple, onion, whole rosemary and thyme and cover with the olive oil.

Place in the oven for 3–4 hours or until the meat comes off the leg bone. Drain the fat, strain and reserve. Any dark cooking juice gathering at the bottom should be kept to add to the terrine. Cool the legs to room temperature. Separate the fat and bones from the meat, and cut half the meat into small regular dice, the other half is combined with the chicken mince (after it has been pressed between paper towel to remove as much of the oil as possible).

Line a terrine mould, 25 cm (10 in) in length and 10 cm (4 in) high and wide with baking paper cut to size, and then layer with the pork or bacon with a lot of overhang; the overhang will close the bottom of the terrine and become the base.

Place the chicken mince, eggs, and any pork belly or bacon trimmings left from lining the terrine in a food processor and pulse until it is well blended. Add the juniper berries, duck meat and juices and pulse further. Add the herbs and finally the cream, salt and pepper.

CONDIMENTS

French cornichons (small gherkins)
Dijon mustard
Baguette

TERRINE PREPARATION CONTINUED Remove immediately from the blender and refrigerate. The mixture should not be wet whatsoever and it is better for it to be more rustic in appearance than finely blended.

Place the potatoes in a shallow container and pour boiling water on top of them until they are submerged. Season with salt and allow to sit for 7 minutes until the potato has lost its raw edge, remove to paper towel and pat dry both sides. Reserve.

TERRINE CONSTRUCTION Preheat oven to 170°C (330°F). Place a layer of filling in the mould followed by a layer of the potato slices, more filling, another layer of potato and finally the rest of the filling, wrap the top of the terrine with the overhanging pork or bacon and press firmly.

Bake the terrine for 45 minutes in a water bath or until an internal temperature of 36°C (97°F) is reached. Set on a wire rack and cool for at least 2 hours under 'weights' by placing a flat board on top of the terrine and a couple of cans for weight.

PRESENTATION Slice and serve at room temperature with the suggested condiments.

✤ ✤
BLUEBERRY VANILLA TART

SERVES 8

SWEET PASTRY
225 gm (7 ½ oz) unsalted butter
100 gm (3 ½ oz) caster sugar
1 egg, beaten
350 gm (11 ½ oz) plain flour

FRANGIPANE FILLING
100 gm (3 ½ oz) unsalted butter
100 gm (3 ½ oz) caster sugar
3 eggs
40 gm (1 ½ oz) plain flour
125 gm (4 oz) ground almonds

VANILLA CUSTARD FILLING
4 cups milk
2 vanilla beans
250 gm (8 oz) sugar
6 egg yolks
40 gm (1 ½ oz) plain flour
40 gm (1 ½ oz) corn flour
3–4 punnets of ripe blueberries, rinsed
    and towel dried

SWEET PASTRY PREPARATION Cream the butter and sugar together in a bowl until very pale, then beat in the egg. Gradually add the flour and mix to a smooth paste. Refrigerate for 1–2 hours. Roll out the pastry to 3 mm (⅛ in) thickness and use to line 8 individual 7.5 cm (3 in) diameter tartlet tins. Chill in the refrigerator for 20 minutes, preheat oven to 180°C (350°F) and blind bake for 10 minutes or until golden brown. Remove from oven add a tablespoon of frangipane filling to each tart and bake for a further 10 minutes or until golden brown.

FRANGIPANE PREPARATION Beat the butter and sugar for 2 minutes then add the eggs, slowly beating until well combined. Stop the mixer. Sift the flour and ground almonds and add to the butter mixture. Beat for 1 minute, transfer to a bowl and refrigerate overnight covered with plastic wrap.

VANILLA CUSTARD PREPARATION Bring the milk, vanilla beans and sugar to the boil, slowly. Cream egg yolks and flours together and pour the slowly boiled liquid into this egg mixture once the vanilla beans have infused well. Mix well. Return the entire mixture to the heat, and cook on moderate heat, stirring until thickening occurs. Continue to mix on low heat and 'cook out' the flour taste for a further 5 minutes. Pass through a sieve and place into a bowl with some baking paper on top to stop a skin from forming. When the mixture has cooled to room temperature, spoon a level amount of the custard into each cooked pastry tart.

PRESENTATION While the vanilla custard is still at room temperature in the tart shells, place the blueberries tightly packed on top of the custard, dust with icing sugar and serve.

My parents used to take us on summer expeditions and the highlight was gathering wild blueberries
and strawberries. I got used to eating the tiny blueberries and, to this day,
I prefer them over the large ones even if my search for them is not always successful.
This blueberry tart is a perfect traveller.

Blueberry Vanilla Tart

Chapter Six
❧ RECIPES ❧
from the sea

We live in an era where it is still possible to consume wild caught fish but, as the years go by, fisheries around Australia and the world are diminishing and are closing to ease pressure on these precious resources. One of the solutions to this is to use species that are less common yet still have plenty of culinary value. So, do not be afraid to substitute the fish in these recipes for something you might not have tried before. Mahi Mahi is a great fish but is underused, probably due to it having the worst commercial name ever given to a fish – dolphin fish – as it does not have anything in common with the dolphin. Tommy ruff, mulloway or jewfish and morwong are some examples of fish that should grace our tables more frequently.

Fish farming is also providing us with a growing range of fresh fish. It is fantastic to see many old and new species like Arctic char, kingfish, barramundi, Murray cod and silver perch being farmed and giving us plenty of options for now, and the future, in our kitchens.

There is certainly an art to cooking fish and the first lesson, apart from selecting the freshest available, is to not overcook it. The fish will continue to cook once off the heat, and until you serve it – you need to factor this into your cooking time. A fillet with a slightly underdone centre will give you much more joy than a firm and fully cooked or overcooked fish. The recipes included here are complex as they come from a restaurant kitchen, but this should not stop you enjoying a simple piece of fish, perfectly cooked at home dusted with sea salt, a squeeze of lemon juice and drizzle of good virgin olive oil.

Steamed Gold Band Snapper

✦ ✦

STEAMED GOLD BAND SNAPPER
WITH RICE NOODLES AND PRAWN

I am not normally a great fan of steaming fish as I mostly prefer gentle poaching but I devised this recipe with Asian influences and it works very well. This is all about soft textures enhanced with the sharpness of coriander, garlic and lemon.

SERVES 8

SEAFOOD

8 portions snapper 170 gm (6 oz) each,
    skin and blood removed
8 large green prawns, peeled and de-veined

BROTH

½ cup each galangal, ginger,
    lemongrass cut into brunoise (tiny dice)
1 large red chilli, de-seeded and sliced
4 cloves garlic
2 tablespoons peanut oil
2 tablespoons palm sugar
1 cup Shao Hsing wine
800 ml (26 fl oz) fish stock
100 ml (3 ½ fl oz) black Chinese vinegar
60 ml (2 fl oz) oyster sauce
100 ml (3 ½ fl oz) soy sauce
1 cup Thai basil, mint and coriander
2 limes, juiced

BROTH PREPARATION In a pot, sauté the galangal, ginger, lemongrass, chilli and garlic in the peanut oil until aromatic. Add sugar and deglaze with Shao Hsing wine. Add all the liquids and bring them to the boil. Skim any froth on the surface of the broth and reduce over medium heat until you have a balanced sweet and sour flavour. Remove from the heat.

Infuse with herbs for 10 minutes (then remove herbs). Finish with lime juice to serve. Keep warm.

NOODLE PREPARATION Cut the noodles into 10 cm x 6 cm (4 in x 2 ½ in) rectangles. You will need 3 per portion so cut 24 rectangles. Plunge the Chinese broccoli into boiling water. Drain when bright green and season. Cool and trim. Layer the broccoli between the noodle pieces. Trim to make even and reserve.

❋ **DELATITE DEAD MAN'S HILL GEWÜRZTRAMINER Mansfield, VIC** A spicy, aromatic wine with lifted rose petal and lychee character.

❋ ❋ ❋ **HIRSCH ZÖBING RIESLING Austria** Delicious dry riesling with a generous bouquet of lime blossoms and citrus peel.

❋ ❋ ❋ **GROSSET POLISH HILL RIESLING Clare Valley, SA** Classy wine with layers of blossoms, lime, mandarin peel. Lovely chalky dry finish.

RICE NOODLES

2 packets 500 gm (1 lb)
   fresh rice noodle sheets
1 bunch Chinese broccoli
   (or Chinese spinach), stems removed
salt and white milled pepper

ASIAN GREMOLATA

1 tablespoon chopped coriander
1 tablespoon chopped parsley
1 tablespoon chopped chives
1 teaspoon very finely grated ginger
1 teaspoon chopped garlic
1 lime, very finely zested

GREMOLATA PREPARATION Mix all ingredients together and reserve for plating.

MAIN PREPARATION Have a 2-tier steaming pot ready on low heat. Place the snapper on a tray and into the steaming pot first, it will take about 6–7 minutes. When it is cooked remove and place in a warm area; this also helps the fish to finish cooking.

Place the noodles and prawns into the steaming pot for 2 minutes.

PRESENTATION Place noodle/broccoli stacks in the centre of each plate. Place the snapper on top and then a prawn on each one. Top with ½ tablespoon of Gremolata. Pour the warm Chinese style broth at the table over each beautifully cooked seafood and noodle stack.

✤

SALMON RILLETTE

Rillette are traditionally made out of pork or duck but I find my salmon rillette a great alternative as a light starter.

SERVES 8

SALMON RILLETTE
1 cup duck fat or olive oil
250 gm (8 oz) butter
550 gm (18 ½ oz) salmon fillet, pin boned, skinned with blood and fat removed
sea salt and white milled pepper
¼ bunch chives, finely chopped
1 cup clarified butter

SALMON PREPARATION To confit the salmon, heat the duck fat or olive oil and butter to a low heat in a heavy-bottomed braising dish. Ensure the braising pot is not much bigger than the salmon itself. Season with a little milled pepper and a pinch of sea salt. Submerge the salmon into the fat and cook at the lowest setting you have on the stove top for 20 minutes. Cool the salmon in the butter and fat liquid.

Once cool, drain, gently break up the salmon into small pieces and season it well with the salt, pepper, chives and some fat.

Set the rillette in small individual pots or in little rings. Refrigerate for 20 minutes and then add a tablespoon of clarified butter on top. Chill again. When ready to serve, if your rillette is in rings, run a hot knife around the ring to remove it and set the rillette on a small plate. Serve with toasted brioche.

Salmon Rillette

Ocean Trout with Seaweed and Spinach

✤ ✤

OCEAN TROUT

WITH SEAWEED AND SPINACH

This trout is an amazing dish, full of sweetness, soft texture, intriguing taste and stunning colour. There is an incredible balance of saltiness and crunchiness from the sea salt. The horseradish sauce dressing adds the necessary acidity.

SERVES 8

OCEAN TROUT
4 x 140 gm (2 oz) ocean trout portions
1 tablespoon shredded nori or other dry seaweed
sea salt

HORSERADISH DRESSING
¼ cup grated horseradish
½ cup grape seed oil
1 tablespoon salt
1 tablespoon white wine vinegar

SEAWEED AND SPINACH PURÉE
1 kg (2 lb) baby spinach
100 gm (3 ½ oz) unsalted butter
5 cloves roasted garlic
salt and white milled pepper
100 gm (3 ½ oz) dried wakame seaweed, soaked

SPINACH AND SEAWEED PURÉE PREPARATION Preheat oven to 150°C (300°F). On a sheet of aluminium foil, drizzle olive oil and sprinkle a pinch of sea salt. Set the garlic cloves on top, wrap up the foil and roast for 10 minutes in the oven. Blanch 1 kg (2 lb) of baby spinach and purée while still hot with the unsalted butter and the roasted garlic. Season well with salt and pepper. Soak the dried wakame seaweed in cold water until it is reconstituted, softly squeeze dry and chop it finely then add it to the spinach purée.

OCEAN TROUT PREPARATION Remove the skin, the thin bones and the grey fat from all sides of an ocean trout fillet. Sprinkle the trout pieces with shredded nori and wrap each in plastic wrap. Place the wrapped fish portions in a small pot of tepid water and heat up to body temperature. Rotate each portion every 5 minutes for 20 minutes to ensure it is evenly cooked. The fish should be cooked with no white protein having escaped from the pink meat. Reserve the portions in the pot (turned off) whilst finishing the dish.

HORSERADISH DRESSING PREPARATION Just before serving, blend all ingredients until smooth.

PRESENTATION Heat the spinach purée and place a dollop in the centre of each plate. Unwrap the trout, trim the sides and cut into two and place it on top of the purée. Sprinkle with sea salt and serve with the horseradish dressing on the side.

❊ **NEPENTHE CHARLESTON PINOT NOIR Adelaide Hills, SA** Juicy, light-bodied wine with sweet plummy fruit. Perhaps even try chilled.

❊ ❊ **YERING STATION ROSÉ Yarra Valley, VIC** A savoury dryish rosé, made from pinot noir.

❊ ❊ ❊ **ATA RANGI PINOT NOIR Martinborough, NZ** Fragrant supple pinot with ripe cherry and plum fruits; complex and rich.

Known as Saint Pierre in France, dory is one of the best eating fish in either continent. Its name derives from the legend that the black thumb-like marks appeared on its sides when St Peter pulled it out of the water. The boudin rose is a refined seafood sausage that is relatively easy to make.

Pan Seared Dory

WINE NOTES

❋ ❋ **KOOYONG ESTATE CLONALE CHARDONNAY Mornington Peninsula, VIC** Newish producer from this region producing very good chardonnays and pinot noirs. This entry level wine is a great introduction.

❋ ❋ **CULLEN SEMILLON SAUVIGNON BLANC Margaret River, WA** Structured blend from this benchmark winery with layers of citrus, toast, vanilla and dried herbs.

❋ ❋ ❋ **HIEDLER GRÜNER VELTLINER MAXIMUM Kamptal, Austria** Hiedler produces wines with wonderful concentration and texture. This wine shows classic pepper and spice.

The barramundi is able to stand strong flavours and this recipe is a play of contrasting ingredients. Each ingredient seems to support the others to create a rich and filling dish that most will enjoy. You could use strips of poached leek to replace the pancetta wrapping.

Bathers' Barramundi

✤ ✤

PAN SEARED DORY
WITH BOUDIN ROSE AND BORSCHT

SERVES 8

DORY

8 x 150 gm (5 oz) dory fillets, trimmed and
  pin boned
60 gm (2 oz) butter
60 ml (2 fl oz) oil

GARNISH

2 beetroot, roasted, peeled and diced
8 scallops, cleaned and trimmed
1 punnet baby amaranth leaves,
  washed and kept chilled

*If you are to use the Borsch, you will need to prepare it five days
prior to use to allow a full fermentation. Alternatively, you could
use a tomato consommé.*

BORSCHT STOCK

(Refer | Basics page 298)

BOUDIN ROSE (PINK SEAFOOD SAUSAGE)

8 outside leaves of Savoy cabbage, blanched and
  pressed (use outside leaves for a brilliant green)
250 gm (8 oz) ocean trout, pin boned and skinned
100 gm (3 ½ oz) green Balmain bugs
  or prawns, de-veined
ice
2 eggs
200 ml (7 fl oz) cream
salt and freshly milled white pepper
50 gm (1 ½ oz) scallops, cleaned and trimmed,
  finely diced

BOUDIN ROSE PREPARATION Place a food processor bowl and blade into the refrigerator for at least
1 hour to chill. Trim the savoy leaves into 10 cm (4 in) square pieces, avoiding the main stem where
possible. Blanch in boiling salted water until they become bright green. Remove and refresh in salted
ice water, pat dry and reserve flat between towels.

For the mousse, cut the prepared trout and bugs into small dice, place into a food processor and pulse
briefly with a handful of ice 2 or 3 times until the mixture becomes more 'mince-like'. Pour the eggs into
the mixture (with the motor running) one at a time until completely incorporated and then quickly pour
in the cream. Be sure not to over-work the mixture as the cream will split and the mixture will be ruined.
Remove the mousse mixture from the processor bowl and season. Rest in the refrigerator for 1 hour.
Fold in the scallop dice and place mixture into a piping bag. Lay plastic wrap on a clean bench, pipe
2 cm diameter x 10 cm (¾ in x 4 in) lengths of the Boudin Rose mix until all the mixture is used. Roll the
mixture in the plastic wrap and tie the ends as if it were a 'lolly', removing all air from inside by running
your hand along each cylinder. Then, tie each end with string. Poach the Boudin in water or until they
float. Remove and plunge in ice water until chilled.

Unwrap the Boudin and pat dry. Wrap each length in a blanched savoy square and keep in the
refrigerator until ready to use. When needed, steam for 1 minute.

BEETROOT DICE PREPARATION Mix the water, vinegar and brown sugar together in a medium pot. Scrub and clean the beetroot whole and place into the pot. Heat the liquid until boiling point, reduce the heat and simmer the beetroot for 30 minutes, or until a thin knife blade pierces the beetroot and is easily removed. The beetroot is ready at this stage. Cool the beetroot in this liquid and, when it is cool enough to handle, peel it. Square the beetroot and cut into large dice, 2 cm square (¾ inch), you will need 5 dice per portion, 40 in total. Reserve the dice with the Borscht Stock until needed for plating.

MAIN PREPARATION Warm the Borscht Stock gently, add a little warm Borscht to the diced beetroot in a separate pot and warm this too. This is the time to steam the boudin as previously explained. Heat two pans to moderately hot, one for the dory and one for the scallop garnish on top. Place half the butter and oil into each pan. Place the fish in one pan and scallops in the other. Cook both until golden brown on one side, turn the scallops over and cook for 1 more minute only, remove and place on absorbent paper until ready to serve. Continue to cook the dory until just under-done. Remove from the heat and reserve in a warm area ready to plate.

PRESENTATION Place two Boudin Rose on each plate, surrounded with a scattering of beetroot. Place the fish and the scallops on top, pour a little of the borscht around and add the amaranth leaf for garnish.

WINE NOTES

❀ PETER LEHMANN SEMILLON
Barossa Valley, SA Consistently a great
buy. This wine has hallmark semillon
character, subtle, lemony with an
underlying minerality and grassy note.

❀ ❀ MEERA PARK ALEXANDER
**MUNROE SEMILLON Hunter Valley,
NSW** Released with around 4 years
bottle age to show clean lemon, subtle
toasty characters.

❀ ❀ ❀ PIEROPAN LA ROCCA SOAVE
Veneto, Italy Top producer in the area.
This is their reserve wine. Restrained in
style with white stone fruits, blossoms
and creamy almonds.

Unfortunately, the days of being able to purchase
a treasured whole Murray cod caught wild in the
fresh water estuaries of our greatest river are over.
Since the wild fish is a protected species, the
farming industry has made this fish available to
all. The combination of risotto and the rice
pasta will surprise you.

Murray Cod Fillet

WINE NOTES

✽ **TERUZZI E PUTHOD VERNACCIA DI** San Gimignana, **Tuscany, Italy** A Mediterranean dish just looking for this light bodied wine with subtle fruit and fresh dry palate.

✽ ✽ **MOUNT HORROCKS SEMILLON** Clare Valley, SA Wonderfully structured wine with lemon and fresh herb palate, a touch of toasty French oak.

✽ ✽ ✽ **SERGE DAGANEAU POUILLY FUMÉ** Loire Valley, **France** Lovely minerally sauvignon blanc with a hint of honeysuckle and ripe fruit.

These are flavours that marry together perfectly. The bitterness of the vongole and peppery taste of the rocket are so well balanced with the sweetness of the fennel and the saltiness of the capers that it makes for a delectable and harmonious fish dish.

Bathers' King Fish

MURRAY COD FILLET
WITH RISO AND RISOTTO RICE

SERVES 8

MAIN INGREDIENTS

8 x 160 gm (5 ½ oz) Murray cod fillets scaled, pin
    boned and skin on
sea salt and white milled pepper
50 ml (1 ½ fl oz) lemon infused olive oil
400 gm (14 oz) baby zucchini, sliced
400 grams (14 oz) snap peas, sliced
2 tablespoons chopped chives

RISO AND RISOTTO

1 tablespoon butter, for sweating
1 medium onion, cut brunoise (tiny dice)
200 gm (7 oz) risotto rice
3 cups vegetable stock
salt and white milled pepper
2 cups cooked riso pasta
100 gm (3 ½ oz) butter, to finish
½ lime, juiced

PEA AND MINT SAUCE (OPTIONAL)

50 gm (1 ½ oz) butter
2 eschalots, peeled and diced
¼ leek, white part only, washed
    and thinly sliced
1 desirée potato, peeled and diced
    1 cm x 1 cm (½ inch x ½ inch)
2 cups chicken or vegetable stock
450 gm (15 oz) peas, blanched
1 bunch mint leaves, picked
2 tablespoons chlorophyll
    (refer | Basics page 309)
salt and white milled pepper

RISOTTO PREPARATION Sweat off the onion with the butter until it is translucent. Add the rice and sweat together on low heat until the rice is warm. Add the warm stock 1 ladle at a time until the liquid is absorbed. Continue until the rice is cooked and fluffy. Season, add the riso pasta, the butter and lime juice and reserve and keep warm.

PEA AND MINT SAUCE PREPARATION Sweat off the eschalots with the leek in the butter. When almost cooked, add the potatoes and the chicken stock and simmer for another ½ hour. Remove from the heat and cool to room temperature. Lastly, blend the peas and mint into the sauce until smooth. When ready to serve, heat the sauce, add the chlorophyll and refine the seasoning.

MAIN PREPARATION Heat a steaming pot for the fish. Season each fillet and lower gently into the steam. Cook the fish for 5–6 minutes then turn off the heat and allow to 'slow cook' for a minute more. Sweat the zucchini in the olive oil in a small pan. Add the snap peas to the zucchini in the pan and warm them.

PRESENTATION Spoon the riso and risotto in the middle of the plate. Place the fish on top and spoon the zucchini and pea mix around the fish. Finish with chopped chives atop the fish. Serve with a sauce boat of pea and mint sauce or a cheek of lemon.

✦ ✦

BATHERS' KING FISH
WITH FENNEL, VONGOLE, CAPERS AND ROCKET PESTO

SERVES 4

SEAFOOD
500 grams (1 lb) vongole/pippies live
4 x 180 gm (6 oz) portions of king fish, skinned
   and de-boned
1 cup white wine
salt and white milled pepper

PESTO
4 garlic cloves
4 cups rocket leaves, picked and washed
150ml extra virgin olive oil

FENNEL COMPOTE
1 large fennel bulb, trimmed and diced
200 ml (7 fl oz) extra-virgin olive oil
6 garlic cloves, peeled
2 leafy twigs basil
1 lemon, juiced
salt and white milled pepper

GARNISH
8 small Kipfler potatoes
 2 Roma tomatoes, peeled, de-seeded and diced
6 tablespoons small salted capers,
   washed and drained
2 tablespoons butter
1 tablespoon finely chopped curly parsley

PESTO PREPARATION, Preheat oven to 180°C (350°F). Roast the garlic cloves in the oven wrapped in aluminium foil with a pinch of salt and a touch of olive oil. When soft, squeeze out the flesh into a small bowl and reserve. Blanch the rocket in salted boiling water then drain. Blend into a thick paste with the olive oil and the roast garlic. Season with salt and white milled pepper.

FENNEL PREPARATION In a pan put the diced fennel, garlic, basil and olive oil and cook on low heat without colour until tender and translucent. Add lemon juice and once cooler remove the garlic and basil, season with salt and white milled pepper.

SEAFOOD AND FINAL PREPARATION AND PRESENTATION Wash then boil the Kipfler potatoes in salted water until tender. Drain and peel while still warm, slice when cool and sauté the potato in some extra butter until they are golden. Season and reserve in a warm place. Steam the vongole with the white wine in a very hot pan with a tight fitting lid for 1 minute. Remove from heat and reserve. Pan-fry the seasoned king fish fillets in the oil/butter on both sides until cooked, about two minutes on each side and 2 minute of resting. Warm the fennel compote over gentle heat. Add the tomato, capers and stir in the butter and parsley then lastly add the drained vongole discarding some of the empty shells. Arrange the potato discs in the centre of the plate and place the king fish on top. Spoon the vongole and fennel compote around the fish. Serve with a side dish of rocket pesto.

We first made this dish with Arctic Char. It is a fish caught wild in the Canadian Arctic but now farmed in Tasmania. A substitute is ocean trout. The recipe is light and demands that the fish flesh is gently warmed through after the skin side of the fish is seared.

Bathers' Arctic Char

✦ ✦

BATHERS' ARCTIC CHAR
WITH PORK AND PRAWN DUMPLING

SERVES 8

MAIN INGREDIENTS
8 x 160 gm (5 ½ oz) arctic char fillets pin boned,
    skin left on and scaled
8 slices of flat pancetta, cut in half
500 gm (1 lb) spinach, stems removed
40 gm (1 ½ oz) butter
salt and white milled pepper

PORK AND PRAWN DUMPLING
50 ml (1 ½ fl oz) peanut oil
50 gm (1 ½ oz) ginger
50 gm (1 ½ oz) galangal
1 garlic clove, peeled and diced
120 gm (4 oz) eschalots
100 gm (3 ½ oz) pork belly
200 gm (7 oz) green prawns, peeled and diced

800 gm (1 ¾ lb) potato, peeled, cooked
    and mashed
150 gm (5 oz) bone marrow
2 eggs
1 egg yolk
170 gm (6 oz) flour

ASIAN MASTER STOCK
(refer | Basics page 298)

CHILLI JAM
(refer | Basics page 304)

MAIN PREPARATION The dumplings should be made beforehand. Start steaming the dumplings, they will be firm when cooked. Allow to cool slightly before slicing and portioning 2 per portion. Heat the Master Stock and keep warm while cooking the other components.

Heat a cast iron pan and place a sheet of baking paper inside it. Place the fish in the pan skin side down and start to cook. Turn the fish over after 1 minute and remove from the heat. Place in a warm area to 'slow cook'. This takes a little patience and a keen eye for consistent colour and tenderness. The fish will look raw but the idea is to warm it through without breaking the protein. Grill 2 slices of pancetta per portion until translucent. Remove and drain on paper towel. Keep warm. Wilt the spinach in a pan over a medium to low heat with the butter, then season.

DUMPLING PREPARATION AND PRESENTATION Heat the peanut oil in a pan and lightly sweat off the ginger, galangal, garlic and eschalots, with the pork and seafood. Then add the potato and fold through the marrow. The ingredients must remain at room temperature once the marrow is added, add the beaten eggs and mix through gently. Gradually add the flour, making sure that the mixture does not become overworked or 'doughy'. Roll into 2 cm (1 in) diameter logs and place in the refrigerator to become firm. Cut into 2 cm (1 in) lengths. Steam for about 15 minutes when ready to serve. Place spinach in the centre of the plate, place the ocean trout fillet on top, dumplings around, pancetta and chilli jam on top and pour the master stock in just prior to serving. We pour at the table for our guests.

✤ ✤
BATHERS' BARRAMUNDI
WITH PANCETTA AND SHIMEJI MUSHROOM

SERVES 4

BARRAMUNDI
4 x 180 gm (6 oz) barramundi portions
12 slices flat pancetta
salt and white milled pepper
¼ cup basil oil (refer | Basics page 303)

CAULIFLOWER CREAM
3 eschalots, peeled and finely diced
2 cloves garlic, peeled and finely diced
200 gm (7 oz) fresh horseradish, grated
½ cauliflower, grated
50 gm (1 ½ oz) butter
200 ml (7 fl oz) chicken stock
150 ml (5 fl oz) cream

SEASONAL VEGETABLES
2 large desirée potatoes
250 gm (8 oz) shimeji mushrooms
100 ml (3 ½ fl oz) chicken stock
250 gm (8 oz) freshly podded peas
4 sticks celery, cut into neat batons
   approximately 5 cm (2 in) long
100 gm (3 ½ oz) butter
2 tablespoons vegetable oil
salt and white milled pepper

BARRAMUNDI PREPARATION Wrap 3 slices of pancetta around each portion of the peppered barramundi making sure the pancetta joins on the bottom of the fillet, set aside. When ready to serve, preheat oven to 180°C (350°F). Sear the fish on both sides in a hot pan with the remaining butter and the oil. Place the fillets on a baking tray and cook in the oven for 5 minutes.

CAULIFLOWER CREAM PREPARATION Gently sauté the eschalots, garlic, horseradish and cauliflower in butter until aromatic. Add the chicken stock and reduce by half. Cover with the cream and reduce again by half. Purée the mixture and adjust the seasoning.

VEGETABLE PREPARATION Cut the potatoes into discs 1 cm high x 4 cm diameter (½ in x 1 ½ inches), place in a saucepan and cover with olive oil. Heat the oil to a gentle heat and then cook the potatoes until tender (approximately 25 minutes). Sauté the mushrooms with a quarter of the butter in a hot pan to give a good colour. Drain on absorbent towel then set aside.

Heat the chicken stock and half the butter in a small saucepan, add the peas and cook for 2 minutes. Add the celery and cook for a further 30 seconds. Drain and season and keep warm for plating.

PRESENTATION Place a tablespoon of the horseradish and cauliflower cream on a plate, then place the potato on top of the cream, surround with the peas, celery batons and mushrooms. Place the fish on top of the potato and drizzle with extra virgin olive oil or basil oil.

Salmon Cooked in Coconut Roti Dough

WINE NOTES

❋ **DOMAINE FENOUILLET CÔTES DU VENTOUX**
Rhône Valley, France Grenache shiraz blend with stewey plum and dark berry fruits with a hint of lavender and thyme.

❋ ❋ **WELLINGTON PINOT NOIR, TAS**
Andrew Hoods' name is synonymous with Tasmanian wine. His Wellington Pinot has dark cherry and plum characters with underlying earthy flavours.

❋ ❋ ❋ **BY FARR PINOT NOIR Geelong, VIC** Garry Farr's newish label delivers a structural style with cherry fruit mixing with undergrowth and herbal notes. Built for food.

Blue Eye Trevalla

WINE NOTES

✳ **TAHBILK MARSANNE Nagambie Lakes, VIC** A classic Victorian wine with tropical honeysuckle palate and a lemony acidity.

✳ ✳ **PEGASUS BAY SAUVIGNON BLANC, SEMILLON Canterbury, NZ** Funky wine from an excellent producer. Has pronounced elderflower, lemon and tropical fruits with creamy mid-palate.

✳ ✳ ✳ ✳ **TYRELL'S VAT 1 SEMILLON Hunter Valley, NSW** Look for a wine with around 10 years bottle age and appreciate the complex honeyed fruits with toast, lanolin and lasting acidity.

Potato Crusted Groper

✦ ✦

SALMON COOKED IN COCONUT ROTI DOUGH

This is a great dish to share with friends at home. The salmon is loved by everyone and the recipe is in a sense quite modern and matches the tastes of today. There is the hint of coconut in the dough and the Indian spice sauce gives the dish a real kick. We enrich the sauce with hollandaise.

SERVES 8

SALMON
8 x 160 gm (5 oz) portions of salmon fillet, skin, blood and fat removed
100 gm (3 ½ oz) ghee

COCONUT ROTI DOUGH
100 gm (3 ½ oz) corn flour
300 gm (10 oz) flour
1 teaspoon salt
2 large eggs
300 ml (10 fl oz) coconut cream
300 ml (10 fl oz) water, approximately

CURRY PASTE
½ onion, peeled and diced
2 garlic cloves, peeled and diced
½ bulb ginger, peeled and diced
5 curry leaves
2 lime leaves
½ bunch coriander roots, scrubbed
1 tablespoon dried shrimp
1 teaspoon shrimp paste
5 red chillies, de-seeded and chopped
1 tablespoon curry powder
1 tablespoon coriander seeds
1 tablespoon cumin seeds
white milled pepper

CURRY PASTE PREPARATION Dry roast the onion and garlic together then place in the bowl of a food processor. Mix the rest of the ingredients in then process in the food processor until a paste consistency is achieved. Refrigerate until needed, freeze the surplus.

SAUCE PREPARATION Put the peanut oil in a pan and slowly cook the onions, leek, carrot and celery until they are tender. Add the curry paste and cook for 2 minutes before deglazing the pan with fish sauce. Add the tomatoes and slowly reduce by half. Add the coconut cream and simmer for 40 minutes. Add the herbs in the last 5 minutes of cooking. Blend the sauce and pass it through a fine sieve. Season with salt and pepper. When ready to serve, finish the sauce with a little lime juice and Hollandaise Sauce to make it rich and frothy.

❀ ❀ YALUMBA EDEN VALLEY
VIOGNIER Eden Valley, SA This wine
delivers what you expect from viognier;
floral, spicy with layers of stone fruit and
quince. The soft acidity lingers.

❀ ❀ ❀ HOWARD PARK SCOTSDALE
SHIRAZ Great Southern, WA Spicy,
aromatic shiraz with red berry fruits and
floral notes. This medium-bodied wine is
elegant and great with food.

❀ ❀ ❀ HUET LE MONT VOUVREY
DEMI SEC Loire Valley, France Exciting
wines made from chenin blanc, this one
made in an off dry style. Even better if
you can find an older one.

INDIAN SPICE SAUCE
2 tablespoons peanut oil
1 cup diced onion, leeks, carrots and celery
1 cup curry paste (see recipe)
2 tablespoons Thai fish sauce
200 gm (7 oz) tin peeled tomato
4 cups coconut cream
½ cup basil, mint and coriander leaves
salt and white milled pepper
1 lime, juiced
½ cup Hollandaise Sauce (refer | Basics page 305)

STIR FRY ASIAN GREENS
2 tablespoons peanut oil
½ bunch spring onions, cut thinly on an angle
4 baby bok choy leaves, cut loosely
1 cup snow pea sprouts, use only the tips
1 cup bean sprouts
1 cup baby spinach or tatsoi
¼ bunch coriander

COCONUT ROTI DOUGH PREPARATION Simply mix all of the ingredients into a smooth paste in the same way as you would mix pancake mix.

SALMON PREPARATION Heat a non-stick frying pan and, when it begins to smoke, add the ghee. Dip the salmon fillets in the coconut roti dough and cook both sides until golden brown and crispy, remove from the pan and rest the salmon for a few minutes on a warm tray.

STIR FRY ASIAN GREENS PREPARATION Heat a wok until smoking hot and add the peanut oil, stir-fry all the vegetables very quickly adding the coriander and seasoning last.

PRESENTATION Heat the Indian spice sauce. Place the stir-fry in the middle of the plate, cut the salmon across the middle and place on top, serve with the hot spice sauce.

POTATO CRUSTED GROPER
WITH ZUCCHINI NOODLE

SERVES 8

MAIN INGREDIENTS
4 medium potatoes, peeled and cut into
  a cylindrical shape, retain in water
4 cups frying oil
8 x 160 grams (5 ½ ounces) groper fillets,
  free from any skin and blood lines
salt and freshly milled white pepper
4 tablespoons olive oil
2 tablespoons butter

VEGETABLES
2 medium green zucchini, trimmed and finely
  sliced into ribbons
2 medium yellow zucchini, trimmed and finely
  sliced into ribbons
2 red capsicum, trimmed, and finely sliced
  into ribbons
2 tablespoons virgin olive oil

SAFFRON SAUCE
5 eschalots, peeled and chopped
100 ml (3 ½ fl oz) white wine
50 ml (1 ½ fl oz) white wine vinegar
400 ml (14 fl oz) fish stock
2 pinches saffron threads or powder
200 ml (7 fl oz) cream
100 ml (3 ½ fl oz) carrot juice (optional)
sea salt
lemon juice

MAIN PREPARATION Remove the potato cylinders from the water and pat dry. Using a Japanese mandolin (or a sharp knife), slice 2 mm (1/8 in) thick circles. Deep-fry in hot oil (150°C/300°F) until they soften. Cool in the oil and the oil will help them stick to the fish and the other potato. Preheat oven to 180°C (350°F). Lay the seasoned potato discs directly onto the fish portions and, when all the portions are done, heat two large pans (for cooking all portions) and add 4 tablespoons of oil and 2 tablespoons of butter to them. Pan-fry the potato crust side for 2–3 minutes until golden brown. Turn over and place in a moderate oven for a further 4–5 minutes or until just cooked. Allow to sit in a warm place for a further 2 minutes.

VEGETABLE PREPARATION While the fish is resting, sauté the vegetables very gently in olive oil until they soften. Season and remove from the pan immediately, they should still be a little crunchy.

SAFFRON SAUCE PREPARATION Place the eschalot, white wine, vinegar, fish stock and saffron in a small pot. Bring to a simmer and simmer until two-thirds of the liquid has evaporated. Add the cream and carrot juice (if using). Strain, season with salt and lemon juice and reserve warm in a separate jug to serve with the fish.

PRESENTATION Place the vegetables in the middle of the serving plates, place the fish on top and finish with a slight sprinkling of sea salt.

BLUE EYE TREVALLA WITH PARSNIP CRUST,

SPINACH DUMPLINGS AND BEETROOT JUS

SERVES 4

MAIN INGREDIENTS

8 eschalots, peeled

1 cup olive oil

½ cup lardons or speck pieces

4 parsnips peeled, avoid using the woody part

4 x 160 gm (5 ½ oz) blue eye trevalla fillets,
    free from any skin and blood lines

1 cup small beetroot leaves

DUMPLINGS/SPAETZLE

375 g (13 oz) flour, sifted

6 whole eggs

2 tablespoons chlorophyll
    (refer | Basics page 309)

180 ml (6 fl oz) cream

60 ml (2 fl oz) milk

BEETROOT JUS

(refer | Basics page 298)

SPINACH DUMPLING PREPARATION Place the flour in a mixing bowl with a beater attachment. Lightly whisk eggs together with the chlorophyll in a separate bowl and slowly add to the flour. Then add the cream and beat very well for 2–3 minutes. Add a little of the milk to reach the consistency of polenta/porridge. Leave the dumpling mixture to rest for 30 minutes before cooking. To cook, force the dumpling mixture through a large colander set over a pot of salted boiling water. When the dumplings are cooked, they will float to the top. Scoop them from the top of the water and refresh quickly in salted iced water then reserve them for the main preparation.

MAIN PREPARATION Place the eschalots in a small pot, cover with olive oil and cook over moderate heat until they are tender. Remove the eschalots and some of the oil from the pot and keep warm on a plate. Blanch the lardons/speck pieces, then drain. Preheat oven to 180°C (350°F). Slice the parsnips lengthways 2 mm (⅛ in) thick then blanch in the olive oil on moderate heat to soften. Take each piece of the blanched parsnip and lay it over the blue eye trevalla fillets, overlapping as you go, approximately six slices of parsnip per serve.

Pan-fry the blue eye trevalla parsnip side down first in a little olive oil then bake in oven for 6–8 minutes. When ready to serve, sauté the lardons in oil until a nice rich colour is achieved. To the same pan, add the dumplings/spaetzle and then the beetroot leaves and season generously.

PRESENTATION Place the dumplings, lardons and beetroot leaves on serving plates, place the fish on top of the dumplings and finish with a drizzle of the beetroot jus and a couple of eschalots.

CRISPY PORK EARS
WITH ABALONE AND JELLY FISH

In my years at Bathers' Pavilion, this dish became quite a hit, especially with our Asian customers who have a great love for abalone. It features a strong play of unusual textures that could challenge some but will reward most.

SERVES 4

INGREDIENTS
300 gm (10 oz) abalone, delicately removed from
    its shell and trimmed
2 pork ears, washed and blanched in salted water
2 litres (32 fl oz) Asian master stock
    (refer Basics | 298)
200 gm (7 oz) black fungus mushrooms
125 gm (4 oz) jelly fish, soaked in cold water

TEMPURA BATTER
2 egg yolks
275 ml (9 fl oz) iced water
200 gm (7 oz) corn flour, sifted
4 cups peanut oil for frying
1 tablespoon Chinese oyster sauce

ABALONE AND PORK EAR PREPARATION Bring the master stock to the simmer and skim the impurities from the surface. Add the abalone and pork ears and simmer skimming from time to time. After one hour remove the abalone and refrigerate but continue to cook the pork ear for another two hours while skimming, topping with water when the level of the liquid gets to low. Once cooked remove the pork ear and skim and strain the stock.

TEMPURA BATTER PREPARATION Place the egg yolks in a bowl and mix the water in gradually. Add all the corn flour and stir briefly (preferably with a pair of chopsticks). Be sure not to mix the batter to a smooth paste, as it should contain small lumps of dry flour. Reserve.

PRESENTATION Thinly slice the abalone into 12 slices and arrange the sliced abalone on four deep plates (3 pieces of abalone overlapping). Cut the pork ears in a fine julienne, lightly flour them, and dip the strips individually in the tempura batter. Fry them in hot peanut oil until crispy. Poach the black fungus mushrooms in the hot master stock for 2 minutes and arrange them on the plate next to the sliced abalone. Scatter the jellyfish next to the mushrooms and place the crispy pork ears on top, drizzle a touch of oysters' sauce on top. Pour a little boiling stock on top of the abalone and serve with fresh hot master stock on the side.

Crispy Pork Ears

Chapter Seven

❧ RECIPES ❧
from the farm

At some point in time, especially when going out for dinner, we all love a real meat dish. There is something quite satisfying in eating a juicy and rich meat course. It is even better when you are very hungry and you have a beautiful wine to accompany the food. Unlike fish, most meat is farmed as very few meats are caught in the wild. There is a huge amount of romanticism about consuming a wild pheasant, quail, deer or wild boar but, in reality, only a few animals are caught in the wild and I personally think it is better to let them enjoy their wild ways.

Beef is probably the meat of choice for many people and the range of cuts is pretty extensive. In a restaurant situation, we seem to put limitations on ourselves in the selection of cuts that we are able to place on the menu. We feel we have to offer only primal cuts as this will offer more value for the customer. Often, however, what the customer is after is a great flavoursome meat dish – no matter what the cut is – and that is a good lesson to remember.

There is a real range of meat dishes over the following pages and it illustrates the complexity of preparing and cooking meat. The sauces are more involved and take longer to achieve – from the preparation of their basic stock to their reduction and finishing – but that is what cooking is all about. Great cooking is about sourcing the product, selecting an appropriate recipe, doing the basic preparation and cooking, finishing and serving the dish. What remains for me is to see my customers truly enjoying their meals.

These days, farmed rabbits are readily available and are a very tender alternative to chicken. We normally only make a few portions of this dish as it is so labour intensive but all the benefit goes to the guests who order it. We try to use all the cuts of one side of the rabbit and this gives a nice contrast of cooking methods.

Assiette de Lapin

✢ ✢ ✢
ASSIETTE DE LAPIN
RACK OF RABBIT WITH ITS LOIN, SHOULDER AND LIVER

SERVES 8

MAIN INGREDIENTS

4 white rabbits, rear legs removed and used in
the terrine recipe
8 slices prosciutto
8 rabbit livers trimmed, cleaned and soaked in
milk for at least 1 hour
4 rabbit kidneys, trimmed, cut in half and soaked
in milk for 1 hour
100 gm (3 ½ oz) butter
8 Rösti potatoes (see recipe over)
200 gm (7 oz) Spinach Purée (refer | Basics page
309 for rocket and spinach purée, replace the
rocket with extra spinach)

LEG TERRINE

rabbit legs (as listed under Main Ingredients)
4 cups olive oil
8 eschalot, peeled, chopped and caramelised in a
pan on the stove with a little oil
¼ bunch picked tarragon leaves
2 tablespoons chopped parsley
salt and milled white pepper

TERRINE PREPARATION Confit the legs by placing in a saucepan with the olive oil and cooking very gently
until the meat falls away from the bone (this may take a couple of hours). Cool down. Remove the meat
from the bones and shred half finely; leave the remaining meat in larger pieces. Mix together with the
eschalots and herbs. Season well (add a little of the oil if necessary to bind) and place in a terrine mould,
press down and let it set overnight. Once set, slice 1 cm (⅓ inch) thick and lay on a tray ready for plating.

RÖSTI POTATO PREPARATION Preheat oven to 180°C (350°F). Grate the potato with a Japanese mandolin
with a fine blade or use a fine grater; soak the potato in a bowl with the salt and hot tap water to cover.
This will help remove the starch and help soften the potato. Soak for 5 minutes. Drain well and pat dry
on a clean kitchen cloth. Grease 8 small metal rings 4 cm (1 ½ in) high and 6 cm (2 ½ in) in diameter.
Place the rings on a tray lined with baking paper and fill with potato – press quiet hard to pack tightly.
Pour some clarified butter over them. Bake for 10–15 minutes. The rösti will be ready when the bottoms
have a nice golden colour. Remove from the oven, wait a minute or two to cool down and press from the
top to compress the potato. Turn over and remove from the mould. The presentation side should be the
nice, flat, golden bottom.

RACK CROWN PREPARATION To create the baby crowns, remove the loin cutting around the ribs as well
to remove both in one piece. Once this is done, cut the loins in half, the smaller of the two loins needs
to be completely cleaned of bones and membranes leaving the bare loin. Wrap this cleaned loin in
prosciutto and roll in plastic wrap. Tie the ends to make it waterproof.

RÖSTI POTATO

4 large désirée potatoes, peeled
2 tablespoons salt
150 ml (5 fl oz) melted clarified butter

SAUCE

30 ml (1 fl oz) olive oil
1 onion, diced into small pieces
1 clove garlic, crushed
¼ teaspoon liquorice powder
½ cup port
½ cup verjuice
forearms of all of the rabbits, roasted
2 cups veal stock
10 black and 10 white peppercorns, crushed

For the crown, make a small incision at the top of the ribs furthest away from the loin and peel the sinew down to reveal the bare ribs, be very careful not to break any. Completely clean the ribs by removing any attached membrane and scrape any loose sinew away.

SAUCE PREPARATION Heat the oil in a heavy-based pot and caramelise the onions and garlic. Add the liquorice powder, deglaze with the port and verjuice. Add the rabbit forearms and veal stock. Bring liquid to the boil and simmer for 20 minutes skimming continuously. Strain and reduce until sauce consistency is achieved. Season and pass through a double muslin cloth. Reserve.

MAIN PREPARATION Pre-heat the oven to 180°C (350°F). Place rösti and sliced leg terrine in the oven until golden brown and crispy. In a pot of hot water, poach the wrapped loin for 4 minutes and rest.

In a hot cast iron pan with a little oil, place the crown upside down to define the shape of the rack whilst giving the top a little colour. Turn it right side up and colour the bottom. Add the butter at this stage and baste the meat until cooked to medium rare. Sear the livers and the kidney in the same pan and rest for 5 minutes before plating. Season well.

Warm up spinach purée and place a dot at the top of the plate to hold the rösti in place. Put some more purée on top of the rösti and the rack on top of that. Place the terrine in front of the rösti and place the poached and sliced prosciutto wrapped loin on top with the liver and kidney to the side. Spoon a little of the sauce over and serve.

Each element of this assiette could easily be served on its own. Duck, like pork, is a very versatile meat that excels served in cold and hot dishes alike. I have always had a fascination with duck, especially during the time I was involved with a friend in raising them.

Duck Rillettes, Pâté, Cured Breast and its Salad

This is a play on the classic Choucroute with all the elements of the dish from Alsace but with my favourite cut and recipes for pork. Homemade black pudding is a far cry from commercial ones and the tatin offers a perfect balance.

Bathers' Pork Flank

WINE NOTES

Try an aromatic white wine such as pinot gris, gewürztraminer or Austrian riesling. Their fruit, spice and textural palate with lingering acidity is a match for such a dish.

❀ ❀ ❀ **GIACONDA SHIRAZ** Beechworth, VIC Exemplary producer making stylish food-friendly wines. This is a beautifully silky aromatic shiraz.

❀ ❀ ❀ ❀ **J.L. CHAVE HERMITAGE** Rhône Valley, France Complex, elegant shiraz from a top producer in the Northern Rhône. This wine's seductive character will enthral from start to finish.

Bathers' Veal Fillet

Everyone loves roast Chinese duck. It is quite exotic to see ducks hanging in the windows of Chinese restaurants or take-away shops. Once in a while, pick up a duck or some glazed pork from Chinatown to have at home. This is one of my easiest and favourite ways to use roast Chinese duck.

Glazed Duck

✦ ✦ ✦ ✦

DUCK RILLETTES, PÂTÉ, CURED BREAST
AND ITS SALAD

SERVES 8

DUCK RILLETTE

1 kg (2 lb) duck legs

1 cinnamon quill, crushed

1 star anise pod, crushed

6 juniper berries, crushed

2 cloves garlic, peeled and finely sliced

2 eschalots, peeled and finely sliced

8 white peppercorns, crushed

4 sprigs thyme

200 gm (7 oz) 'flossy' salt (pickling salt)

2 kg (4 lb) duck fat or olive oil

DUCK LIVER PARFAIT

500 gm (1 lb) duck livers, trimmed

60 gm (2 oz) duck fat

6 eschalots, peeled and finely sliced

2 cloves garlic, peeled and finely chopped

½ teaspoon picked thyme

160 gm (5 ½ oz) butter, soft

2 tablespoons brandy

80 gm (3 oz) foie gras, optional

1 teaspoon truffle oil, optional

½ teaspoon salt

white milled pepper, to taste

JELLY FOR DUCK LIVER PARFAIT

1 cup cranberry juice

¼ punnet of blueberries

½ cinnamon quill

2 star anise pods

2 cardamom pods

1 tablespoon cabernet sauvignon vinegar

2 gelatine leaves, soaked in cold water

CURED DUCK BREAST

2 large duck breasts

100 gm (3 ½ oz) sea salt

75 gm (2 ½ oz) raw sugar

5 juniper berries, crushed

1 teaspoon smoked paprika

½ small bunch thyme

10 black peppercorns, crushed

1 clove garlic, peeled and crushed

You should start preparing this dish a couple of days before it is needed.

RILLETTE PREPARATION **Mix all of the marinade ingredients except the fat and saving two sprigs of thyme for later. Rub the marinade ingredients over the duck legs liberally and leave to marinate in the refrigerator *overnight*. The next day, wash off the duck pieces and pat dry. Preheat oven to 120°C (250°F). Heat the fat in a deep roasting pan on the stove and submerge the duck legs in it. Cover with a lid or foil and place into oven to cook gently until the flesh can be pulled away easily from the bone.**

When the meat has achieved this state, cool in the fat until it reaches room temperature. Drain the duck pieces from the fat and gently pull the duck apart into thin strips. Once shredded, divide the meat in two piles. Process half the meat in a food processor until you have a fine paste.

GREEN OLIVE TAPENADE

100 gm (3 ½ oz) large green olives, pitted

2 tablespoons extra virgin olive oil

½ eschalot, peeled and chopped

1 anchovy fillet, chopped

1 clove garlic, peeled and chopped

1 teaspoon baby capers, washed

1 teaspoon chopped continental parsley

DUCK CONFIT WITH APPLE AND ROCKET SALAD

2 duck legs

½ apple, chopped

1 small onion, chopped

12 parsley stalks

1 clove garlic

2 tablespoons 'flossy' salt (pickling salt)

2 cups standard olive oil

1 cup baby leaves or celery leaves

2 apples, thinly sliced

1 tablespoon basic vinaigrette
  (refer | Basics page 302)

RILLETTE PREPARATION CONTINUED Mix the fine paste with the remaining half of coarse duck and add a little of the duck fat — just enough to bind the meat together. Season with milled white pepper and the leaves from the reserved thyme. Press into a terrine mould lined with plastic wrap and leave overnight.

PARFAIT PREPARATION Heat a cast iron pan to very hot, sauté the livers in the duck fat until they are cooked to rare, adding the eschalots, garlic and thyme. Remove from the heat when the mix becomes aromatic. Blend this mixture whilst the livers are still hot adding the soft butter, brandy, foie gras, truffle oil and seasoning. Pour this mixture into little individual bottomless rings (alternatively, you could set your parfait in an egg holder or a little demi tasse cup) filling them to 80% full. Once the liver parfait is set, pour the cold jelly over the parfait to the rim then refrigerate again.

JELLY PREPARATION Place all of the ingredients in a heatproof bowl except for the gelatine. Place over a saucepan with a little water to make a double boiler on medium heat until the berries are cooked and have released their flavour. Squeeze the excess water from the soaked gelatine when soft. Melt the gelatine and add to the jelly liquid. Pass through a fine muslin cloth and cool until nearly set then use to top the parfait.

CURED DUCK PREPARATION Mix all the marinade ingredients together well. Rub the mixture onto both sides of the duck breasts and leave them to marinate *overnight*. The next day, rinse off the marinade and pat dry. In a hot frying pan, shallow fry the breasts, with the skin side down, over a medium heat to render the fat. This should take about 5 minutes. Turn the breasts over and cook for a further 2 minutes. Allow them to rest in the pan off the heat. When cool, slice thinly and reserve until you set your plate.

recipe continues over

GREEN OLIVE TAPENADE PREPARATION Pit and roughly chop the olives. Heat a small saucepan and add the olive oil, lightly sweat off the eschalot and anchovy. Allow cooling. Using a food processor purée the olives, eschalot, anchovy, garlic and capers to create a smooth paste, if necessary add extra olive oil. Season with milled black pepper and add chopped parsley to taste.

DUCK CONFIT PREPARATION Place the trimmed duck legs in a wide ovenproof pot. Marinate the duck with the apple, onion, parsley stalks, garlic and salt overnight.

The next day, preheat oven to 120°C (250°F). Cover the mix with the olive oil. Place in the oven for 3–4 hours or until the meat falls away from the bone easily. Drain the fat and allow the legs to cool to room temperature. Separate the fat and bones from the meat, and pull the meat into small regular strips, reserve. Alternatively, just cook a couple of extra duck legs with the rillette recipe.

PRESENTATION Slice the rillette terrine, place a slice on each plate and sprinkle sea salt and ground black pepper on top. Next to the rillette, place the liver parfait. Plate the cured duck, thinly sliced and topped with the green olive tapenade. Mix the duck confit with the baby leaves and thinly sliced apples into the vinaigrette and place on the plate, pushing slightly in a neat pile.

WINE NOTES

❀ ❀ ROARING FORTIES PINOT NOIR TAS Made by Andrew Hood, combining flavours of sweet fruit and undergrowth beautifully.

❀ ❀ BINDI PINOT NOIR Macedon, VIC Well made pinot with great fruit length and structure. Excellent reserve wine 'Block Five' also worth seeking out.

❀ ❀ ❀ ❀ VIEUX TÉLÉGRAPHE CHÂTEAUNEUF-DU-PAPE Rhône Valley, France Classic label from Southern Rhône, blending predominately grenache and shiraz. Try and find an older vintage for this dish.

GLAZED DUCK
WITH SCALLOPS AND SALSIFY

SERVES 8

MAIN INGREDIENTS
1 whole Peking duck (Chinese roast duck)
8 scallops, cleaned and trimmed
2 tablespoons peanut oil
salt and milled white pepper

STOCK
1 tablespoon hoisin sauce
1 tablespoon shao hsing wine
1 cup chicken stock or consommé
½ cup water

SALSIFY
8 salsify, peeled trimmed and blanched
4 cups water
¼ cup white vinegar
1 tablespoon salt

GARNISH
1 punnet baby coriander

STOCK PREPARATION Combine all the ingredients and warm only slightly before serving.

SALSIFY PREPARATION Peel the salsify, put in water and vinegar mix for a few minutes. Remove the salsify, transfer the water and vinegar mix to a saucepan and bring to the boil. Once the water is boiling, add the salsify and cook until tender; this could take 10–20 minutes depending on the size. Drain and cool. When ready to serve reheat either by sautéing in a touch of butter or by steaming.

DUCK PREPARATION Preheat oven to 160°C (320°F). Carefully remove the legs, thighs and breasts; remove the bones from the legs and thighs carefully without cutting into the meat too much so that the pieces retain their shape. Before serving, warm the duck pieces in the oven for 5 minutes. Slice (where necessary) and arrange in a warm bowl.

PRESENTATION Brush each scallop with peanut oil, season well on both sides and sear in a pan. Rest on paper towel briefly. Reheat the salsify and place on top of the duck, add a little baby coriander to garnish the dish, pour the stock at the table for your guests.

BATHERS' VEAL FILLET
WITH MARRON TAIL AND HOLLANDAISE

All chefs probably have their own version of Surf and Turf – a favourite of the 1970s. Mine involves a beautiful marron tail and a tender veal fillet. What makes this dish come together is the rocket and hollandaise; the peppery element of the rocket just gives enough bite to make the dish exciting.

SERVES 4

MAIN INGREDIENTS
2 veal fillets middle cut, tied and rolled
    (130 gm/4 oz raw weight per portion)
8 Australian live marrons
400 gm (14 oz) mushroom duxelle
    (see over)
4 cups court bouillon (see over)
olive oil
1 tablespoon of soft butter
2 handfuls picked rocket
salt and pepper, to taste

HOLLANDAISE SAUCE
Refer | Basics page 305

RED WINE SAUCE
Refer | Basics page 306

COURT BOUILLON PREPARATION Cut all vegetables in rough dice. Place all ingredients together in a heavy based pot and bring to boil, simmer for 30 minutes.

VEAL FILLET PREPARATION From the middle cut of the veal fillet, trim any silver skin and remove the tail end. Wrap the fillet in plastic wrap, ensuring it is tight, to give the fillet a more defined cylindrical shape. Refrigerate for a minimum of 2 hours but preferably overnight.

MARRON PREPARATION Put the marrons in the freezer for 5 minutes. Remove the heads. Put the marron in the court bouillon and gently poach until the shells just start to turn red. Remove the tails and place them on a draining tray to cool in the refrigerator (don't refresh in water as you will wash off the flavour). When cool, peel the shell very carefully pulling the centre tubes (gut/vein) out with the tail and remove the meat from the claws. Reserve.

DUXELLE PREPARATION Heat olive oil in a medium-sized pan and sweat the eschalots. When soft, add the garlic and cook for 1 minute or until the garlic is soft. Add the butter, increase the heat and add the field mushrooms. Cook until the mushrooms are soft and most of the moisture has evaporated. Add the porcini, season with salt and pepper and reserve.

FINAL PREPARATION Preheat oven to 170°C (330°F) and preheat a griller to medium heat. In a thick-based pan add a little oil, season the veal fillet and add it to the pan basting with a little butter. When a golden

✽ ✽ ORLANDO STEINGARTEN
RIESLING Eden Valley, SA A wine which
ages well, showing pear, buttered toast
and spice character at around five years
of age.

✽ ✽ ✽ BY FARR CHARDONNAY
Geelong, VIC A newish label from
Gary Farr, ex-Bannockburn winemaker.
Tight, structured chardonnay with citrus,
blossoms and white stone fruit.

✽ ✽ ✽ ✽ YVES CUILLERON
CONDRIEU Rhône Valley, France
Condrieu to many is what viognier is all
about. Treat yourself to a bottle from this
top producer.

COURT BOUILLON

1 small leek, washed and cleaned
1 carrot, peeled
1 onion, peeled
1 stick celery, washed, leaves removed
2 cloves garlic, crushed
1 sprig each thyme, rosemary, bay leaf, parsley
2 star anise pods
100 ml (3 ½ fl oz) white wine
1 teaspoon sea salt
½ teaspoon white peppercorns
4 cups water

MUSHROOM DUXELLE

2 tablespoons olive oil
4 eschalots, finely chopped
3 cloves garlic, finely chopped
100 gm (3 ½ oz) diced butter
12 field mushrooms, peeled, stems removed and
    finely chopped in a food processor
1 tablespoon dried porcini mushrooms, soaked
    and chopped finely
salt and pepper

brown crust is achieved, place veal on a rack in a baking dish and cook in the oven until medium rare, about 15–20 minutes. Remove from the oven and allow to rest in a warm place. Gently heat the red wine sauce. Cut the veal into medallions (you should have two medallions per portion) and place the warm duxelle on top in a dome shape. Keep aside. Brush the marron tails with a little soft butter and very quickly sauté them in a pan. Keep warm. In a clean pan, melt the butter and wilt the rocket in it. Season with salt and pepper and reserve.

PRESENTATION On warm plates, set the veal medallions, a good portion of the rocket and, finally, the tail and claw meat. Drizzle with a little red wine sauce and serve with the hollandaise.

✢ ✢ ✢

BATHERS' PORK FLANK
WITH BLOOD PUDDING AND APPLE TARTE A TATIN

SERVES 8

PORK FLANK

3 kg (6 lb) trimmed pork flank, skin on
12–16 cups Asian Master Stock (refer | Basics
   page 298)

BOUDIN NOIR (BLOOD PUDDING)

1 onion, finely chopped
8 cloves garlic, finely chopped
1 tablespoon vegetable oil
2 teaspoons mixed spice
4 teaspoons English mustard
1.2 litres (42 fl oz) pig's blood
500 gm (1 lb) veal sweetbreads (blanched, fried
   until crispy and diced)
100 gm (3 ½ oz) cooked veal tongue
100 gm (3 ½ oz) diced pancetta
100 gm (3 ½ oz) oats
salt and white milled pepper
250 gm (8 oz) butter, softened

PORK FLANK PREPARATION *You need to start the pork flank preparation the day before it is needed.* Preheat the oven to 180°C (350°F). Trim the flank of any excessive membrane and fat. Heat a thick-bottomed braising pan and seal the flank on both sides. With the skin uppermost, add sufficient Asian Master Stock to submerge. Braise for 1–2 hours (depending on the size of the piece) until the meat is tender. The flank must be cooled in the same liquid to room temperature.

Once cool the flank must be 'pressed'. To do so, find two containers where one fits inside the other, place the flank and a little stock for the piece to sit in and, with a double piece of plastic wrap to separate the meat from the containers, place the second container on top. Place cast iron weights heavy enough to firmly press the meat on top. Press overnight.

Uncover the next day, and slice into pieces, each weighing about 150 gm (5 oz). Preheat oven to 180°C (350°F). To serve, reheat 600 ml (1 pint) of fresh Asian Master Stock. Place each portion of the flank in the oven for 6 minutes. Remove from oven and submerge the pieces of flank in the hot stock (off the stove).

BOUDIN NOIR PREPARATION Sauté onions and garlic in vegetable oil and cook until translucent and soft. Add spices and cook for 1–2 minutes until aromatic. Add pig's blood and warm over a very low heat *constantly stirring* until blood coagulates, approximately 20–25 minutes.

APPLE TARTE A TATIN
100 gm (3 ½ oz) butter, soft
200 gm (7 oz) onions, peeled and thinly sliced
100 gm (3 ½ oz) sugar
8 apples, peeled and cored
350 gm (12 oz) short crust base (you can use
   a good quality frozen pastry)

CHOUCROUTE
half a savoy cabbage, cut finely (white part only)
1 head radicchio, cut finely
1 tablespoon vinegar
1 tablespoon verjuice

BOUDIN NOIR PREPARATION CONTINUED Remove from heat, add diced meats (sweetbread, tongue, pancetta) and oats and season with salt and white milled pepper. Fold in a little softened butter for a smoother texture. Whilst still warm, pipe onto plastic wrap and roll into thick sausage shape. Leave to rest for 2 hours before cooking. Preheat oven to 85°C (185°F). To cook the boudin noir, place in a bain-marie and cook with a light steam for 20 minutes. Leave to cool then slice 2 cm (1 in) thick.

APPLE TARTE A TATIN PREPARATION Preheat oven to 220°C (425°F). Melt a quarter of the butter in a sauté pan and add the sliced onions. Caramelise them with a quarter of the sugar until they are very soft and golden brown. Mix the remaining sugar and butter together smearing the bottom and the sides of 6 x 4.5 cm (2 in) diameter moulds. Cut the apples into regular cylinders (like corks) with an apple corer and neatly pack the apples in the moulds. Place in oven and allow the apple and sugar to caramelise and cook through. Remove them from the oven and cool to room temperature. Once cool, cover the apples with the sliced onions and roll the short crust pastry to 3 mm (1/8 inch) thick. Cut pastry into circles measuring the same diameter as the moulds. Tuck the pastry inside the edges of the tin and ensure the onions and apples are contained. Reduce the oven temperature to 200°C (400°F) and bake the tatin for approximately 15–20 minutes. Remove from the moulds while the tarts are still hot and stand so that the pastry is at the bottom.

CHOUCROUTE PREPARATION This recipe can only be cooked in readiness for plating and not before. The recipe method is in a light Japanese style, very light and fresh and briefly cooked so the cabbage and radicchio are still crunchy. Mix together the cabbage and raddichio and cook lightly in a saucepan to wilt gently. Add the vinegar and verjuice. Remove from the heat, season and reserve.

PRESENTATION Place the warm pork flank on hot plates, set the tatin and boudin noir on the side. Top the pork with the choucroute and drizzle with a touch of reduced Asian Master Stock.

This dish is all about the Chartreuse, a fascinating form and something I enjoyed developing. It is demanding to make, but with a bit of practice it could become one of your signature dishes.

Bathers' Guinea Fowl

WINE NOTES

❊ **CHRISTA ROLF SHIRAZ GRENACHE Barossa Valley, SA** A juicy blend from the Barossa. Alternatively look for a Côtes du Rhône.

❊ ❊ **PASANAU GERMANS CEPS NOUS GRENACHE, MERLOT, MAZUELO Priorato, Spain** Medium-bodied wine, with lovely dark berry sweetness, liquorice and underlying meatiness.

❊ ❊ ❊ **PARINGA ESTATE PINOT NOIR Mornington Peninsular, VIC** Produces excellent pinot for the region, with black cherry, plum fruits and spice and is wonderfully textured.

WINE NOTES

❀ **TORBRECK WOODCUTTERS
SHIRAZ Barossa Valley, SA** A great
introduction to the wines of Torbreck.
Juicy black fruits, liquorice and spicy.

❀ ❀ ❀ **HAUTES CANCES CAIRANNE
TRADITION Rhône Valley, France**
Grenache-based wine from the Côtes
du Rhône. Savoury, meaty with plenty of
sweet, dark fruits.

❀ ❀ ❀ **BROKENWOOD
GRAVEYARD SHIRAZ Hunter Valley,
NSW** A single vineyard classic Hunter
shiraz. Stylish, savoury and spicy. Built
for food.

In the past I made this recipe with braised beef
brisket but I find oxtail a better option even if more
labour intensive. You could omit the beef tenderloin
if you increase the amount of oxtail and you could
even bake this in a gratin dish sprinkled with
breadcrumbs and melted butter.

Beef Tenderloin

✦ ✦ ✦

BATHERS' GUINEA FOWL
WITH POTATO CHARTREUSE

SERVES 8

GUINEA FOWL

8 guinea fowl, legs removed for confit, breast
  retained on saddle

2 tablespoons cold butter, chopped

salt and white milled pepper

1 cup red wine

2 cups chicken stock

CHARTREUSE FILLING

8 guinea fowl leg confit (refer | Basics page 304)

2 tablespoons butter

8 eschalots, peeled and chopped

½ savoy cabbage or 16 Brussels sprouts, chopped
  in small dice

1 clove garlic, peeled and crushed

1 cup cream

salt and white milled pepper

POTATO CHARTREUSE

8 large désirée potatoes, peeled

8 metal dariole moulds

8 baking paper circles of 4 cm (1 ½ in) diameter
  (to line the bottom of the dariole moulds)

2 tablespoons butter

4 cups oil for frying (peanut or vegetable)

ESCHALOT PURÉE

500 gm (1 lb) eschalots, peeled

2 cups chicken stock

2 tablespoons butter

salt and white milled pepper

PEA COMPOTE

500 gm (1 lb) peas removed from the pod

1 heart cos lettuce

1 tablespoon butter

salt and white pepper

CHARTEUSE FILLING PREPARATION Shred the meat from the guinea fowl leg confit and reserve. Melt the butter in a heavy pan and sauté the eschalots until soft. Add the cabbage and cook until the cabbage is wilted. Add the garlic, cook a little longer and add the cream. Cook until the liquid reduces and then add the shredded leg and remove from the heat. Season with a touch of salt and some pepper and cool in the refrigerator. Reserve to fill the chartreuse.

POTATO CHARTREUSE PREPARATION Slice the potato on a mandolin to 2 mm (⅛ in) thickness. Cut 16 circles 4 cm (1 ½ in) in diameter with a small round cutter. Cut the rest for an A (or an A frame) like a triangle with pointy tip cut off (2 cm/1 in at the top 3 cm/1 ½ in at the base and approximately 7 cm/2 ¾ in long). Deep-fry the potato slices in hot oil (150°C/300°F) until they soften then remove them and allow to cool. They will be quite greasy but that is needed for this recipe. Drop the circles of baking paper in the bottom of the buttered dariole moulds. Put one small potato circle in the bottom. On a clean board, lay the flat remaining potato pieces with the large part at the bottom and overlapping them slightly (like an open set of playing cards). You will need about 10 flaps. Pick this up gently and line the side of the mould with the thinner ends at the bottom. Fill the chartreuse with the filling, press the flaps down towards the centre and top with the other potato circle to close.

POTATO CHARTREUSE PREPARATION CONTINUED Press again to achieve a good seal. Repeat to line and fill all moulds.Preheat oven to 150°C (300°F) and set the darioles on a rack set in a tray. This will help prevent the bottom burning. Cook the dariole with the open end at the top for about 20 minutes. Take care that the potato doesn't burn and reduce heat if necessary. After 20 minutes, remove from the oven and try to remove one from the mould to check if the potatoes are browned enough. If not, increase the heat and cook until they are golden brown. The chartreuse should be cooked half an hour before you serve dinner so they cool down a little and you can remove them from the mould. They can then be gently reheated in the oven at the same temperature.

ESCHALOT PURÉE PREPARATION Cook the eschalots in stock until tender. Drain and purée with the butter. Season and adjust thickness with the reduced chicken stock until you have a smooth purée.

PEA COMPOTE PREPARATION Blanch the peas. Add the lettuce to a pan with the melted butter and toss for a few minutes. Add the peas and season.

GUINEA FOWL SADDLE PREPARATION Bring the guinea fowl saddles to room temperature by resting, covered in a tray, for about half an hour prior to cooking. Preheat oven to 200°C (400°F). Smother the saddles with butter and season with salt and white pepper. Sear the breasts and any other unused part of the guinea fowl (neck, back, etc) in a non-stick pan until they are golden. Place in a baking tray and roast for 12–15 minutes. Remove from oven, remove the saddles from the pan and rest for 10 minutes before carving. On the stove top at high heat, deglaze the pan with the red wine, add 2 cups of chicken stock and reduce until the sauce thickens. Season and strain into a small pot. Add 2 tablespoons of cold butter while whisking slowly. Reserve warm.

PRESENTATION On a warm plate, set the chartreuse on a touch of eschalot purée to prevent it from sliding. Set another large spoon of purée beside the chartreuse and set the carved breast on top. Drizzle with the pan juice sauce and serve with the peas.

✤ ✤

BEEF TENDERLOIN
WITH WILD MUSHROOMS

SERVES 8

BRAISED OXTAIL

3 kg (6 lb) oxtail, cut in large pieces
½ cup vegetable oil
2 onions, peeled and cut into quarters
2 carrots, peeled and cut into quarters
2 garlic cloves, peeled
2 sprigs thyme
6 bay leaves
salt and ground black pepper
cold water to cover
1 cup dry red wine

BEEF TENDERLOIN

1.5 kg (3 lb) beef tenderloin, tournedo/centre
    cut, trimmed
2 tablespoons vegetable oil
50 gm (1 ½ oz) butter
1 teaspoon sea salt
milled black pepper

OXTAIL PREPARATION Preheat oven to 180°C (350°F). In a cast iron or other heavy pot, sear the oxtail on high heat with the oil until well coloured. Drain any excessive oil and add the vegetables, garlic, herbs, salt and pepper and lightly brown. Cover with cold water and bring to the boil, remove any scum from the surface and cover with a lid. Braise in the oven for 3 hours or until the meat comes away from the bone easily. Cool the meat in the stock. Remove the oxtail from the liquid and shred into strands taking care to remove any fat or gristle. Place the oxtail into a ring form, filling to one third of the ring's height. Add the potato purée and refrigerate to set. Strain the stock from the vegetables into a saucepan and reduce the stock with the red wine until jus consistency. Strain through a very fine strainer and reserve for plating.

POTATO PURÉE PREPARATION Preheat oven to 180°C (350°F). Roast potatoes in their skins until cooked through. Scoop the flesh and pass through a rice presser or fine sieve. Add the cold butter and mix. Adjust seasoning with the salt, pepper and a touch of grated nutmeg then add some hot cream until you have a firm but smooth and workable textured potato purée. Ensure potato is firm enough to hold the weight of the oxtail and the beef. There is no standard recipe for the perfect purée, everything depends on the quality and variety of potato used and the time of year it is grown.

BEEF TENDERLOIN PREPARATION Preheat oven to 180°C (350°F). Season the trimmed tenderloin and sear on all sides in hot vegetable oil in a hot, thick-bottomed pan. Place in the oven adding the butter to the pan and baste every 5 minutes. Roast the beef until it is cooked rare, approximately 6–8 minutes. Remove from the oven and rest the tenderloin in a warm place on a rack until ready to plate.

POTATO PURÉE

500 gm (1 lb) désirée potato
100 gm (3 ½ oz) cold diced butter
100 ml (3 ½ fl oz) hot cream
salt and milled white pepper
nutmeg

MUSHROOMS AND SPINACH

60 gm (2 oz) butter
1 garlic clove, peeled
2 punnets morel mushrooms, cleaned
1 punnet black trumpet mushrooms, cleaned
1 punnet chanterelle mushrooms, trimmed
    (use any other mushrooms available if you
    cannot source these wild mushrooms)
salt and milled white pepper
60 gm (2 oz) butter, extra
2 bunches English spinach

MUSHROOMS AND SPINACH PREPARATION In a heavy-based pan, heat up the butter and sauté the garlic clove. First add the morels to the pan, then add the trumpets and cook for 2 minutes. Finally, add the chanterelles and cook gently. Season with salt and pepper. Remove and reserve the garlic clove and place the mushrooms in a warm place to rest.

In the same pan, add the butter and the reserved garlic clove. Add the spinach and wilt at high heat. Drain, discard the garlic clove and season with salt and pepper.

PRESENTATION Preheat the oven to 180°C (350°F). Warm the oxtail and potato in the rings in the oven. Heat the beef tournedos in the same oven for 5 minutes. Plate the parmentier and remove the ring, place spinach and beef on top, then place mushrooms on top and scattered around the plate. Season with the sea salt and black milled pepper, pour the sauce and serve.

Bathers' Sweetbreads

The season for pheasant is short but it is a meat I love using. Chestnuts are in season at the same time and are perfect teamed with pheasant. It is better to cook the leg separately either as a confit or in a soup like the chestnut soup of this book.

Bathers' Roast Pheasant

* *

BATHERS' SWEETBREADS
WITH CARAMELISED ONIONS, POTATO AND MÂCHE

If you are into sweetbreads, this is the dish for you. It is full of softness, crispiness and sweetness at the same time. Veal sweetbreads are not that easily found but are well worth the trouble to order them in advance. Otherwise, you could always fall back on lamb sweetbreads.

SERVES 8

SWEETBREAD INGREDIENTS

1 kg (2 lb) veal sweetbreads, trimmed and rinsed
1 onion, peeled
1 stalk celery
1 carrot, peeled
15 white peppercorns, crushed
2 sprigs thyme
2 bay leaves
½ bunch parsley stalks
salt
200 ml (7 fl oz) white wine
4 cups chicken stock
2 tablespoons olive oil
50 gm (1 ½ oz) butter
100 ml (3 ½ fl oz) veal jus, reduced
   (refer | Basics page 301)

CRISP POTATO

2 potatoes, Idaho or désirée potato
4 cups vegetable oil for deep-frying
salt

CARAMELISED ONIONS

50 gm (1 ½ oz) butter
4 onions, peeled and sliced thinly lengthwise
2 tablespoons palm sugar
2 cloves garlic, chopped
1 cup port
350 ml (12 fl oz) red wine
salt and milled white pepper

VINAIGRETTE

½ teaspoon salt and white milled pepper
½ teaspoon Dijon mustard
100 ml (3 ½ fl oz) white wine vinegar
150 ml (5 fl oz) grape seed oil

SALAD

2 handfuls baby mâche leaves, washed
   and drained
2 tablespoons vinaigrette (see method over)

❋ ❋ T'GALLANT PINOT GRIS
Mornington Peninsula, VIC A label
that forged the way for this variety in
Australia. Combines sweet, savoury
and texture of pinot gris well.

❋ ❋ ❋ LEO BURING LEONARY
RIESLING **Eden Valley, SA** A classic
Australian label. A 10th year vintage of
this wine with some creamed lemon,
honeyed palate is noticed here.

❋ ❋ ❋ ❋ DOMAINES OTT ROSE
Côtes de Provence This wine is not easy
to find. Elegant, food-friendly styles, with
gentle red berry fruites and a textural
palate, finishing with subtle tannins.
Best if not served too cold.

SWEETBREAD PREPARATION Wash sweetbreads thoroughly in cold salted water and soak for 30 minutes. While these are soaking, place the onion, celery and carrot in a food processor and chop finely. Add them to the herbs and peppercorns in a pot and season with salt. Add white wine and cold chicken stock. Bring to the boil and simmer for 15 minutes. Add the sweetbreads and cook them for 10 minutes on a slow simmer. Cool the sweetbreads in the cooking liquid draining well once chilled. Remove and discard the membranes and skin. Reserve the trimmed sweetbreads after drying with paper towel, chill.

CRISP POTATO PREPARATION Cut potato into very thin slices with a mandolin and deep-fry on moderate heat until they are golden and crisp. Drain on paper towel, sprinkle with salt and reserve.

CARAMELISED ONION PREPARATION Melt the butter and sweat the onions in a wide-bottomed pot until soft. Add the palm sugar and the garlic and cook on a medium heat to caramelise the onions. Increase the heat and deglaze the pan with a quarter of the port. When the pan is nearly dry, add the next quarter and so forth until all the port is finished. Repeat this process with the red wine in the same pot. The caramelised onion should be thick and nearly dry. Season and cool at room temperature. Refrigerate until ready to use.

VINAIGRETTE PREPARATION Simply mix the salt, pepper, mustard and vinegar, incorporate the oil while whisking vigorously. Refine the seasoning.

PRESENTATION Cut the sweetbreads into 1 cm (½ in) slices, season and sear them in the hot oil and butter until they are golden and crisp. On a warm plate, arrange the sweetbreads and drizzle with a little warmed veal jus. Garnish with the crisp potato and the caramelised onions. Place some mâche leaves tossed with a touch of vinaigrette.

✤ ✤ ✤

BATHERS' ROAST PHEASANT
WITH CHESTNUT PURÉE

SERVES 4

PHEASANT

2 saddle of pheasant (legs reserved for the confit)

salt and milled black pepper

1 tablespoon olive oil

6 eschalots, peeled and chopped

8 whole peeled chestnuts (roast them with
    the chestnuts for the purée to make them
    easier to peel)

100 gm (3 ½ oz) butter, half diced and cold, and
    half at room temperature for basting

100 ml (3 ½ fl oz) madeira or brandy

200 ml (7 fl oz) chicken stock

12 dried morels, soaked in the madeira

½ cup broad beans, blanched and peeled

CHESTNUT PURÉE

2 cups chestnuts

2 tablespoons olive oil

100 gm (3 ½ oz) butter at room temperature

6 eschalots, peeled and chopped

1 clove garlic, peeled and crushed

3 cups chicken stock

salt and pepper

PHEASANT CONFIT

4 legs of pheasant

100 gm (3 ½ oz) rock salt

a few sprigs parsley, rosemary, tarragon

1 teaspoon whole black peppercorns

1 knob ginger, sliced

1 orange, peel only

3 star anise

2 cups duck fat or olive oil

FRIED SALSIFY

4–8 salsify, depending on the size

1 lemon, cut in half

¼ cup clarified butter

1 clove garlic, crushed with husk still on

1 tablespoon butter

1 branch rosemary

salt and white milled pepper

PHEASANT PREPARATION Season the pheasant inside and outside and bring it to room temperature before roasting it. Preheat oven to 180°C (350°F). In a hot pan, seal and lightly brown the pheasant on all sides. Set in a roasting tray with the eschalots and the 8 peeled chestnuts and baste with the soft butter. Bake in the oven for 15–20 minutes, keeping breast side up. Remove from oven and rest (breast side down to allow the juices to return to the breast) for at least 10 minutes covered with buttered aluminium foil.

On the stove top, heat up the roasting tray and deglaze the pan with a touch of madeira or brandy (reserve the morels). Add the chicken stock, boil for a few minutes and transfer to a small pot to finish the sauce. Reduce the liquid by half while skimming and degreasing the top from time to time, season and strain the sauce. Add 50 gm (1 ½ oz) of cold butter while whisking gently to enrich the sauce just before serving. Reserve the chestnuts for the garnish.

CHESTNUT PURÉE PREPARATION Preheat oven to 200°C (400°F). Score the chestnuts starting at their base with a paring knife, all the way around (be very careful!). Lightly rub with olive oil and place on a baking tray. Roast in oven until the chestnuts start to split open, approximately 5–7 minutes.

Peel the chestnuts while still hot (they are much easier to peel). Gloves might also be needed. Roughly slice the roasted chestnuts. In a medium-sized pot, add the butter and gently sweat off the eschalots, garlic and chestnuts until the mix is nicely caramelised. This should take about 8–10 minutes. Add the chicken stock and bring up to the simmer. Cook until all ingredients are soft; this will take about 30 minutes. Strain and blend the chestnuts in a blender adding a touch of the liquid to achieve a smooth purée texture. Adjust the seasoning and keep warm.

PHEASANT CONFIT Marinate the pheasant legs with the dried ingredients for at least 6 hours, covered in the refrigerator. Heat up the duck fat if you are using this, the olive oil can be at room temperature. Brush all the solids from the legs and set them in a pot packed closely but with some room left. Add the warm duck fat or olive oil or a combination of the two just to cover the legs and place on the stove at very low heat. Cook at this very low heat until you are able to pull the meat easily away from the bone. Cool in the fat for 1 hour. Drain and remove the meat from the bones making sure you don't have any skin or sinew. Shred the meat by hand and add a touch of fat to bind. Set the mix in small rillettes using rings or roll like a sausage in plastic wrap. Refrigerate until firm then cut in small portions (if you made a sausage shape) 3 cm (1 in) long.

FRIED SALSIFY PREPARATION Peel the salsify and plunge into a bowl of cold water with the 2 lemon halves squeezed into the water to prevent the salsify from discolouring. Once all the salsify are peeled, cut them in small sticks (the size of a small finger) and plunge them again as you do this in the lemon water.

In a cast iron or heavy-bottomed pan, heat the clarified butter with the garlic clove. Drain the salsify and dry on a tea towel. Once the butter is hot, fry the salsify with the branch of rosemary. Cook for 3–4 minutes until tender and then drain the clarified butter off. With the salsify still in the pan, add the tablespoon of butter and cook for a further minute or two. This butter will help the salsify gain colour and will improve the taste. Drain again, season and serve in a small bowl to the side of the pheasant.

PRESENTATION Preheat oven to 200°C (400°F). Heat the confit rillettes and the whole chestnuts for 5 minutes. Heat up the sauce and add the soaked morels. Bone the pheasant breast. Place hot chestnut purée on warm plates with the rillettes topped with the chestnut, a garnish of pommes fondant (refer Basics page 307), some broad beans, the morels and a touch of the sauce.

WINE NOTES

❊ ❊ **MONTE ANTICO SANGIOVESE**
Tuscany, Italy A fragrant wine which
captures the essence of sangiovese.
Medium-bodied, with cherry fruit,
leather and black olive.

❊ ❊ ❊ **BALNAVES CABERNET
SAUVIGNON Coonawarra, SA**
Family-owned winery producing
excellent cabernets. Delicious cassis
fruit, liquorice and dusty tannins.

❊ ❊ ❊ ❊ **CHÂTEAU MARGAUX**
Bordeaux, France One of the best
expressions of cabernet you will find.
Refined and long living.

There are three elements in this recipe that
could each be used on their own as well.
The lamb in pastry is a popular element and
can easily be reproduced at home.

Loin of Lamb 'Aux Trois Façon'

✤ ✤ ✤

LOIN OF LAMB 'AUX TROIS FAÇON'

SERVES 4

LAMB IN PASTRY

2 large loins of lamb from the rack, trimmed of all
    fat and silver skin

salt and white milled pepper

200 gm (7 oz) mushroom duxelle with porcini
    (refer | Basics 309)

2 thin herbed crêpes (see recipe opposite)

2 sheets puff pastry, rolled out to ¼ cm (or use
    a good quality frozen puff pastry)

1 egg, mixed with a teaspoon of water
    for the egg wash

HERB CRÊPES

1 egg

100 ml (3 ½ fl oz) milk

2 pinches salt

75 gm (2 ½ oz) flour

1 tablespoon chopped herbs (parsley,
    chives, tarragon)

RACK OF LAMB

2 racks of lamb, trimmed French style and
    seasoned

salt and black milled pepper

1 tablespoon olive oil

1 teaspoon butter

POACHED LAMB LOIN

2 loins of lamb from the rack, trimmed of all fat
    and silver skin

2 cups chicken stock

200 gm (7 oz) chicken breast

200 gm (7 oz) lamb sweetbreads, cleaned and
    trimmed (or more chicken breast)

1 egg white

100 ml (3 ½ oz) cream

salt and white milled pepper

nutmeg, freshly grated

2 teaspoons chopped fresh mint

LEEK PURÉE

1 tablespoon olive oil

2 eschalots, peeled and sliced

1 clove garlic, peeled and finely chopped

2 large leeks, cleaned and chopped

2 tablespoons butter, soft

1 small désirée potato, peeled and cubed

1 cup vegetable stock

1 cup cream

salt and white milled pepper

VEGETABLE GARNISH AND JUS

16 baby Dutch carrots, peeled and blanched

100 gm (4 oz) borlotti beans, cooked until tender

200 ml (7 fl oz) lamb jus (refer | Basics page 301
    but replace the veal for lamb)

LAMB IN PASTRY PREPARATION Season the lamb loin well and sear all over in a hot, oiled pan. Cool. Cover the loin with the duxelle and wrap it in the crêpe. Trim to neaten ends and wrap the parcel in puff pastry. Seal the edges then make a cross pattern with the point of a knife on top. Preheat oven to 180°C (350°F). Brush the pastry with egg wash. Place the lamb in pastry into the oven and bake for 10 minutes, until pastry is golden and cooked. Rest on a rack in a warm place ready for plating.

HERB CRÊPE PREPARATION Mix the egg, milk, salt and flour together until smooth. Add the herbs and mix. Test the mix in a lightly greased pan. If it is too thick, add a little milk; if it is too fragile, add a little flour. You will need a 20 cm (8 in) pan to make the large crêpes needed for this recipe. Cook crêpes in the lightly buttered pan by pouring a small amount of mix in and swirling it to spread. When bubbles appear on the surface of the crêpe, flip it over and cook the other side until golden brown as well. Continue until crêpe mixture is used.

RACK OF LAMB PREPARATION Preheat oven to 180°C (350°F). Season the rack all over with the salt and pepper and sear in a hot pan with the oil and butter. Place the rack in a baking dish and roast to medium rare for approximately 8–10 minutes. Rest the rack in a warm area for 10 minutes before slicing.

LAMB LOIN PREPARATION Poach the lamb loins in the chicken stock just below simmering point for 2 minutes. Remove from pot and let it cook with the remaining heat for another 5 minutes then allow to cool. In a cold food processor, process the chicken breast and sweetbreads, then egg white and finish by slowly adding the cream. Season well with salt, pepper and a small grating of nutmeg and finish with the mint. On a piece of plastic wrap, spread some of the mousse in a rectangle to cover the loin completely. Set the cold poached loin on top and wrap with the plastic wrap. Refrigerate and rest until needed. When ready, poach the lamb loin in simmering stock for approximately 4 minutes, remove, discard plastic wrap, rest and slice each loin into 4 portions.

LEEK PURÉE PREPARATION Pour the oil into a pan and sweat the eschalots and garlic. Add the leek and butter and cook gently for 5 minutes. Add the potato and the stock and simmer for another 5 minutes. Drain and add the cream. Boil until the cream is absorbed. Purée in a food processor and season with salt and white pepper.

PRESENTATION Spoon purée on serving plates, place poached lamb on top, plate the lamb in pastry and lamb rack. Arrange the warmed up vegetables on plates and serve with lamb jus.

Chapter Eight
❧ Wine Lovers' ❧
MENU

Caviar on Potato Rösti
Poached Tail of West Australian Marron with Parsnip Brandade
Roast Duck with Beetroot and Sautéed Spinach
Roast Truffled Guinea Fowl with Artichokes and Broad Beans
Bathers' Skirt Steak with Beef Brisket Flan and Roast Garlic
Milawa Washed Rind Cheese on Date, Fig and Walnut Bread
Mango Bavarois with Almond and Star Anise Tuile

One of the most pleasant and fulfilling aspects of my work is creating menus for many special occasions. These happen mostly at Bathers' but often I am asked to visit a wine region, like the Barossa Valley, Margaret River or the Hunter Valley, and work with some of our best wine producers to create fun lunches or great dinners. I just love working with winemakers and matching their wines with some of my dishes. There is a real challenge in trying to understand the wine and then match it with a dish that will enhance the food and wine experience for everyone. The results are often sublime.

My general approach with matching food to a particular wine is very much to let the wine take precedence over the food. I never try to challenge a wine; I find it much better to find flavours, textures and produce that will harmonise with that particular wine. Often the simplicity of a dish is essential in achieving this. On other occasions with a more robust wine I like to use a more traditional even rustic dish. The overriding factor is to create a balanced menu in harmony with the wine, one that will have a natural crescendo of flavours to match with your more fulsome and precious wine.

I have done many special dinners for Len Evans; most of them were to match extraordinary wines. Len's achievements in the Australian wine industry are legendary. His lunches, dinners and tastings are always celebrated occasions. I was privileged to cook for Len and his friends for many dinners and none were more special than the gathering of the 'Single Bottle Club'.

The following menu was one that I created and cooked to match wines that everyone attending brought along. These wines were unique - selected by the individual after an extensive search, they were often bought from some of the great wine auctions of Europe. Maybe only one of these bottles was left in the world so special they could be. On one particular occasion the wines revolved around the 1930s because it was one of Len's special birthdays. How can you match food to such extraordinary wine? In this case, because several wines were served with each course catering to a wide range of tastes, the best approach was to make food that matched generally the type of wine served. Here I have used some unique produce like caviar and truffles to match the occasion but my goal was to have the right flavours to match extraordinary wines.

CAVIAR ON
POTATO RÖSTI

WINE NOTES

1929 Pommery and Greno Natur

1929 Bollinger

1911 Perrier Jouet

1847 Duke Of Wellington's Sherry

CAVIAR ON POTATO RÖSTI

Caviar is an expensive and rare food. Wild harvested caviar used to be plentiful but is now off our list of imported products. A good alternative is caviar from farmed sturgeon. Caviar's uniqueness, its taste and texture make it more evocative than any other food and an ideal starter for very special meals.

SERVES 8

MAIN INGREDIENTS
250 gm (8 oz) caviar
100 gm (3 ½ oz) crème fraîche

POTATO RÖSTI
800 gm (1 ¾ lb) Idaho potatoes, peeled
salt and white milled pepper
1 eschalot, peeled and finely diced and sautéed in
    clarified butter until translucent
180 gm (6 oz) clarified butter, warmed

POTATO RÖSTI PREPARATION Finely grate the potatoes on a micro-plane or fine julienne. Place them immediately into just boiled water for 1 minute only, strain. Season with salt and pepper, add sautéed eschalot and pour half of the warmed clarified butter in. Pack the potato firmly into metal rings 7 ½ cm (3 in) in diameter. Turn over and press firmly.

Heat a heavy cast iron frying pan, add the remaining clarified butter. Place the rösti, still in their metal rings, into the pan and cook to a beautiful golden brown colour on both sides, remember the potato is already cooked. You can also place the rösti in the oven to crisp it evenly on both sides.

PRESENTATION Place the warm rösti in the centre of serving plates, add a spoonful of crème fraîche off centre, then a big dollop of wonderful caviar.

POACHED TAIL OF
WEST AUSTRALIAN MARRON

WINE NOTES

1929 Forster Kirchenstück

1921 Niersteiner

1887 Marcobrunner

✦ ✦ ✦

POACHED TAIL OF WEST AUSTRALIAN MARRON
WITH PARSNIP BRANDADE

A brandade is an old French recipe that may or may not have potato in it. I use parsnip and crab meat in it to vary its taste and to adapt it better to the marron. The marron is the closest crustacean we have to an Atlantic lobster and a perfect match for an aged white wine.

SERVES 8

MARRON INGREDIENTS
3 eschalots, peeled and sliced
1 small carrot, peeled and sliced
1 stick celery, peeled and sliced
4 parsley stalks
1 bay leaf
1 cup dry white wine
2 litres (4 pints) water
8 x 250 gm (8 oz) Marron or 4 lobster tails
½ bunch sorrel, picked and finely cut into julienne,
    to garnish

PARSNIP BRANDADE
200 gm (7 oz) dry salt cod, soaked overnight
    in cold water
6 medium sized potatoes, washed and peeled
    (désirée or sebago variety)
1 parsnip, peeled and cored
4 cloves garlic, peeled
150 ml (5 fl oz) cream
salt and white milled pepper
100 gm (3 ½ oz) crab meat

PARSNIP BRANDADE PREPARATION Soak the salt cod pieces overnight in cold water. Strain the salt cod pieces from the soaking water and poach for 10 minutes in fresh water. Cool. Once sufficiently cool, drain and clean the cod free of skin and bones. Flake into small pieces ready to add to the mashed potato.

Cut the potatoes and the parsnips into quarters and place them in a pot with the garlic, cover with cold salted water and simmer until tender and fully cooked. Drain and mash with the garlic; use warm cream to achieve the right consistency in the mashing process. Season. Add the cod to the warm mashed potato, adjust the consistency with warm cream and a touch of the cod poaching liquid, refine the seasoning and fold the crab meat into the brandade. Reserve.

MARRON PREPARATION Place the eschalots, carrots, celery, parsley stalks, bay leaf, white wine and water in a pot to make a *court bouillon* (a poaching liquid for the cooking of delicate meats). Bring to the boil and simmer for 30 minutes. Strain the liquid and discard the solids, return the stock to a clean pot and re-boil briefly.

CHAMPAGNE CREAM

6 eschalots, peeled and sliced

2 cloves garlic, peeled and thinly sliced

60 ml (2 fl oz) olive oil

1 cup Champagne or sparkling wine, reduced
    over heat to ⅓ cup

100 ml (3 ½ fl oz) white wine

200 ml (7 fl oz) fish stock

a few stalks of parsley, sorrel and thyme stalks

12 black peppercorns, cracked

400 ml (14 fl oz) cream

salt and white milled pepper

2 tablespoons whipped cream

MARRON PREPARATION Put the marron in the freezer for 5 minutes. Drop the marron/lobster in the boiling stock, bring the stock to a gentle simmer and poach seafood for 4–6 minutes, depending on the size. Plunge into salted iced water briefly to stop the cooking process.

Once chilled twist the head from the torso, cut the belly with kitchen scissors and remove the tails whole. Remove the gut tract. If you need to reheat, wrap in plastic wrap and steam gently for 3 minutes.

CHAMPAGNE CREAM PREPARATION Sweat the eschalot and the garlic in the olive oil without colouring it. Add the wine and reduce by half, then add the reduced Champagne and bring to the boil, then the fish stock and reduce by a third of the volume. Add the herbs and the peppercorns then the cream and reduce it by half the volume until you achieve a creamy sauce consistency. Season, strain and re-season. Just before serving, add the whipped cream to achieve a frothy consistency for the plate.

PRESENTATION Arrange the brandade in serving bowls. Garnish the brandade with the marron or half a lobster tail. Froth the sauce with a hand-held mixer or small sauce whisk and drizzle around the brandade. Finish with a julienne of sorrel. Serve hot.

ROAST TRUFFLED GUINEA FOWL

WINE NOTES

1924 Château Pavie

1919 Château Graud – Larose En Magnum

1918 Château Latour

1918 Château Lafite

1900 Château Haut – Bailly

✦ ✦ ✦

ROAST TRUFFLED GUINEA FOWL
WITH ARTICHOKES AND BROAD BEANS

There is something quite evocative about this recipe as I love the slow roasting technique and the classic addition of the truffle under the skin. In the old days, the bird would have been wild; these days, as most birds are farmed, you could use a free range chicken, a pheasant or the guinea fowl.

SERVES 8

GUINEA FOWL INGREDIENTS
4 guinea fowl
celery stalks, for stuffing birds
1 or 2 winter truffle, thinly sliced (optional)
100 gm (3 ½ oz) butter
2 cups oil
2 carrots, peeled and sliced
1 celery heart, cut in two
6 eschalots, peeled

CARAMELISED WITLOF
1 cup sugar
1 cup water
8 whole red witlof
100 ml (3 ½ fl oz) sherry vinegar
150 ml (5 fl oz) brandy
2 blood oranges, peeled and juiced

CARAMELISED SHERRY SAUCE
100 gm (3 ½ oz) caster sugar
1 tablespoon water
100 ml (3 ½ fl oz) brandy
1 cup dry sherry
10 juniper berries
4 cups strong chicken stock

VEGETABLES
4 globe artichokes rinsed, trimmed and halved
½ cup clarified butter
salt and milled white pepper
1 cup shelled broad beans

GUINEA FOWL PREPARATION Preheat oven to 170°C (320°F). Rinse each guinea fowl in cold water and drain well. Pat dry with a paper towel and stuff with celery stalks to retain the flavour and shape.

Find an opening between the skin and the flesh to insert the sliced truffles; place the truffle slices close to the wing and lower breast area on both sides. Insert some of the butter in the same way. Truss the birds by tying the wings together on the back of the bird, cross the twine over and wrap each length of twine around each leg and tie together.

Heat the oil to 'smoking point'. While the oil heats, pat the guinea fowl dry completely. Sit the birds on a wire rack over a deep dry baking dish ready to coat in the oil. Using a medium-sized ladle, pour the hot oil over the skin of the birds to get a really beautiful even golden brown colour.

GUINEA FOWL PREPARATION CONTINUED Repeat several times until you have achieved the desired colour. In a roasting/casserole dish, sauté the carrot, celery hearts and eschalots with a touch of oil and butter for 5 minutes to soften them. Set the birds on top and place in the oven for 20 minutes or until the juices run clear when the leg is pierced. Remove the leg to prepare the sauce and reserve the rest of the fowl in a warm place for 15 minutes prior to carving and removing the celery from the cavity.

CARAMELISED WITLOF PREPARATION Preheat oven to 180°C (350°F). Place the sugar and water in a pot over heat. When it turns a golden dark caramel, add the red witlof, stir, deglaze with the vinegar, brandy, and then add blood orange juice. Cover with baking paper and place in oven for 15–20 minutes. Remove from oven and cool. Strain and reduce cooking liquor by half the volume and set aside to warm the witlof in at the last minute. Cut the witlof in half and remove the hearts just prior serving. They should be a beautiful red colour.

CARAMELISED SHERRY SAUCE PREPARATION Place the sugar in a pan, add the water and cook until a golden caramel colour is achieved. Deglaze the pot with brandy, add sherry and juniper berries. Reduce by half and add the chicken stock and roasted legs. Bring to the boil, skim and simmer for 20 minutes. Strain the sauce and then reduce until sauce consistency is achieved. Strain through a fine strainer lined with cheesecloth and keep warm.

VEGETABLE PREPARATION Trim the artichokes and remove the choke, rinsing in lemon juice wherever a cut has been made. Sauté in clarified butter until golden brown and season well when needed for plating. Always store the artichokes in lemon water until cooking but make sure you pat them dry prior to placing in hot butter for safety from burns.

For the broad beans, simply blanch them in salted water for 1 minute only at the last minute, toss lightly in a little clarified butter and season just prior to plating.

PRESENTATION Carve the bird according to the desires of your guests, serve each portion with an artichoke, some seasoned beans and a braised witlof. Pour the sauce over the guinea fowl and enjoy.

✤ ✤

BATHERS' ROAST DUCK
WITH BEETROOT AND SAUTÉED SPINACH

SERVES 4–6

DUCK INGREDIENTS
2 tablespoons olive oil
2 tablespoons butter
1 leek, washed and sliced
1 carrot, peeled and diced
1 potato, peeled and diced
4 Spanish onions, peeled and left whole
10 cloves garlic, peeled
2 number 20 ducks (legs removed)
salt

SAUCE
300 ml (10 fl oz) game jus or veal jus
2 teaspoons Jerez vinegar or verjuice
½ cup sherry

SPINACH
4 bunches English spinach, stalks removed,
    rinsed in cold water
2 tablespoons salted butter
salt and white milled pepper

BEETROOT
6 medium beetroots, trimmed and washed
500 gm (1 lb) rock salt

DUCK PREPARATION Preheat oven to 150°C (300°F). In a large roasting pan, sauté the vegetables in the oil and butter until lightly caramelised. Add the duck and sprinkle with salt. Place in the oven for 1 hour, turning the duck and mixing the vegetables from time to time. For the last 5 minutes, increase the temperature to 180°C (350 °F) to give the duck a nice colour. If the vegetables look well cooked at this stage, remove them before increasing the temperature. Remove the pan from the oven, reserve the duck in a warm place. Put vegetables back into the tray (if necessary) except the onion. Put the roasting pan on the stove top and caramelise the vegetables for a minute or two. Deglaze the pan with the sherry and vinegar, reduce to half, and add the jus. Simmer for 15 minutes, then add the sherry, reduce to half, and add the us. Simmer for 15 minutes, then add the Jerez vinegar. Strain well and season the game jus. You might need to skim off any fat. Reserve for presentation.

BEETROOT PREPARATION Preheat oven to 180°C (350°F). Scrub the beetroot with a light brush. Spread rock salt to ½ cm (¼ inch) thick in a baking dish and place the beetroot on top. Bake for 30–40 minutes until the skins come away easily with a firm pinch. Peel the beets retaining the stalks for presentation. Cut in quarters and reserve. Keep warm.

SPINACH PREPARATION In a large pan, heat up 1 tablespoon of butter and add the spinach. Sauté until the spinach wilts. Season with salt and pepper. Drain and add back to the pan with another tablespoon of butter. Reserve.

PRESENTATION Carve the duck into portions. Place the beetroot and spinach on plates. Arrange duck and pour over the jus.

BATHERS' ROAST DUCK

WINE NOTES
1929 Château Carbonnieux
1929 Château La Lagune
1929 Château Rouget
1929 Château Margaux

BATHERS' SKIRT STEAK

WINE NOTES
1928 Château Phélan-Ségur
1928 Château Cos d'Estournel
1928 Château Haut Brion

MILAWA WASHED RIND CHEESE ON
DATE, FIG AND WALNUT BREAD

(*See Basics* / *page 310*)

WINE NOTES

1930 K.W.V. Muscatel

1900 Muscatel

1834 Roriz

⚜ ⚜

BATHERS' SKIRT STEAK
WITH BEEF BRISKET FLAN AND ROAST GARLIC

One day skirt steak will become a fad food; at the moment it is under-used and you should take advantage of this. The secret of this steak is to give it a long period of resting. The meat can withstand strong sauces like eschalot, pepper or a strong wine sauce.

SERVES 6

SKIRT STEAK
1 kg (2 lb) skirt steak
1 tablespoon vegetable oil
3 tablespoons butter
12 eschalots, peeled and chopped
salt and milled white pepper
2 cups red wine (preferably shiraz)
2 sprigs fresh tarragon
1 cup veal jus (refer to Basics page 301)

BRISKET FLAN
500 gm (1 lb) beef brisket, trimmed and cut
    into 5 cm (2 in) cubes
2 tablespoons oil
2 white onions, finely chopped
1 medium carrot, peeled and finely chopped
1 stalk celery, washed, string removed, finely
    chopped
4 garlic cloves, peeled
2 bay leaves
1 litre (32 fl oz) beef stock
1 kg (2 lb) Idaho potatoes, washed, peeled and
    trimmed into cylinders
1 cup clarified butter

GARLIC CONFIT
1 bulb garlic
2 cups olive oil

SKIRT STEAK PREPARATION Depending on the thickness of the skirt steak, either slice it in two or if you have a thinner steak cut it into manageable pieces. In a hot pan add the oil then a tablespoon of butter, sear the seasoned steak and cook at a high heat on both sides. Remove from the pan and baste with 1 more tablespoon of butter.

In the same pan, add the eschalots and the remaining butter to start the sauce preparation. Cook the eschalots until they are soft (about 3 minutes) then add the red wine, reduce by half. Add half the fresh tarragon and the veal jus, simmer for 30 minutes, skimming the impurities from the surface and reduce to sauce consistency.

Preheat oven to 170°C (320°F). Remove the skirt steak from the pan and place on a rack of a roasting pan. Place in the oven and cook for 5–8 minutes depending on your taste and the thickness of the steak. Remove from oven and rest in a warm place.

SKIRT STEAK PREPARATION CONTINUED Just prior to serving, strain the sauce through a very fine strainer into a small saucepan, bring the sauce to the boil and add the rest of the tarragon without breaking it or cutting it up, and infuse this for 10 minutes off the heat. Strain and bring to the boil again then serve immediately. Remember to season well prior to the last 'boil' and do not season again after this.

FLAN PREPARATION Preheat oven to 150°C (300°F). Trim the beef brisket pieces of sinew and membrane. Seal the beef in a pan with the oil until well coloured. Add the mirepoix (onion, carrot and celery), garlic and bay leaves and cook until coloured. Pour in boiling stock and bring to the boil. Place a piece of baking paper on the surface of the submerged beef and braise in the oven for 2–3 hours depending upon the size and thickness of the cut. When the meat is falling apart — similar to the lamb shank philosophy of falling off the bone — remove from oven and cool in the stock. When cool, remove the meat from the stock and shred with your fingers or a fork. Lightly knead the meat with the heel of your hand, pour in a little of the braising stock liquid to loosen the mixture. Season and reserve for the flan assembly.

Slice the potatoes very thinly, and soak them in just boiled water to remove a little of the starch and soften the potato. Strain the water and pat potatoes dry on a paper towel.

Assemble in 7½ cm (3 in) straight-sided flan tins by shingling the potato on the bottom and sides allowing the potato slices to overhang the edges. Brush with clarified butter and fill with shredded beef brisket. Fold over the overhanging potato, placing more shingled potato slices to cover the beef completely and brush with clarified butter. Place the flans into the oven at 150°C (300°F) in their tins to brown and heat through.

GARLIC CONFIT PREPARATION To make the garlic confit, separate the cloves of garlic from the bulb, retain the skin of each clove and rinse in water. Pat dry and place into the olive oil and cook on the stove top at low temperature for 1 hour or until soft. Cool in the oil. Remove the base of each clove with the tip of a sharp paring knife retaining the skin layer to make it easier for your guests.

PRESENTATION Slice the skirt steak thinly and plate as shown on page 208 with the remaining components.

MANGO BAVAROIS
WITH ALMOND AND STAR ANISE TUILE

SERVES 6

MANGO GARNISH AND SALAD
4 gelatine leaves
1 cup mango purée, strained
2 mangoes, peeled, stoned and finely diced
20 ml (¾ fl oz) muscat wine
1 tablespoon sifted icing sugar

BAVAROIS BEAUMES-DE-VENISE
125 g (4 oz) caster sugar
125 ml (4 fl oz) Beaumes-de-Venise or a light
  sweet wine
5 egg yolks
3 gelatine leaves
1 cup cream, slightly whipped

ALMOND AND STAR ANISE TUILE
refer | page 260

MANGO BAVAROIS GARNISH AND SALAD PREPARATION Lightly oil bavarois moulds. Soak the gelatine leaves and then squeeze the excess water from them. Warm the mango purée in a saucepan over moderate heat and add gelatine to melt the leaves into the liquid. Once melted, pour 1 tablespoon of this purée into the bottom of each oiled mould, refrigerate. Then make the sabayon for the bavarois.

Place the remaining two-thirds of the finely diced mango into a bowl, add the muscat and icing sugar and macerate for 20 minutes prior to serving with the bavarois.

BAVAROIS PREPARATION Start to boil the sugar and wine, whisk the egg yolks in a bowl and add the boiling sugar and wine into the egg. Soak the gelatine leaves in water until soft, and whisk until combined and melted. Cool and then fold the slightly whipped cream into the bavarois. Fill the moulds to the rim with the bavarois and refrigerate for 4 hours before serving.

PRESENTATION When it is time to serve, run moulds under warm water and unmould bavarois into small bowls. Place the marinated mango around and serve with the tuile.

This recipe is easy to love; fresh mango and a sweet wine from the Rhône Valley is a superb match. You can put this dish together fairly quickly when it is time to serve it. It would also work perfectly well with diced peaches and a local sweet wine.

MANGO BAVAROIS WITH ALMOND
AND STAR ANISE TUILE

WINE NOTES
1919 Château Rayne – Vigneau
1917 Château d'Yquem
1770 Sauternes

Chapter Nine

❧ RECIPES ❧
from the pastry kitchen

In a kitchen usually you are either a chef cooking savoury dishes or you are a pastry chef dedicated to preparing sweets and various desserts. I elected a long time ago not to specialise in desserts. I am not sure exactly why but I certainly felt that spontaneity was more suited to me and I like the freedom to create on the spot and follow my own instincts.

A pastry chef is often not able to work in a spontaneous fashion. A pastry chef follows precise recipes and methods of preparation and has great attachment to classic dishes and ways. For me, the exactitude and the discipline required to be a pastry chef never quite got me as thrilled as working on the stove during a fiery service in a restaurant kitchen. Still, I love creating a dessert that follows my own style and vision, and working with my pastry chef devising new desserts using different approaches with an edge to captivate my customers. It does help that I adore desserts and have a passion for them.

Most of my desserts are quite original and use skills and equipment that are specific to them. You might have to improvise a little if you do not have the same moulds and forms but the basic recipe and method should not really change. You could interchange some biscuits, bases and sponges between the various recipes and you could certainly purchase good quality ice-cream, puff pastry and sponges to cut down on the preparation. With good quality purchased ingredients, putting some of these desserts together will certainly lift your dinner party to another level and make you a very popular host.

Star Anise Blancmange

WINE NOTES

❋❋ **MARENCO BRACHETTO D'ACQUI PINETO Piedmonte, Italy** This is a sweet, red sparkling wine with a strawberry coloured tinge. It is a fun, lively wine, with flavours of pears, roses and red fruits. Also lovely with chocolate.

❋❋❋❋ **INNISKILLIN CABERNET FRANC ICE WINE Niagara, Canada** This producer has an outstanding range of iced wine made from different grape varieties. They are not cheap, due to the extreme conditions needed to produce them, however are well worth the experience to seek out.

STAR ANISE BLANCMANGE
WITH POACHED CHERRIES

SERVES 8

STAR ANISE BLANCMANGE
400 ml (14 fl oz) milk
300 ml (10 fl oz) cream (35%)
3 star anise
1 vanilla bean, scrapped
3 egg yolks
70 gm (2 ½ oz) sugar
3 leaves gelatine, soaked in cold water

POACHED CHERRIES
400 ml (14 fl oz) water
350 gm (12 oz) sugar
25 ml (¾ fl oz) lemon juice
24 cherries, pitted

TUILES
125 gm (4 oz) plain flour
125 gm (4 oz) icing sugar
2 egg whites

BLANCMANGE PREPARATION Simmer the milk and the cream with the star anise and vanilla, remove from heat and allow it to infuse for 1 hour. In the meantime, mix the egg yolks with the sugar until light and creamy. Re-boil the milk and whisk into the egg and sugar mixture. Return to the saucepan, place on the stove and cook it very gently (without boiling) until it thickens into a light custard consistency. Add the soaked gelatine leaves into this mixture and stir to melt them in. Pass through a fine sieve and cool to room temperature. Just before the gelatine sets the mixture, pour into small moulds filling them to the top.

CHERRY PREPARATION Bring the water, sugar and lemon juice to the boil. Carefully poach the cherries until tender. Cool down in syrup. When the liquid becomes homogenous, strain, cool and pour back over the cherries. Refrigerate.

ALMOND TUILE PREPARATION Mix all ingredients together and refrigerate for 1 hour. Make a stencil out of thin hard plastic in a triangle shape (about 8 cm/3 ¼ in long and 5 cm/2 in at the base). The plastic should be about 2 mm (⅛ in) thick. Preheat oven to 180°C (350°F).

With a flat metal spatula, spread some of the tuile mix over the cut-out stencil and then place the tuile triangle on a non-stick baking tray. Make as many tuiles as you have mix for by repeating the procedure with the same stencil. Bake in the oven for 5–8 minutes or until golden. Remove from the oven and quickly fold the tuile over the round of a rolling pin. Cool for a few minutes and store them in a dry place until you are ready to use.

PRESENTATION Run the blancmange moulds under tepid water and then slide out onto serving plates. Spoon the cherries and some syrup around and garnish with a tuile.

SUMMER BERRIES
WITH CITRUS SABLÉ, FROMAGE BLANC ICE-CREAM

SERVES 8

CITRUS SABLÉ
100 gm (3 ½ oz) soft butter
50 gm (1 ½ oz) icing sugar
1 egg yolk
1 lemon and 1 lime, zested
120 gm (4 oz) plain flour

FROMAGE BLANC ICE-CREAM
1 cup milk
100 gm (3 ½ oz) glucose
5 egg yolks
150 gm (5 oz) caster sugar
500 gm (1 lb) fromage blanc or cream cheese
120 gm (4 oz) mascarpone cheese

BERRIES
1 punnet raspberries
1 punnet strawberries
1 punnet blackberries
1 punnet blueberries
½ punnet red currants
1 tablespoon sugar
1 tablespoon water

CITRUS SABLÉ PREPARATION Cream the butter and icing sugar until smooth. Gradually add egg yolk and zests. Mix in the flour to form a soft paste. Chill slightly.

Preheat oven to 180°C (350°F). Roll out pastry on a lightly floured surface. Cut 16 rectangular shapes of 10 cm x 4 cm (4 in x 1 ½ in) from the mixture, place on a tray and bake for approximately 10 minutes. If necessary, turn tray around once for even colour and cooking.

ICE-CREAM PREPARATION Warm the milk and add the glucose. When the mix reaches a little over blood temperature (40°C/104°F), mix in the yolks and the sugar. Keep stirring until the mix reaches a temperature of 85°C (185°F) or until it starts to thicken. Pass through a fine sieve and cool. Blend this mixture into the fromage blanc and mascarpone in larger bowl until homogenous. Churn in an ice-cream machine then transfer to a tray lined with plastic wrap. The mix should be to a depth of 2 ½ cm (1 in) in the tray. Set in the freezer. Just before serving, cut rectangles of 10 cm x 4 cm (4 in x 1 ½ in) from the slab and return them to the freezer to firm.

BERRY PREPARATION Gently wash the berries and dry. Slice the strawberries into a small bowl. Add the sugar and water, mix and marinate for 1 hour before serving.

PRESENTATION Place a sable biscuit on serving dishes. Place a rectangle of the ice-cream on top and then another sable biscuit. Arrange the marinated strawberries and then the rest of the berries on the top and on the sides of the sable. Dust with a touch of icing sugar and serve immediately.

This is a striking dessert with the powerful aroma and taste of the fresh raspberry and sorbet. The cooked cream is like a crème brûlée that can easily absorb the strong flavours of the raspberry. Just choose a time when raspberries are abundant to enjoy the best of their season.

Raspberry Chiboust Tart

❀ ❀ MT HORROCKS CORDON CUT RIESLING Clare Valley, SA This dessert wine is made by cutting the cane of the vines, allowing the grapes to hang and raisin on the vine. An elegant dessert wine with citrus and spice flavours and lingering acidity.

❀ ❀ CHÂTEAU DU PAVILION St Croix du Mont, France The appellation of St Croix du Mont looks across to Sauternes from opposite banks of the Garonne. The wines are somewhat less expressive than sauterne, offering a simpler, but none the less delicious alternative. Light apricot, honey and light toasted almond flavours.

❊ ❊ **MACULAN DINDARELLO VENETO, Italy** This producer from Northern Italy makes excellent sweet wines. Made from moscato grapes, as is traditional in this region, dried and made into a concentrated dessert wine, with a floral, grapey bouquet and luscious palate.

❊ ❊ ❊ **VEUVE CLIQUOT PONSARDIN DEMI-SEC Champagne, France** Champagne is such a great versatile food wine, suited for any time of day and any occasion. This demi-sec is a sweeter style of champagne which is delicious with fresh berries and lighter desserts.

This is a dessert that reflects summer so beautifully – use any berries you are able to put your hands on. There is a certain crescendo to the berry season and the peak is when all the berries are available in abundance, if you are lucky you might find some currants.

Summer Berries

♣ ♣

RASPBERRY CHIBOUST TART

SERVES 8

SHORT SWEET PASTRY
250 gm (8 oz) plain flour
125 gm (4 oz) icing sugar
pinch fine salt
125 gm (4 oz) unsalted butter, diced
1 whole egg
10 egg yolks

CRÈME BRÛLÉE
200 ml (7 fl oz) cream
3 egg yolks
100 gm (3 ½ oz) caster sugar
30 fresh raspberries
1 vanilla bean

CHIBOUST CREAM
75 gm (2 ½ oz) crème fraîche
75 ml (2 ½ fl oz) milk
1 vanilla bean
4 egg yolks
75 gm (2 ½ oz) caster sugar
75 gm (2 ½ oz) corn flour
2 leaves gelatine, soaked in water
40 gm (1 ½ oz) caster sugar, extra
6 egg whites

SWEET PASTRY PREPARATION Sift the flour, icing sugar and salt together. Rub in the diced butter until a crumbly consistency is reached. Add the whole egg and egg yolks and mix until you have a smooth paste. *Chill for 1 hour.* Preheat oven to 180°C (350°F). Roll the pastry to 2 mm (⅛ in) thick and place on a baking tray. Bake until golden brown. Cut while still warm into 8 cm (3 ¼ in) circles.

CRÈME BRÛLÉE Preheat oven to 120°C (240°F). Pour brûlée mix into 8 cm (3 ¼ in) diameter round Sil-pat moulds to a height of about 1 cm (½ in), and cook for 25 minutes. *Cool and refrigerate the day before use.*

CHIBOUST CREAM PREPARATION Place the crème fraîche and milk in a small heavy-based saucepan. Split the vanilla bean and scrape the seeds from the centre then add vanilla to the milk and crème fraîche mixture. Slowly bring to the boil over a gentle heat.

Whisk the egg yolks and 75 gm (2 ½ oz) sugar together in a bowl until pale and creamy, add the corn flour and mix to a smooth paste. Add half the boiling milk mixture and whisk until smooth, return the pot to the heat and stir in the remaining milk, re-boil stirring constantly. Cook for a further 1–2 minutes until thick. Add the previously soaked gelatine, mix through and cool.

RASPBERRY SORBET

60 gm (2 oz) caster sugar
6 tablespoons water
350 gm (12 oz) raspberries
juice of 1 lemon

GLASS BISCUIT

30 gm (1 oz) butter
30 gm (1 oz) caster sugar
30 gm (1 oz) plain flour, sieved
30 gm (1 oz) glucose syrup

CHIBOUST PREPARATION CONTINUED Whisk the 40 gm (1 ½ oz) of caster sugar with the egg whites to a stiff meringue. Fold into previously cooked cream mixture, very carefully. Pipe into 8 cm (3 ¼ in) diameter rings, smooth the top and freeze.

SORBET PREPARATION Place the sugar and water in a saucepan over a low heat and warm until the sugar has dissolved then bring to the boil. Remove from the heat and cool completely. Place the raspberries and lemon juice together in a blender and pureé. Pass through a fine sieve and stir into the cooled sugar syrup. Churn the mixture in an ice-cream maker, and freeze.

GLASS BISCUIT PREPARATION Preheat oven to 170°C (330°F). Mix all the ingredients into a smooth paste and *refrigerate overnight before use*. The next day, roll the mix between two sheets of greaseproof paper, refrigerate again for 20 minutes. Peel off the top paper layer and place the bottom paper on a baking tray. Bake in the oven until golden brown. Place a sheet of greaseproof paper on top and roll out thinly with a rolling pin whilst the mixture is still hot from the oven. Cut 8 cm (3 ¼ in) diameter discs with a metal ring cutter.

PRESENTATION Place sweet pastry in the middle of a plate, place crème brûlée on top of the disc. Then the chiboust cream on top of that, and to finish top with a Glass Biscuit. Arrange 12 fresh raspberries on top of the chiboust cream per plate and a quenelle of raspberry sorbet to finish in the centre.

The 'floating island' is a classic French dessert that I have modified to suit our summer ingredients. The sorbet can be made of raspberry for a more vibrant colour and the garnish could then be poached strawberry and rhubarb if mango is out of season. However, my constant is the superb Sauternes Anglaise.

Mango and Passionfruit 'Ile Flottante'

This is a highly perfumed dessert, and because of its lightness and
freshness it is an ideal summer dessert.

Lychee and Gooseberry Soup

MANGO AND PASSIONFRUIT 'ILE FLOTTANTE'
WITH GUAVA SORBET AND SAUTERNES ANGLAISE

SERVES 8

FLOATING ISLAND
200 gm (7 oz) egg whites
300 gm (10 oz) sugar

GUAVA SORBET
500 gm (1 lb) fresh guava
250 ml (8 fl oz) water
250 gm (8 oz) sugar
50 ml (1 ½ fl oz) lemon juice

SAUTERNES ANGLAISE
100 ml (3 ½ fl oz) cream
50 ml (1 ½ fl oz) passionfruit juice (no seeds)
50 ml (2 fl oz) Sauternes
2 egg yolks
40 gm (1 ½ oz) sugar

ORANGE AND SESAME BISCUIT
125 ml (4 fl oz) orange juice
250 gm (8 oz) icing sugar
2 oranges, zested
90 gm (3 oz) cake flour
125 gm (4 oz) sesame seeds
90 gm (3 oz) butter, melted and warm

MANGO AND PASSIONFRUIT SALAD
1 ripe mango, still firm enough to dice
3 passionfruit

FLOATING ISLAND PREPARATION Preheat oven to 150° (300°F). Add the sugar to the egg whites and whisk in a bowl over hot water until the sugar is dissolved. Place into a mixer, whisk on high speed until the meringue has reached firm peaks.

Lightly spray 8 soufflé moulds with non-stick spray. Pipe the meringue into the centre of the moulds in one continuous motion to avoid any air bubbles. Flatten the surface with a palette knife and run your finger around the edge to remove any excess mixture and to help the meringue rise. Place the moulds in a deep-sided tray and fill the tray with hot water to half way up the side of the moulds.

Place the dish into the oven. Bake for 15 minutes and rotate the dish (to allow for even cooking), bake for a further 15 minutes. Remove from oven and cool.

Pour cold water over the meringue gently until they separate from the moulds, remove some of the core with the help of a small ice-cream scoop and place onto a wet cutting board. Use a pastry cutter dipped into hot water to trim the sides so that they are nice and even. Reserve the meringues onto a tray drizzled with water to avoid them sticking.

GUAVA SORBET PREPARATION Blend the guava in a food processor or a blender and strain through a fine sieve. Weigh it to make sure you have 500 gm (1 lb) and set aside. Bring the water and sugar to the boil until the sugar has dissolved then cool. Add this sugar syrup to the guava and mix in the lemon juice. Let stand for 15 minutes and then churn in an ice-cream maker. Pour into a chilled container and set in the freezer.

SAUTERNE SAUCE PREPARATION In two separate pots, bring the cream to the boil, and the juice and wine to the boil. Whisk the egg yolks and sugar and stir in the hot cream followed by the wine and juice. Return the mixture to the stove and cook stirring constantly until the mixture covers the back of a spoon and becomes thicker. Strain and cool.

BISCUIT PREPARATION Mix the orange juice into the icing sugar to make a smooth batter. Add all the other dry ingredients with the warm melted butter last. Chill in the refrigerator overnight. Preheat oven to 180°C (350°F). Pipe the mixture onto trays lined with baking paper and bake until golden brown. Let cool slightly and mould into desired shape. Store in an airtight container until ready to use.

PRESENTATION Place a small scoop of the guava sorbet onto the middle of a deep soup plate (on a small piece of sponge or biscuit if you have it to prevent it moving on the plate). Spoon a little diced mango around and place a floating island over the sorbet, push down lightly. Pour some Sauternes Anglaise around it and drizzle the top of the floating island with fresh passionfruit and a little extra mango. Dust a sesame biscuit with icing sugar and place it onto the floating island.

WINE NOTES

✽ ✽ MARGAN BOTRYTIS SEMILLON Hunter Valley, NSW
Andrew Margan has had great success with this style which blends late harvest and botrytis infected fruit, to produce a lighter fresher style of sweet wine.

✽ ✽ SAROCCO MOSCATO D'ASTI Piedmonte, Italy For those yet to be charmed by these Italian sweet wines, Sarocco is a great example. Fresh, fruity, floral and lightly 'frizzante', is perfect with fruit plates or lighter desserts. Best when drunk young.

CARAMELISED PINEAPPLE AND GINGER TART

SERVES 8

PINEAPPLE CUSTARD

325 ml (11 fl oz) pineapple juice
1 vanilla bean
85 gm (2 ½ ounces) sugar
1 tablespoon corn flour
1 tablespoon flour
4 egg yolks
300 ml (10 fl oz) fresh cream, whipped

CARAMEL SAUCE AND GARNISH

1 cup caster sugar
1 cup water
1 cup small dice of pineapple

PINEAPPLE AND GINGER CONFIT

1 golden or Betonga pineapple, peeled and cut in
  small dice
2 apples, peeled and cut in small dice
200 gm (7 oz) sugar
1 tablespoon butter
1 tablespoon candied ginger, chopped

TART SHELLS

12 filo pastry sheets
1 cup melted butter
1 cup icing sugar, sifted
8 metal rings of 8 cm (3 ¼ in) diameter
  x 3 cm (1 in) high sides or use small
  individual soufflé dishes

CUSTARD PREPARATION Bring the pineapple juice, vanilla bean and sugar to the boil, then reduce heat to a simmer. Remove a little pineapple juice and mix it with corn flour, flour and egg yolks. Add this mixture to the warm juice and whisk thoroughly for 5 minutes whilst boiling. Remove from heat and strain, cool and refrigerate. Before using, add 1 part whipped cream to 1 part custard and fold together ready for piping, this will lighten the custard.

PINEAPPLE AND GINGER CONFIT PREPARATION Combine all ingredients and bring to the boil then simmer until thick and no liquid is left, the consistency of a sweet jam.

TART SHELL PREPARATION Preheat oven to 180°C (350°F). Lay a sheet of filo on a clean bench and brush with melted butter repeat for the next two sheets and dust the third with icing sugar. Repeat with the next three sheets only brushing with butter in between each sheet. Cut the sheet in squares about 15 cm (6 in) on each side. Make another batch with the remaining filo.

Fit a square of filo sheets into a greased ring. Press the filo well to reach the edge and the bottom of the ring. Use scissors to trim the excess filo pastry that sits over the top of the edge of the rings.

TART SHELL PREPARATION CONTINUED If you are using soufflé bowls, you will need to cut the filo into a large circle of 14 to 15 cm (6 in) diameter) to fit inside the bowl. Set the tarts aside for 20 minutes before you bake them. Repeat this process with the rest of the filo pastry to fill all the moulds.

Fill each mould with a layer of plastic wrap overlapping the side and then fill with raw rice or baking beans and fold the plastic wrap over the beans to form a little bundle in the tart. The plastic wrap will not burn when you cook the tart. Blind bake for 15 minutes while checking regularly to ensure they brown evenly. When golden brown, remove from the oven, cool and then remove the plastic wrap bundles. Return to the oven and cook until the bases are golden. Remove from the oven and from the moulds and place on a rack to cool.

CARAMEL SAUCE PREPARATION Combine the sugar and the water in a pot and bring to the boil. Continue to boil until a caramel is achieved. Add a little water to adjust to a sauce-like consistency and reserve.

PRESENTATION Put 2 tablespoons of pineapple confit in each tart shell, level it to fill the bottom and pipe the custard on top to fill the tart shells to the rim. Flatten with a metal spatula. Sprinkle with plenty of sugar then caramelise with a blow torch until golden brown adding a little more sugar if the caramel starts to burn. Place the caramelised pineapple tart on a plate, you may need a little custard under to prevent it from sliding. Set a spoonful of diced pineapple on the side and on top of the pineapple place a slice of the ice-cream terrine (see recipe page 230). Drizzle a touch of the caramel sauce around the plate.

COCONUT AND PINEAPPLE TERRINE

SERVES 4–6

1 triangle terrine dish or a terrine of any shape
for the ice-cream

PINEAPPLE SORBET
300 ml (10 fl oz) fresh golden pineapple purée
(purée in a blender)
75 gm (2 ½ oz) sugar
30 gm (1 oz) glucose
¼ cup water

COCONUT ICE-CREAM
500 ml (16 fl oz) milk
600 ml (1 pint) cream
150 ml (5 fl oz) coconut cream
120 gm (4 oz) sugar
3 egg yolks

PINEAPPLE SORBET PREPARATION Bring everything to the boil in a pot, strain and cool then churn in an ice-cream machine once you have cooled your mix.

COCONUT ICE-CREAM PREPARATION Bring the milk, cream and the coconut cream to the boil. Combine sugar and yolks and add some hot milk mixture to the yolk mixture, stirring continuously. Then add the egg mixture to the hot milk mixture and cook at medium heat, stirring until it coats the back of a spoon. Strain and cool on ice. Once the mixture is cold, churn in an ice-cream machine and store in freezer.

TERRINE ASSEMBLY Line a triangular terrine mould first with greaseproof paper and then with plastic wrap and create even layers of pineapple sorbet and coconut ice-cream by placing first a finger deep of sorbet, then a layer of ice-cream then sorbet again and finish lastly with the ice-cream. *Freeze the terrine overnight prior to serving.* You will need to remove the greaseproof paper and plastic wrap before you cut the terrine. If you are using the whole terrine, cut what you need first before you unwrap it.

✦ ✦

APPLE GÂTEAUX
WITH CALVADOS CHANTILLY CREAM

SERVES 4–6

APPLE GÂTEAUX
12 Granny Smith apples, peeled and cored

APPLE AND RAISIN COMPOTE
75 ml (2 ½ oz) apple cider
150 g (5 oz) caster sugar
2 green apples, peeled, cored and diced
    into brunoise
2 tablespoons sultanas

CALVADOS CHANTILLY CREAM
1 cup double cream
1 tablespoon Calvados
1 tablespoon caster sugar

APPLE GATEAUX PREPARATION Preheat oven to 125°C (240°F). Butter the bottom of a 15 cm (6 in) baking tray and line it with greaseproof paper. Using a sharp mandolin, thinly slice the apples. Lay the apples over the bottom of the tray, and repeat the same process until you have 20 layers. Bake in the oven for 4 hours, with a sheet of baking paper and another tray on top. Cool, refrigerate overnight, still with the top tray in place.

APPLE AND RAISIN COMPÓTE PREPARATION Reduce the apple cider by half in a saucepan over moderate heat. Add the sugar to the cider and mix. Continue the reduction until it coats the back of a spoon. Add the apple dice and the sultanas. Cool and refrigerate.

CALVADOS CHANTILLY PREPARATION Lightly whisk the cream and caster sugar to soft-peak stage. Fold in the Calvados and refrigerate for at least 1 hour.

PRESENTATION Slightly warm the apple gateaux in the oven. Slice the gateaux into 3 cm x 7 cm (1 in x 2 ¾ in) rectangles. Place gateaux pieces onto serving plates off centre. Add a small pool of the cider sauce and a quenelle of the chantilly cream.

✦ ✦

APRICOT FRANGIPANE
WITH LIME SABAYON

SERVES 6

FRANGIPANE MIX
100 gm (3 ½ oz) unsalted butter
100 gm (3 ½ oz) caster sugar
2 whole eggs
100 gm (3 ½ oz) ground almonds
1 tablespoon plain flour

LIME SABAYON
120 gm (4 oz) sugar
100 ml (3 ½ fl oz) water
100 ml (3 ½ fl oz) white wine
6 egg yolks, beaten
2 limes, juiced

APRICOT COMPOTE
12 apricots
50 ml (1 ½ fl oz) water
400 gm (14 oz) sugar
400 ml (14 fl oz) water
125 ml (4 fl oz) sweet wine
2 vanilla pods

PUFF PASTRY
1 kg (2 lb) puff pastry (frozen is fine)

FRANGIPANE PREPARATION Cream the butter and sugar together until pale using an electric mixer and flat beater, gradually beat in the eggs until evenly incorporated. Fold the ground almonds and flour in. Chill for a few hours before use.

APRICOT COMPOTE PREPARATION Blanch the apricots in boiling water for 1 or 2 minutes, chill in iced water and peel the skin away. Cut in half and remove the stone. Make a light caramel with the 50 ml (1 ½ fl oz) water and the sugar. Add the rest of the water when a nice golden colour is achieved. Then, add the wine and the vanilla bean. In a larger pot, place the apricots and cover with the syrup. Cook slowly for 15–20 minutes or until tender but still holding their shape. Cool in the syrup.

PUFF PASTRY PREPARATION Preheat oven to 180°C (350°F). On a lightly floured surface, roll out the pastry to approx 3 mm (⅛ inch) thick, fork the pastry, spread a thin layer of frangipane mixture on top and then an apricot half keeping a small space between each apricot. Cut using a round 7 cm (3 in) diameter cutter to make neat circles. Lift these discs and put them on a flat oven tray and bake for about 10 minutes or until the edges are golden. Alternatively, you can cook the whole apricot sheet and cut the circles after baking.

LIME SABAYON PREPARATION AND PRESENTATION Place the sugar and water in a saucepan and heat until the sugar dissolves to form a sugar syrup. Let the syrup cool to room temperature then place the white wine and the beaten egg yolks in a bowl and whisk over a pot of gently boiling water until nice and fluffy. Add the lime juice and mix. Serve with the apricot frangipane. Warm the little tarts in an oven if necessary. Pour a ladle of lime sabayon on each serving plate and stack the tarts on top of the sabayon. Dust with icing sugar and serve.

This dessert has a concentrated apricot flavour that will burst in the mouth. The apricots are effectively cooked twice and this enhances their colour and flavour. The crispness of the frangipane tart with the tartness of the lime sabayon will melt resistance away.

Apricot Frangipane

WINE NOTES

❀ ❀ **DOMAINE DE DURBAN MUSCAT BEAUMES-DE-VENISE Rhône Valley, France** Fresh, fragrant style of dessert wine, grapey, floral with tropical fruit and a hint of honey.

❀ ❀ **PELLEGRINO MOSCATO DI PANTELLERIA Sicily, Italy** From the tiny island of Pantelleria, made from the Zibibbo grape. Fresh style with light raisin flavour and hints of citrus and rose petals.

The Poached Figs in Beaume de Venise makes an excellent combination that will pleasantly surprise the diner.

Poached Figs in Beaume de Venise

WINE NOTES

❉ ❉ **WELLINGTON ICED RIESLING TAS** An excellent style
from the talented winemaker Andrew Hood. Flavours of
pineapple and lime, with refreshing acidity.

❉ ❉ ❉ **DOMAINE PICHOT VOUVRAY MOELLEUX Loire
Valley, France** Domaine Pichot produces great value, age
worthy sweet wines from chenin blanc grapes. Flavours
include honeysuckle, pear, stone fruits and spice with
characteristic clean acidity.

Pineapple is a difficult fruit to turn
into a dessert. Still, this is perfectly
balanced with the ginger and coconut.
There is plenty of preparation but
a quick plate up will help when the time
comes to serve it.

Caramelised Pineapple and Ginger Tart

Coconut and Pineapple Terrine

The composition of this dessert makes
it quick and easy to make.

Apple Gâteaux

WINE NOTES

❉ ❉ ❉ **SAUVEROY COTEAUX DU LAYON CUVÉE
NECTAR Loire Valley, France** Sweet wine made from
chenin blanc, whilst deliciously sweet it balances out with a
palate-cleansing acidity.

❉ ❉ ❉ **CHÂTEAU JOLYS JURANÇON South-West
France** From the foothills of the Pyrenees, this wine displays
pear and spice characters with a rancio edge. Lovely with
desserts that are not too sweet.

✦ ✦ ✦

POACHED FIGS IN BEAUME DE VENISE
WITH GLASS BISCUITS

SERVES 6

SABAYON BEAUME DE VENISE
125 gm (4 oz) caster sugar
125 ml (4 fl oz) Beaume de Venise
5 egg yolks
3 leaves gelatine
1 cup cream, slightly whipped

POACHED FIGS IN BEAUME DE VENISE
300 gm (10 oz) caster sugar
50 gm (1 ½ oz) butter
1 cup Beaume de Venise
1 cup water
6 fresh figs, quartered lengthways

GLASS BISCUITS
100 gm (3 ½ oz) fondant
75 gm (2 ½ oz) liquid glucose

NOUGATINE
250 gm (8 oz) flaked almonds
325 gm (11 oz) caster sugar
50 gm (1 ½ oz) butter

SABAYON PREPARATION Boil the sugar and wine together, whisk the egg yolks in a bowl and when the boiling sugar reaches 120°C (245°F) add it to the egg yolks whisking the whole time. Then add the soaked gelatine leaves and whisk until cold. Fold in the slightly whipped cream. Place 6 rings 4 cm (1 ½ in) diameter x 3 cm (1 ¼ inch) high on a tray. Fill the rings with the mix and freeze.

POACHED FIGS PREPARATION Place the sugar in a pan over low heat and caramelise to a light blond caramel. Add butter and deglaze with the wine and water. Add the figs, with the peel intact, cook slowly reducing the liquid until the figs are cooked but still hold their shape. Reserve.

GLASS BISCUITS PREPARATION Heat and blend the fondant and glucose until the mixture reaches a temperature of 160°C (325°F). Pour onto a greaseproof paper sheet and cool. Cut into 7 cm (2 ¾ in) diameter rounds. This is used to make a 'roof' for the dessert.

NOUGATINE PREPARATION Preheat the oven to 180°C (375°F). Toast the flaked almonds until light brown. Cook the sugar in a pan over low heat stirring gently and continuously with a wooden spatula until it dissolves and colours to a light golden caramel. Add the butter, and stir until dissolved. Add the almonds and stir them in over a low heat, for 1 minute. Pour the nougatine onto a tray with greaseproof paper placing another sheet on top; roll out the nougatine thinly and cut into 7 cm (2 ³/₇ in) diameter round discs with a cutter.

PRESENTATION Arrange each sabayon on a nougatine disc in the middle of each plate, arrange 4 fig quarters around the sabayon with a little drizzled sauce; place the glass biscuit nicely on top of the dessert.

⚜ ⚜

LYCHEE AND GOOSEBERRY SOUP
WITH MINT AND BASIL ICE-CREAM

SERVES 4

SOUP
100 gm (3 ½ oz) caster sugar
1 cup water
16–20 gooseberries
40 lychees
½ lemon, juiced

BASIL JELLY
1 bunch fresh basil leaves
1 cup mineral water
1 tablespoon caster sugar
2 leaves gelatine

MINT AND BASIL ICE-CREAM
¼ cup fresh mint leaves (reserve tips for garnish)
¼ cup fresh basil leaves
500 ml (16 fl oz) milk
150 ml (5 fl oz) cream
1 tablespoon milk powder
30 gm (1 oz) glucose
100 gm (3 ½ oz) caster sugar

SOUP PREPARATION Place the sugar and water into a saucepan and bring to the boil. Add the gooseberries and cook for 5 minutes, then remove them and allow to cool. Peel and de-stone the lychees and cook in the syrup with the lemon juice added. Cook for 20 minutes until the lychees are soft. Strain and reserve some of the lychees for plating. Blend the remaining lychees until you have a smooth pulp. Pass through a fine sieve. Keep adding some syrup to the pulp until a soup consistency is reached.

ICE-CREAM PREPARATION Wash mint and basil leaves well with cold water. Drain and place in a saucepan with the milk and cream and allow the flavours to infuse. Add the milk powder, glucose and sugar and heat to near boiling point. Strain and leave in its liquid state for 24 hours. The next day, freeze in an ice-cream machine.

BASIL JELLY PREPARATION Blanch the leaves and chill them in iced water. Process leaves in a food processor, with the mineral water and sugar. Strain and then heat some of the basil water to melt the soaked and drained gelatine. Mix this into the rest of the basil water, strain again, leave to cool in a container and then set in the refrigerator.

PRESENTATION In deep bowls, place a few lychees and gooseberries with the jelly and mint leaves. Pour some syrup over. Serve the ice-cream separately in a small dish.

I think there is no better fruit than peaches and other stone fruit when they are in full season. The first time you wish to prepare this dessert, I suggest you just concentrate on one element to absorb the technique. This dessert is really several desserts so just choose your favourite part and enjoy preparing it.

Roasted Vanilla Peach

WINE NOTES

 LILLYPILLY BOTRYTIS SAUVIGNON BLANC Riverina, NSW Lillypilly make beautiful sweet wines that are good value and manage that fine balancing act of sweetness without being cloying.

✳ ✳ ✳ **CHÂTEAU DERESZLA 5 PUTTONYAS TOKAJI Hungary** Tokaji is a unique world-renowned style from Hungary. Rich, unctuous, complex style with stone fruit and citrus peel.

This is one of the easiest desserts of this book and will never disappoint – firstly because it is chocolate, secondly it is warm and fills the house with an addictive chocolate smell. And, lastly, because it tastes great. You could just serve only the chocolate sauce but then have some whipped cream or ice-cream ready as well.

Bathers' Chocolate Pudding

WINE NOTES

❀ ❀ **WESTEND ESTATE 3 BRIDGES 'GOLDEN MIST' BOTRYTIS SEMILLON Riverina, NSW** Rich, with apricot, honeyed flavours, vanilla and spice. Manages the fine balancing act of sweetness and acidity very well.

❀ ❀ ❀ **GRANDE MAISON CUVÉE DU CHÂTEAU MONBAZILLAC South-West France** A worthy alternative to the more expensive option of Sauternes. Rich and luscious with concentrated fruits and non-cloying finish.

I love the flavour of caramel, butterscotch and, in that same line, maple syrup. In winter, if you have the chance to be beside a fire place, this would be a great dessert to serve. The log is easy to serve, just place it on a platter, slice it in front of everyone and wait for the comments.

Butterscotch Caramel Log

WINE NOTES

❀ ❀ **CAMPBELLS CLASSIC RUTHERGLEN TOKAY Rutherglen, VIC** Tokay is to lose its naming as it falls into line with the regulation allowing only the sweet wines of Hungary to carry the name Tokaji. A completely different style to those wines, this is a fortified wine made from Muscadelle grapes and done particularly well in Northern Victoria. Its complexity and richness depends on the age of the base material used in the blending. This is a style made from younger material, with a lighter, fresher palate, and delicious tea, roasted coffee, toffee and nutty flavours.

❀ ❀ **TELMO RODRIGUEZ MR MOSCATEL Spain** Telmo Rodriguez makes a number of terrific wines, reflecting the modern Spain whilst respecting its heritage. The MR moscatel is an aromatic dessert wine, with floral scents and sweet grapey palate.

✢ ✢ ✢

ROASTED VANILLA PEACH
WITH PARFAIT, NOUGATINE AND APRICOT COMPOTE

SERVES 8

PEACH PARFAIT
4 peaches, blanched, peeled and cut in halves
apricot sauce (see recipe below)
3 egg yolks
150 gm (5 oz) caster sugar
1 vanilla bean, cut and scraped
420 ml (14 fl oz) cream, semi-whipped

APRICOT COMPOTE AND SAUCE
8 apricots cut in half
100 ml (3 ½ fl oz) sweet wine
1 cup water
100 gm (4 oz) sugar
1 vanilla bean
1 cinnamon stick
1 orange, cut in wedges
1 lemon, cut in wedges

ALMOND NOUGATINE
300 gm (10 oz) sugar
300 gm (10 oz) glucose
200 gm (7 oz) butter
300 gm (10 oz) flaked almonds

PEACH JELLY
400 gm (14 oz) peach purée, strained
80 gm (2 ½ oz) sugar
1 lemon, juiced
4 gelatine leaves, soaked in cold water

ROASTED PEACH
4 large peaches for roasting
1 vanilla bean, cut in eight to make the stalks
2 tablespoons caster sugar

PEACH PARFAIT PREPARATION This recipe will fill one triangular terrine mould with 8 cm (3 ¼ in) sides. Line the dish with non-stick baking paper and then plastic wrap. Poach the peach halves in the apricot sauce (see below) for 20 minutes. Drain and blend to make a purée. Whisk the yolks with sugar over a saucepan of simmering water until they are creamy. Remove from heat, add the vanilla bean scrapings and whisk until cold and fluffy. Add the purée then fold in the semi-whipped cream. Fill the terrine mould and freeze overnight.

APRICOT COMPOTE AND SAUCE PREPARATION Preheat oven to 150°C (300°F). Blanch the apricots in boiling water for 1 minute. Refresh in iced water. Remove the skins. Place the apricot halves into a baking dish, bring all the other ingredients to the boil and pour over the apricots. Cover with aluminium foil and bake in oven until just tender.

Save the best 8 apricot halves for the garnish and blend the rest to make a fine purée. Add a little cooking syrup to achieve a thin sauce. Strain through a fine sieve.

ALMOND NOUGATINE PREPARATION Preheat oven to 180°C (350°F). Caramelise sugar and glucose in a saucepan over gentle heat until a golden caramel. Incorporate the butter with a wooden spoon whilst still on the heat. Remove from the heat and mix in the almonds, spread thinly onto a tray lined with baking paper and place in the oven until fully melted (about 15 minutes). When hot and pliable, place another sheet of baking paper on top, roll as thinly as possible with a rolling pin. Cut into triangles the same size as the terrine while it is still warm.

PEACH JELLY PREPARATION Bring the peach purée to the boil with the sugar and lemon juice. Remove from the heat. Squeeze excess water from the gelatine and stir in. Strain and pour into a tray with 1 cm (½ in) high sides. Refrigerate the jelly in the tray and then cut out circles with an 8 cm (3 ¼ in) cutter. Place the jelly discs on small pieces of baking paper until you are ready to serve. If the jelly is very soft, you might have to freeze it until just ready to plate, it will soften very quickly.

ROASTED PEACH PREPARATION Blanch the peaches in boiling water. Refresh in ice water. Remove the skin from the peaches and cut them in half. Skewer with a 'vanilla stalk' and set aside. Best to do this just before you serve the dessert.

Preheat oven to 220°C (450°F). Dust the peach with caster sugar and bake quickly in oven and/or caramelise under the grill. Set aside while you assemble your other elements.

PRESENTATION Set 8 nougatine biscuits on a flat tray that fit in the freezer. Peel the baking paper off the parfait and cut in 2 cm (¾ in) thick slices and immediately place each slice on a biscuit. Top with the other nougatine biscuit and return to the freezer immediately.

Place the jelly circles in middle of the serving plates. Place an apricot half on the side and drizzle with the apricot sauce. Arrange the nougatine and parfait on the jelly, then the peach on top. Lastly, scoop some apricot sorbet or vanilla ice-cream or apricot sorbet on top of the apricots and serve.

BATHERS' CHOCOLATE PUDDING
WITH TWO SAUCES

SERVES 8

CHOCOLATE PUDDING

150 gm (5 oz) dark chocolate

100 gm (3 ½ oz) soft butter, plus butter
   to grease moulds

100 gm (3 ½ oz) chocolate cake crumbs

50 gm (1 ½ oz) ground hazelnuts

50 gm (1 ½ oz) plain flour

4 eggs, separated

50 gm (1 ½ oz) icing sugar

50 gm (1 ½ oz) caster sugar, plus sugar
   to line moulds

PASSIONFRUIT AND ORANGE SAUCE

200 ml (7 fl oz) passionfruit juice, seeds strained

200 ml (7 fl oz) orange juice

100 gm (3 ½ oz) caster sugar

2 tablespoons cold water

1 tablespoon corn flour

CHOCOLATE SAUCE

300 gm (10 oz) caster sugar

425 ml (14 fl oz) water

125 gm (4 oz) dark cooking chocolate

250 ml (8 fl oz) fresh cream

CHOCOLATE PUDDING PREPARATION Grease 8 cup-size moulds, and then sprinkle with caster sugar. Tap out excess sugar and set aside. Melt chocolate and butter in a double boiler. Mix together chocolate cake crumbs, ground hazelnuts and plain flour.

Beat together egg yolks and icing sugar then add chocolate butter mix. Beat egg whites until stiff, then slowly add caster sugar continuing to beat the mixture until a soft meringue is formed. Do not over-beat.

Add dry ingredients to the chocolate egg yolk mixture, then add a little meringue. Mix gently, then gradually fold in the rest of the meringue. Pour mixture into prepared moulds and cook in a steamer for 30 minutes. Turn puddings out and serve warm with the sauces.

PASSIONFRUIT AND ORANGE SAUCE PREPARATION Combine juices and sugar, boil for 5 minutes. Whisk water and corn flour until the flour dissolves. Pour onto hot sauce and whisk until it thickens.

CHOCOLATE SAUCE PREPARATION Combine all ingredients in a saucepan and boil gently for 20 minutes, stirring from time to time.

PRESENTATION Pour the passionfruit–orange sauce into serving bowls, place the pudding on top and then pour the chocolate sauce over the pudding.

⚜ ⚜

BUTTERSCOTCH CARAMEL LOG

SERVES 6

CARAMEL ICE-CREAM
150 gm (5 oz) caster sugar
1 tablespoon water
100 gm (3 ½ oz) liquid glucose
1 litre (32 fl oz) cream, warmed
6 egg yolks

BUTTERSCOTCH GLAZE
200 gm (7 oz) caster sugar
1 tablespoon water
100 gm (3 ½ oz) golden syrup
1 cup cream
1 leaf gelatine, soaked

SPONGE SHEET
2 egg yolks
½ egg (lightly beat and pour half into a bowl)
60 gm (2 oz) caster sugar
2 whole eggs, extra
60 gm (2 oz) plain flour, sieved

ICE-CREAM PREPARATION Caramelise the sugar and water in a saucepan over gentle heat until a light gold colour is achieved. Mix constantly to avoid burning and mix in the glucose. Deglaze the mix with warm cream, stirring the whole time. Cook for 5 minutes. Pour the mixture onto the egg yolks, whisk and cook until a custard consistency is reached. Strain, then let cool completely. Churn in an ice-cream maker and freeze overnight.

The next day, take the ice-cream out of the freezer and form a log on a sheet of greaseproof paper. Freeze again for 2 hours. When firm, remove the paper and roll the ice-cream in the prepared sponge (see below) to form a perfect log. Trim any excess sponge and freeze again.

SPONGE SHEET PREPARATION Preheat oven to 220°C (425°F). Line a 38 cm (15 in) square baking tray with baking paper. Whisk the 2 egg yolks with the ½ egg together with slightly warmed sugar. Whisk in the additional 2 eggs until the mixture doubles in volume. Carefully fold in the flour. Pour the mixture into the prepared tin and cook until the sponge springs back to the touch.

BUTTERSCOTCH GLAZE PREPARATION Caramelise the sugar in a saucepan with the water, stirring to avoid burning. Add the golden syrup and deglaze with the cream. Squeeze excess water from the gelatine, add to the butterscotch, mix. Remove from the heat and set aside to cool.

FINAL PREPARATION AND PRESENTATION Remove the log from the freezer. Place on a wire rack and coat with the glaze. Return to the freezer to firm again until ready to serve.

These little hedgehog cakes are ideal for a birthday party if you serve them in addition to a fruit dessert. There are only two major components to assemble. Do not forget to eliminate the rum if you are serving children. You could serve this with a vanilla anglaise or a strawberry coulis.

Chocolate Hérisson Cake

DESSERT

There is quite a technique in making these beautiful chocolate sheets but you can achieve this quite easily if you get the acetate sheet from a professional kitchen equipment supplier. The trick is mostly in choosing the timing of when the chocolate is ready to be cut and to be peeled from the acetate paper.

Chocolate Mille Feuille

Ménage à Trois des Chocolats

Quince Cake with Maple Syrup ice-cream

* * *
QUINCE CAKE
WITH MAPLE SYRUP ICE-CREAM

Quinces are a bit of a treat and are also an under-used fruit. This recipe is ideal for the winter season, served warm with a special maple syrup sauce. These flavours remind me of my childhood visit to the 'Cabane a Sucre' where the maple syrup is produced in small cabins in the forests of Québec.

SERVES 8

QUINCE COMPOTE
4 cups water
500 gm (1 lb) sugar
½ bottle white wine
1 cinnamon stick
1 star anise
2 cloves
2 fresh bay leaves
1 lemon
3 quinces, scrubbed well

QUINCE CAKE
100 gm (3 ½ oz) butter
125 gm (4 oz) sugar
2 eggs
125 ml (4 fl oz) cream
1 teaspoon vanilla essence
125 gm (4 oz) plain flour
1 teaspoon bi-carbonate of soda
½ teaspoon baking powder
1 teaspoon ground cinnamon
1 pinch ground clove powder
1 pinch ground ginger

QUINCE PREPARATION Prepare the poaching liquid by placing all the ingredients together in a large baking tray except the quince. Peel, quarter and core the quince and add to the prepared poaching stock. Gather the quince peelings, put them in a bag made of muslin cloth and place in the poaching liquid. Cook for 1 hour or until they are soft and full of flavour. Cool overnight and drain the next day. Cut some of the quince to fit in your cake rings. Dice the rest for the garnish and add a little cooking syrup to this.

CAKE PREPARATION Preheat the oven to 180ºC (350ºF). Cream the butter and sugar until light. Beat in the eggs and fold in the cream and the vanilla essence. Sift in the flour, bi-carbonate of soda, baking powder and the spices. Grease 8 metal rings (3 ½ cm/1 ½ in diameter x 4 cm/1 ¾ high) and place them on a baking tray lined with baking paper. Arrange 2 pieces of cooked quince at the bottom of each ring, you might have to trim them. Fill the rings three-quarters of the way with the cake mixture. Cook in oven for 20 minutes or until they spring back to the touch.

MAPLE SYRUP ICE-CREAM PREPARATION Boil the milk and the maple syrup with the cream and combine the sugar and the yolks. Add the boiling milk and cream to the sugar mixture and cook over a double boiler to the ribbon stage (as for a light custard). While still hot, strain the mixture. Cool down in an ice bath and churn in an ice-cream maker. Put the maple syrup ice-cream in a baking dish and freeze.

MAPLE SYRUP ICE-CREAM
125 ml (4 fl oz) milk
125 ml (4 fl oz) cream
150 ml (5 fl oz) maple syrup
75 gm (2 ½ oz) sugar
2 egg yolks

MAPLE SYRUP SAUCE
200 gm (7 oz) caster sugar
200 ml (7 fl oz) maple syrup
80 gm (2 ½ oz) butter
150 ml (5 fl oz) cream

NUTTY TUILE
100 gm (3 ½ oz) sugar
100 gm (3 ½ oz) glucose
50 ml (1 ½ fl oz) maple syrup
50 ml (1 ½ fl oz) glucose syrup
50 gm (1 ½ oz) butter
50 gm (1 ½ oz) pistachio nuts, toasted
    and chopped
80 gm (2 ½ oz) flaked almonds, toasted
    and chopped

MAPLE SYRUP SAUCE PREPARATION Caramelise the sugar and maple syrup in a saucepan over low heat.
Add the butter. Boil for 5 minutes until completely incorporated. Add the cream and boil for a further
5 minutes. Allow sauce to cool. Re heat when ready to serve.

NUTTY TUILE METHOD Preheat oven to 180°C (350°F). Line a baking tray with baking paper. Mix all the
ingredients together except the nuts and bring to the boil. Add the nuts and mix until the caramel forms
and it has reached a nice golden colour. Pour the mixture immediately onto the paper-lined baking tray.
Spread out thinly and evenly. Bake in the oven for 15–20 minutes being careful not to burn the crust.
When ready, remove from the oven and remove from the baking tray to avoid overcooking. Allow to cool
before cutting. When ready to serve, cut into pieces 2 cm (¾ in) wide x 7 cm (2 ¾ in) long. You may have
to peel the paper from the tuiles before you use them. These can be stored in an airtight container in a
cool place until needed.

PRESENTATION When ready to serve, cut the ice-cream into pieces 2 cm (¾ in) wide x 7 cm (2 ¾ in) long
the same as the nutty tuile. Return to the freezer to firm up. Warm the cakes in an oven set at 150°C
(300°F) for 10 minutes and warm the maple syrup sauce. Set the cakes on serving plates, sandwich the
ice-cream slices between two layers of nutty tuile and set on the plates. Spoon some quince compote and
maple sauce syrup around and serve.

CHOCOLATE MILLE FEUILLE
WITH HAZELNUT MOUSSE

SERVES 4

CHOCOLATE DIAMOND
200 gm (7 oz) bakers chocolate
1 tablespoon icing sugar, for the dusting

VANILLA PASTRY CREAM
1 vanilla bean
2 cups milk
110 grams (3 ½ oz) caster sugar
4 egg yolks
45 gm (1 ½ oz) corn flour
25 gm (1 oz) unsalted butter

HAZELNUT MOUSSE
125 gm (4 oz) cool vanilla pastry cream
   (recipe below)
60 gm (2 oz) unsalted butter, room temperature
30 gm (1 oz) hazelnut paste (or Nutella)

CHOCOLATE DIAMOND PREPARATION Melt the bakers chocolate in a heatproof bowl over hot water and stir until smooth. Pour the chocolate on to an acetate plastic sheet and spread out as thinly as possible using a pastry spatula. Leave until the chocolate is set and pliable (5 minutes in cool area) then cut out 12 diamond-shaped chocolate sheets about 10 cm (4 in) square and set them aside in a cool place.

VANILLA PASTRY CREAM PREPARATION Split the vanilla bean and scrape the inside with the tip of a knife. Add the bean and the seeds to the milk. Add half the sugar and bring to the boil in a heavy sauce pan. Beat the egg yolks with the remaining sugar and the corn flour until it is light and fluffy. Whisk a little hot milk into the egg mixture. Pour the egg mixture into the milk mixture saucepan and bring to a simmer. Cook for about 3 minutes until thick, without boiling. Remove from the heat and whisk in the butter. Transfer to a shallow dish and refrigerate to cool rapidly.

HAZELNUT MOUSSE PREPARATION Slowly beat the vanilla pastry cream with the soft butter, add hazelnut paste and blend until smooth.

PRESENTATION Place a tiny amount of mousse on the centre of a plate, set one sheet of chocolate on it and press down. Pipe some little mounds of hazelnut mousse to cover the base, top with a second layer of chocolate diamond and repeat for the final layer. Dust with icing sugar if desired.

WINE NOTES

❀ ALL SAINTS RUTHERGLEN MUSCAT Rutherglen, VIC
All Saints has a great cellar door to visit; set in an 1800s castle setting with an array of fortified wines to try, ranging up to 80 years base material. This one is the younger style, with grapey appeal, rose petal aroma and raisin sweetness.

❀ ❀ ❀ CHÂTEAU DOISY-DAËNE Barsac, France This wine is made as a lighter, more delicate style. Its sweeter palate can have apricot, floral, citrus and lightly baked apple flavours and is balanced with fresh racey acidity.

꙳ ꙳

CHOCOLATE HÉRISSON CAKE

SERVES 8

CHOCOLATE SPONGE
10 egg yolks
100 gm (3 ½ oz) sugar
5 egg whites
60 gm (2 oz) sugar
80 gm (2 ½ oz) flour, sifted
2 tablespoons cocoa powder
6 tablespoons rum
extra cocoa powder, to serve

CHOCOLATE GANACHE
600 gm (20 oz) dark chocolate, chopped
100 gm (3 ½ oz) butter
300 ml (10 fl oz) cream

CHOCOLATE GANACHE PREPARATION Break the chocolate into a bowl. Add the butter and melt over a double boiler. Boil the cream and add to the chocolate. Mix until you have a smooth and silky ganache. Allow to cool before you use it.

CHOCOLATE SPONGE PREPARATION Preheat oven to 180°C (350°F). Beat the egg yolks with the sugar until white and fluffy, set aside. Beat the egg whites and sugar until stiff. Fold the sifted flour and the cocoa powder into the egg yolk mixture. Then fold in the beaten egg white mixture. Spread the chocolate mixture ½ cm (¼ in) thick on baking paper and bake until slightly firm, it should only take about 5 minutes. To make sure it is cooked, just press with the tip of your finger; it should be firm but springy.

Cool the cake and peel away from the baking paper. Have 3 round cutters in decreasing size ready to cut the cake — start with 7 cm (2 ¾ in), then 5 cm (2 in) and finally 3 cm (1 in). Cut 8 rounds of each size. Put the larger circles on a clean kitchen bench or on a piece of greaseproof paper. Sprinkle each cake layer as you build them with the rum diluted in a little bit of water or sugar syrup (refer | Basics page 309) if you have this. Spread the ganache between each layer before adding the next size cake layer. Finally cover the external surface of the cake to give it a bombe shape. To make the spike effect, pull the ganache with a flat spatula (touch and pull). When you are ready to serve, sprinkle with the extra cocoa powder. You can store these cakes in the refrigerator but allow the external moisture to dry before you apply the cocoa powder.

WINE NOTES

꙳ ꙳ ꙳ **CLOS DE PAULILLES BANYULS RIMAGE** Roussillon,
France Grown on barren looking terraced vineyards, close to
the Spanish border, these sweet red wines offer an alternative
style to accompany chocolate. Concentrated with dark berry
flavours and richly textured.

✢ ✢ ✢

MÉNAGE À TROIS DES CHOCOLATS

This is now a signature dessert at Bathers' Pavilion. The elements often change but two that keep coming back are the cone and the chocolate tart. The tart was inspired long ago by Stephanie Alexander and the chocolate cone by Christine Manfield.

SERVES 12

CHOCOLATE ICE-CREAM CONE
750 ml (26 fl oz) milk
450 ml (15 fl oz) cream
300 gm (10 oz) sugar
7 egg yolks
200 gm (7 oz) dark chocolate couverture,
    finely chopped
6 tablespoons chocolate ganache (use
    the ganache from the tart recipe, you
    should have enough)

CHOCOLATE TART BASE
120 gm (4 oz) butter
115 gm (4 oz) sugar
pinch of salt
dash of vanilla essence
50 gm (1 ½ oz) cocoa powder
120 gm (4 oz) plain flour

GANACHE FILLING
400 ml (14 fl oz) cream
525 grams (17 oz) chocolate

ICE-CREAM CONE PREPARATION Boil the milk with the cream, and combine the sugar and the yolks. Add the boiling milk and cream to the sugar mixture and cook over a double boiler, stirring, to reach the ribbon stage (as for a light custard). While still hot, strain the mixture over the chopped couverture and mix until it is combined. Cool in an ice bath and churn as a normal ice-cream in an ice-cream maker.

Prepare some baking paper cones and secure with a stapler, about 12 cm (5 in) high and 5 cm (2 in) in diameter at the opening. You might need to put these cones in tall glasses to hold them (like a Champagne glass). Pipe the soft ice-cream with the help of a piping bag into the cones filling them nearly to the top. Shake the cone slightly to remove any air bubbles. Freeze them immediately and when the ice-cream is firm add half a tablespoon of warm chocolate ganache to form the base. Freeze for 8 hours before you use them. You will have some ice-cream left over, I am sure you will find someone to enjoy it.

TART BASE PREPARATION Pre heat the oven to 180°C (350°F). Cream the butter and sugar. Add the rest of the ingredients and mix to a dough. Roll to 3 mm (⅛ in) thick and line a greased tart ring 24 cm (9 ½ in) in diameter and 3 cm (1 in) deep. Bake blind for 8–10 minutes. Allow to cool and fill to the top with the ganache filling. To serve, slice the tart into 12 pieces using a hot knife. If you are serving the tart on its own, you could serve it with ice-cream or whipped cream.

WINE NOTE

❋ ❋ VILLA MARIA RESERVE NOBLE
RIESLING Marlborough, NZ A delicious
dessert wine worthy of laying down a few
years to gain in richness. Citrus, pear, apricot
and honey characters.

CHOCOLATE MARQUISE
180 gm (6 oz) butter
165 gm (5 ½ oz) sugar
110 gm (4 oz) cocoa
8 egg yolks
65 gm (2 oz) clear honey
40 ml (1 ½ fl oz) water
95 gm (3 ½ oz) dark chocolate, melted
300 ml (10 fl oz) semi whipped cream
chocolate sponge cake (refer | Basics page 310)
1 cup frozen raspberries

CHOCOLATE MARQUISE GLAZE
100 ml (3 ½ fl oz) water
125 ml (4 fl oz) cream
25 ml (1 fl oz) glucose syrup
300 gm (10 oz) dark cooking chocolate, chopped

GANACHE FILLING PREPARATION Bring the cream to the boil, pour over the chocolate and whisk until smooth.

MARQUISE PREPARATION Cream the butter, sugar and cocoa until very smooth. Add the egg yolks, honey, water and warm chocolate and mix. Once the mix has cooled to room temperature, fold through the semi-whipped cream. Line a baking tray with plastic wrap. Cut a piece of the chocolate sponge to fit the baking tray. Sprinkle the chocolate sponge with the raspberries. Spread the chocolate mixture over the raspberries. Place in the refrigerator until set, approximately 30–45 minutes. Remove from the refrigerator and top with the chocolate glaze (see below). Return to the refrigerator until you are ready to serve. To serve cut each portion into pieces 2 cm (¾ in) wide x 7 cm (2 ¾ in) long.

CHOCOLATE GLAZE PREPARATION Warm the water, cream and glucose. Fold in the chopped chocolate. Stir until smooth.

MÉNAGE À TROIS DES CHOCOLATS PRESENTATION Make sure your serving plates are as cold as possible without putting them in the refrigerator. Firstly set the chocolate tart slice on the plate, then the raspberry slice and lastly peel the paper off the cone and place it on the plate (as shown on page 244) serve immediately. At the table you could pour a touch of sauce anglaise (refer | Basics page 310) in the middle of the plate if desired.

Chapter Ten
❦ Petits Fours ❦
RECIPES

Clockwise from left: Cigarettes with Orange Cream (page 256), Rosewater Turkish delight (page 257), Candied Orange Friand (page 257), Apricot Pâte de Fruit and Almond Star Anis Tuiles (page 261). Opposite page, Macaroons (page 256).

LIME TURKISH DELIGHT

MAKES ABOUT 20 PIECES

INGREDIENTS

3 leaves gelatine

100 ml (3 ½ fl oz) hot water

200 gm (7 oz) caster sugar

1 lime, zest only

a few drops of lime oil

1 tablespoon icing sugar, for dusting

1 tablespoon cornflour, for dusting

PREPARATION AND PRESENTATION Soak gelatine leaves in the water with the lime zest, until they are softened. Add the sugar and bring to the boil. Remove from the heat. Cool, strain and add the lime oil and pour into lightly oiled tray. When set, cut into rectangles 4 cm x 2 cm (1 ½ x ¾ in), roll in icing sugar mixed with the corn flour and serve.

From left, Pistachio Nougat and Nuts, Raspberry Sponge, Lime Turkish Delight and Lemon Tartlet

Petits fours, little treats and mignardises – are all part of the wonderful world of confectionery. Every culture has its little treats, more morsels than desserts – the marzipan fruit of Thailand, the sugar candy of America, the Middle Eastern baklava, the chocolate of Belgium, and the nougat of France. In France, petits fours generally fall into two main categories – either they are a style of cookie like Madeleine, macaroon, palmier or sablé; or they are glazed petits fours like marzipan, fondant fruit or iced cakes. But, then again, there are so many others – dipped and moulded chocolates, the pâté de fruit, the bonbons, fudge, and praline – that categorising is far too difficult. Only one thing is certain – everyone loves to finish a dinner with a last little sweet offering.

♣ ♣
CIGARETTES WITH ORANGE CREAM

MAKES APPROXIMATELY 20 PIECES

ORANGE CREAM FILLING
75 gm (2 ½ oz) sugar
3 eggs
1 orange, juiced and zested
75 gm (2 ½ oz) unsalted butter, cut into cubes

CIGARETTE TUILE
125 gm (4 oz) plain flour
125 gm (4 oz) icing sugar
3 egg whites
50 gm (2 oz) flaked almonds

For this recipe you will need to create a plastic stencil which is 3cm wide x 5 cm long for the tuile. This could be done with a plastic ice cream container lid.

ORANGE CREAM PREPARATION Put the sugar, eggs, zest and juice in a saucepan and cook over a very gentle heat, whilst constantly stirring until mixture thickens. Do not allow to boil or it will curdle. Remove from the heat and whisk in the butter a few pieces at a time. Allow the filling to cool.

CIGARETTE PREPARATION Preheat the oven to 180°C (350°F). Mix all the ingredients together until you form a smooth paste.

Place a sheet of baking paper on the baking tray. Put the stencil on to the baking paper and spread the tuile mix with a palette knife on top of the stencil. Smooth out the mixture. Then remove the stencil and repeat. Sprinkle each tuile with flaked almonds. Bake in the oven for approximately 8 minutes until golden brown.

Remove from the oven and immediately roll each tuile into a cigarette shape. The almond side will be on the outside of the finished cigarette.

PRESENTATION Fill a piping bag with a small nozzle with the orange cream and pipe into the scrolls. These may be stored in an airtight container until needed.

♣ ♣
MACAROONS

MAKES APPROXIMATELY 50 PIECES

MAIN INGREDIENTS
4 egg whites
25 gm (1 oz) caster sugar
250 gm (8 oz) icing sugar
125 gm (4 oz) almond meal

PREPARATION Whisk the egg whites and caster sugar at medium speed until they form firm peaks. Sieve the icing sugar and almond meal together. Fold the egg white into the almond and sugar mix with a spatula.

Transfer the meringue to a piping bag with a 1 cm (¼ in) nozzle and pipe the mix onto baking paper lined trays in perfect little domes, about the size of a 20 cent coin. Rest them for 20 minutes.

Preheat oven to 170°C (330°F). Bake for 10–12 minutes or until crisp. Remove from oven and cool

PRESENTATION Once cold, you can sandwich each of them with a little jam or chocolate ganache.

VARIATIONS You can flavour and colour the macaroons if you wish. Here are some suggestions:
  pistachio add 1 tablespoon pistachio paste
  raspberry add 1 tablespoon raspberry purée
  chocolate replace 25 gm (¾ oz) almond meal with
    25 gm (¾ oz) cocoa powder
  coffee add 1 teaspoon instant dried coffee granules
  citrus add the zest of half a lemon and half a lime,
    grated on a micro plane

ROSEWATER TURKISH DELIGHT

MAKES ABOUT 20 PIECES

INGREDIENTS

3 leaves gelatine

100 ml (3 ½ fl oz) hot water

200 gm (7 oz) caster sugar

1 tablespoon rosewater

1 drop red food colour

1 tablespoon icing sugar, for dusting

1 tablespoon corn flour, for dusting

PREPARATION AND PRESENTATION Soak gelatine leaves in the water, until they are softened. Add the sugar and bring to the boil. Remove from the heat. Cool and add the colouring and the rosewater and pour into a lightly oiled tray. When set, cut into rectangles 4 cm x 2 cm (1 ½ x ¾ in), roll in icing sugar mixed with the corn flour and serve.

CHOCOLATE LOG

MAKES 20–25

INGREDIENTS

65 ml (2 fl oz) cream

250 gm (8 oz) dark chocolate, roughly cut

40 gm (1 ½ oz) unsalted butter

15 ml (½ fl oz) brandy

100 gm (3 ½ oz) dark chocolate, roughly cut

50 gm (1 ½ oz) dark chocolate, shavings

PREPARATION AND PRESENTATION In a medium-sized pot, bring the cream to a simmer. Add the 250 gm (8 oz) dark chocolate, stir until smooth and glossy. Then add the butter and brandy. Allow to cool at room temperature. Line a baking tray with non-stick baking paper. Place the cooled chocolate mixture in a piping bag with a 5 mm (¼ in) nozzle. Pipe 3 cm (1 in) logs onto the tray and refrigerate for 30 minutes.

CHOCOLATE LOG CONTINUED Place the 100 gm (3 ½ oz) chocolate in a bowl over a saucepan of simmering water and melt it, stirring continuously until it reaches a smooth and glossy texture. Using a fork, dip the chocolate logs in the melted chocolate. Drain the excess chocolate and gently roll them in the chocolate shavings. Serve immediately or store in a cool dry spot.

CANDIED ORANGE FRIAND

SERVES 20

INGREDIENTS

200 gm (7 oz) icing sugar

80 gm (2 ½ oz) almond meal

60 gm (2 oz) flour

1 pinch salt

6 egg whites

150 gm (5 oz) unsalted butter, melted

2 tablespoons chopped orange peel

1 tablespoon soft butter (to grease mould)

2 tablespoon of honey

1 tablespoon lemon juice or water warm

¼ cup pistachio nuts, peeled

PREPARATION AND PRESENTATION Preheat oven to 170°C (330°F). Place all the dry ingredients in the bowl of an electric mixer except the orange peel and mix at low speed for a minute. Add the egg whites and mix for 3–4 minutes until smooth. Add the melted butter, mix for another minute and lastly add the orange peel and mix until all combined. Spoon the mix into small individual greased moulds of your choice. Bake in oven for about 10–15 minutes. Cool for a few minutes and un-mould. Glaze with the honey diluted with the lemon juice or water and garnish with a pistachio nut.

✤ ✤
BERRY FINANCIER

MAKES APPROXIMATELY 40

INGREDIENTS

100 gm (3 ½ oz) plain flour
100 gm (3 ½ oz) ground almonds
300 gm (10 oz) caster sugar
2 drops vanilla essence
1 pinch salt
8 egg whites
150 gm (5 oz) unsalted butter, melted

GARNISH

2 punnets strawberries
2 tablespoons honey
1 tablespoon hot water
2 punnets raspberries

PREPARATION AND PRESENTATION Preheat oven to
200°C (400°F). Place the flour in a mixing bowl, add the
almonds and the caster and vanilla sugar and mix well.
Add a pinch of salt to the egg whites and whisk them until
very stiff peaks form. Fold them very carefully into the cake
mixture and quickly mix in the tepid melted butter. Spoon
a little of this mixture into small buttered and floured tins
and bake for 10–12 minutes, or until the financiers are
golden brown. Remove from oven and set on a rack. Wash,
dry and hull the strawberries and set one on top of each
financier. Glaze with the honey diluted with the warm
water and top with a raspberry.

✤ ✤
RASPBERRY SPONGE

MAKES APPROXIMATELY 40

INGREDIENTS

100 gm (3 ½ oz) plain flour
100 gm (3 ½ oz) ground almonds
300 gm (10 oz) caster sugar
2 drops vanilla essence
1 pinch salt
8 egg whites
2 punnets raspberries
150 gm (5 oz) unsalted butter , melted

PREPARATION AND PRESENTATION Preheat oven to
200°C (400°F). Butter the moulds with soft butter (you
can purchase flexible moulds that are ideal and easy to use
to bake these interesting shaped petits fours). Place the
flour in a mixing bowl, add the almonds and the caster
sugar and vanilla essence and mix well. Add a pinch of salt
to the egg whites and whisk them until very stiff peaks
form. Fold the egg whites very carefully into the cake
mixture and quickly mix in the tepid melted butter. Put one
raspberry in each mould and top with the mixture. Bake for
10–12 minutes, or until the cakes are golden brown.
Remove from oven and cool on a rack.

✤ ✤

PISTACHIO AND NUTS NOUGAT

MAKES APPROXIMATELY 48

INGREDIENTS
200 gm (7 oz) whole almonds
100 gm (3 ½ oz) whole hazelnuts
100 gm (3 ½ oz) pistachio nuts, peeled
180 gm (6 oz) honey
120 gm (4 oz) glucose
1 egg white
300 gm (10 oz) fondant
40 gm (1 ½ oz) glucose
rice paper sheets

PREPARATION AND PRESENTATION Preheat oven to 150°C (300°F). Roast the nuts (except almonds) in the oven for 10 minutes or until they brown slightly. Roast the almonds separately and chop in a food processor until you have a rough texture.

You will need a sugar thermometer to make this recipe. Boil the honey and the 120 gm (4 oz) glucose until it reaches 128°C (245°F). With an electric mixer, whip the egg white until firm peaks form. Pour your hot honey–glucose mix on top and mix for 10 minutes.

While the meringue is in the mixer, boil the fondant and the 40 gm (1½ oz) glucose to 138°C (250°F) and then pour on the meringue. Whisk for a further 10 minutes. At low speed, add the nuts. Pour the mix on a table lined with overlapping rice paper and cover with more rice paper. With a rolling pin, smooth the surface to achieve an even thickness of 2 cm (¾ in). Let it set overnight then cut in rectangles 4 cm x 2 cm (1½ x ¾ in). (If you do not have rice paper, use plenty of icing sugar on the table and on top of the nougat instead.)

✤ ✤

APRICOT PÂTÉ DE FRUIT

MAKES 60

INGREDIENTS
250 gm (8 oz) apricot purée (see recipe below)
250 gm (8 oz) caster sugar
1 teaspoon glucose
1 teaspoon lemon juice
1 teaspoon caster sugar
1 teaspoon pectin
granulated sugar for coating

APRICOT PURÉE
12 ripe apricots
1 lemon, juiced
2 tablespoons water

APRICOT PURÉE PREPARATION Cut the apricots in half and remove the stone. Chop roughly and place in a saucepan over heat with the lemon juice and water. Stew until the mix resembles a compote. Cool and purée in a blender or pass through a sieve.

MAIN PREPARATION AND PRESENTATION Place the apricot purée in a heavy-based saucepan and reduce by half to concentrate the natural pectin. Be careful *not* to burn the purée. You will need a sugar thermometer to make this recipe. Heat the 250 gm (8 oz) batch of sugar, the glucose and lemon juice in another saucepan until it reaches the 'soft crack' stage at 130°C (270°F). When this temperature has been achieved, add the apricot purée, 1 teaspoon sugar and the pectin. Stir until smooth with a temperature of 106°C (223°F).

Pour the mixture immediately into a tray lined with baking paper. Allow to set for 2 hours, cut into a variety of shapes and tumble through granulated sugar.

GIN AND LIME MERINGUE TART

SERVES 10

SWEET PASTRY
(refer | Basics page 311)

LIME FILLING
100 gm (3 ½ oz) caster sugar

3 whole eggs

2 limes zested finely

2 tablespoons lime juice

75 gm (2 ½ oz) unsalted butter, cut into cubes

1 tablespoon gin

LIGHT ITALIAN MERINGUE WITH GIN
250 gm (8 oz) sugar

50 ml (1 ½ fl oz) water

4 egg whites, semi-whipped to soft peaks

1 tablespoon gin

2 tablespoons clear honey

1 tablespoon water

FILLING PREPARATION Place the sugar, eggs, zest and juice in a saucepan and cook over a very gentle heat, whisking constantly until the mixture thickens — *do not allow to boil*. Remove from the heat and whisk in the butter, a few pieces at a time, and then the gin. Allow the filling to cool then spoon into the tartlet cases.

ITALIAN MERINGUE PREPARATION Boil the sugar with the water until it reach 121°C (250°F). Pour onto the egg whites whipped to soft peaks and beat at medium speed until the mix reaches room temperature, about 10 minutes. Add the gin and mix a little more. Pipe a bulb of meringue on top of each lime tartlet and lightly brown in a hot oven 180°C (350°F). Warm up the honey and water in a small pot and glaze the tartlets over a wire grill set on a tray.

ALMOND AND STAR ANISE TUILES

MAKES ABOUT 48 TUILES

INGREDIENTS
235 gm (7 ½ oz) sliced almonds

50 gm (1 ½ oz) whole star anise

235 gm (7 ½ oz) caster sugar

65 gm (2 ¼ oz) plain flour, sifted

125 ml (4 fl oz) egg whites

50 gm (1 ½ oz) butter, melted

1 tablespoon vanilla essence

PREPARATION AND PRESENTATION Preheat oven to 170°C (330°F). Mix sliced almonds and star anise with sugar. Add the sifted flour and egg whites. Mix well. Add the melted butter. Lastly, add the vanilla essence and mix all together. This mixture can last for up to 5 days, covered, in a refrigerator. Roll in a sausage shape of 5 cm (2 in) diameter. Roll in greaseproof paper and then roll in aluminium foil. Bake in the oven for 30–45 minutes. Cool and refrigerate overnight.

The next day, preheat oven to 170°C (330°F). Slice the sausage shapes thinly using a mandoline and place them on a tray lined with baking paper. Dry them in the oven for 5 minutes then remove from the oven and rest over round moulds (rolling pin, water glass) to form the tuile shape.

Opposite, Petits Fours plate: clockwise from top left, Chocolate Log (page 257), Macaroon (page 256), White Chocolate Fudge (page 261), Berry Financier (page 258), and Gin and Lime Meringue Tart (page 260)

✦ ✦

LEMON TARTLET

MAKES 25–30

LEMON CURD
100 gm (3 ½ oz) sugar
2 eggs
85 ml (2 ½ fl oz) lemon juice
50 gm (1 ½ oz) unsalted butter
1 gelatine leaf, soaked in cold water
pastry (see recipe Basics p 311)

LEMON CURD PREPARATION AND PRESENTATION Mix
sugar, eggs and lemon juice in a large metal bowl. Slowly cook
over a saucepan of simmering water until mixture slightly
thickens. Add cold diced butter to the hot egg mixture.
Squeeze excess water from the gelatine and mix into the curd.
Pass through a fine strainer and allow to cool. Dust the holed
out pastry discs with icing sugar and place on top of the full
discs. Fill a piping bag with lemon curd and pipe a small
dollop in each shell. Use a hot pallet knife to flatten the curd.

✦ ✦

WHITE CHOCOLATE FUDGE

MAKES 20

INGREDIENTS
250 ml (8 fl oz) glucose syrup
60 gm (2 oz) butter
310 ml (10 ½ floz) cream
750 gm (1 ½ lb) sugar
350 gm (12 oz) white chocolate

PREPARATION AND PRESENTATION Combine the
glucose, butter, cream and sugar in a saucepan over medium
heat. Bring to the boil and cook until the mixture reaches
120°C (250°F) or until the consistency is a creamy fudge
texture. Place the chocolate in a large bowl. Pour the hot sugar
mixture over the chocolate and mix until smooth. Pour the
mixture onto a tray lined with baking paper (about 30 cm/12
in square tray or chocolate mould). Allow to cool for
3–4 hours. Once set, cut into 2 cm (¾ in) x 4 cm (1 ½ in)
rectangles and serve.

Chapter Eleven
❦ Romantic Wedding ❦
MENU

Making people happy is very important to me. We try to make
every occasion at Bathers' Pavilion special and each wedding is unique
and requires careful discussion and planning. The Bathers' Pavilion boasts a
dream location – with a view through the heads of the harbour, the nearby
Rocky Point Island and the Rotunda – ideal for the exchange of vows. The
white sandy beach is perfect for a stroll before dinner and is a stunning
photographic backdrop. The historical and sophisticated architecture of the
building makes it a compelling location for a wedding.

These are smart little morsels. Most people love basil and these are also crispy and salty – two elements that people crave when hungry – so these little pasta pillows are just perfect for a canapé before a meal.

Fried Basil Ravioli

CELEBRATION MENU

canapes
cured salmon with citrus, corn soup,
fried basil ravioli, crab sandwich

prawn salad with green mango
and pawpaw

scallop timbale with zucchini flowers

veal rack with porcini sauce, asparagus
and wood mushrooms

bathers' wedding cake

raspberry vacherin

Once in a lifetime the biggest occasion of all will grace a lucky couple That very special occasion is a wedding, and food will be a part of that celebration. It is a day that most men feel nervous apprehension about and many are happy to let their partner take care of the preparations for the day. To me, the wedding day is a day when women blossom and relish the planning and organising of all the little details. The venue, the food, the setting and the service offered on that day are very important.

After the union of the couple has been blessed, our roles and experience at functions come into play. Food is such an integral and important part of the celebration that I like to devise menus expressing the sophistication of the restaurant but enjoyable and pleasing for all of the guests. Beautifully crafted food is what we excel at making – each dish and menu is balanced to leave a lasting impression.

THE BATHERS' PAVILION MENUS AND RECIPES

Curing is a very easy process and the home-cured product will prove a much less expensive option than buying ready prepared. You can purchase a side of salmon or ocean trout and have a great amount of lovely gravalax made in one day.

Cured Salmon with Citrus

Corn Soup

WINE NOTES

LOUIS ROEDERER BRUT PREMIER NV, Reims, Champagne, France Their blend has a higher proportion of pinot noir to chardonnay and has a full-flavoured complex palate, which delivers apples and pear fruits and biscuity complexity. A long time favourite at Bathers' Pavilion, Louis Roederer Brut Premier NV has been the Champagne offered by the glass for many years.

BILLECART-SALMON ROSE NV Mareuil-Sur-Ay, Champagne, France Their Brut Rose style is a blend of chardonnay, pinot noir and pinot meunier, with the addition of a small amount of red wine added to the mix. This champagne has a lovely salmon coloured hue, with aromas of red fruits, rose petal and fresh pears. The palate is very fine with lingering fruit palate.

DOM PÉRIGNON Epernay, Champagne, France The fruit is sourced primarily from Premier Cru sites in Hautvillers and the result is a very fine, sophisticated drink. The flavours are so complex, refined and complete, its mouthfeel is pure elegance.

I find a little sandwich is always a crowd pleaser. This recipe can be made with crab for a special occasion or with chicken if it is a more casual affair. Have the softest and freshest bread possible when making these and use homemade mayonnaise for the best results.

Crab Sandwich

✦

CURED SALMON WITH CITRUS

SERVES 8

MAIN INGREDIENTS
320 gm (11 oz) cured salmon
32 pieces of brioche, 5 cm (2 in) x 2 cm (¾ in),
    4 per person
32 segments pink grapefruit
32 amaranth leaves or chervil, for garnish

CURED SALMON
1–1.5 kg (2–3 lb) side of salmon, skin on
2 tablespoons vodka (optional)
100 gm (3 ½ oz) sea salt
100 gm (3 ½ oz) sugar
2 cloves garlic, finely chopped
1 tablespoon finely chopped ginger
2 limes, zest only
1 tablespoon white peppercorns

CURED SALMON PREPARATION Remove the pin bones
from the salmon using tweezers. Clean with paper towel
and wet with vodka if using. Lay the salmon skin side
down on a tray. Mix all dry ingredients, garlic, ginger
and lime zest together and cover the salmon with
the mix. Cover with plastic wrap and refrigerate for
24 hours. The next day, brush the marinade mix away,
pat dry and slice in the desired way.

MAIN PREPARATION Just prior to guests arriving,
assemble the salmon fingers in the following order.
Slice the salmon into pieces ½ cm (¼ in) x 4 cm
(1 ½ in). Keep cold for as long as possible. Toast the
brioche fingers under a grill or in the oven at 180°C
(350°F) until golden brown. Rinse the amaranth leaves
in ice cold water and drain on absorbent paper towel.
Lay a salmon sliver on each toasted brioche finger, a
grapefruit segment on top and an amaranth leaf to
garnish. Try not to assemble too far ahead of schedule
as the grapefruit will make the toasted brioche soggy.

✦

CORN SOUP

SERVES 12

SOUP INGREDIENTS
8 cobs fresh corn
100 ml (3 ½ fl oz) olive oil
6 eschalots, peeled and finely chopped
2 cloves garlic, peeled and crushed
6 cups vegetable stock
salt and white milled pepper
50 gm (1 ½ oz) butter, to finish

SOUP PREPARATION Husk and clean the corn,
removing the outer layers and the silk, cut kernels
(flesh) from the cobs.

Heat the olive oil in a heavy-bottomed casserole or
saucepan, add the corn kernels, eschalots and garlic
and cook gently for about 15 minutes or until the corn
is cooked. Add the stock and bring to the boil. Cook
for about 2 minutes and remove from the heat.

Strain and blend the solids to achieve a fine purée.
Strain the purée back into a pot and add some of the
cooking liquid until you reach a nice consistency.
Season with salt and pepper and whisk in the finishing
butter. Serve in small bowls or demitasse cups.

FRIED BASIL RAVIOLI

SERVES 8

BASIL PESTO FILLING
50 ml (1 ½ fl oz) olive oil
6 garlic cloves, peeled and roughly chopped
100 gm (3 ½ oz) pine nuts
200 gm (7 oz) basil, picked and roughly chopped
freshly ground black pepper
1 tablespoon grated Parmesan cheese

PASTA
500 gm (16 oz) pasta dough coloured with
    1 tablespoon chlorophyll (refer | Basics page 309)
1 egg, beaten for egg wash
table salt
2 litres oil for deep-frying

BASIL PESTO FILLING PREPARATION Pour the olive oil
into a blender, add the garlic and blend for 5 seconds.
Add the pine nuts and blend for 10 seconds or
until crushed in a paste. Add the chopped basil and
blend for 5 to 10 seconds until you have a chucky
texture. Season with the black pepper and mix in the
Parmesan cheese.

PASTA PREPARATION Roll out the pasta dough
into sheets. Egg-wash the sheets entirely and place
teaspoons of the basil pesto in two continuous rows
leaving a 4 cm (1 ¾ in) gap around each small pile
of filling. Add another sheet of pasta on top making
sure that it is sealed tightly around the filling. Cut
into little ravioli using a crinkled cutting wheel. Chill
for one hour. Deep-fry in the hot oil until they are
crispy, drain on absorbent paper. Serve immediately
dusted with fine salt.

CRAB SANDWICH

SERVES 8

SANDWICH INGREDIENTS
400 gm (14 oz) picked spanner crab meat
½ avocado (ripe), mashed
¼ cup mayonnaise
1 tablespoon crème fraîche
¼ bunch chives, finely snipped
¼ bunch watercress, rinsed and bruised with salt
    in a mortar and pestle
table salt and fresh milled pepper
24 slices white or light brown bread, crusts
    removed
1 punnet baby cress, for garnish

SANDWICH PREPARATION Mix the crab meat with
the avocado, mayonnaise, crème fraîche, chives,
watercress and seasoning.

Cut out rounds of the bread with a pastry cutter 5 cm
(2 in) in diameter. Spread the mixture liberally on the
bread rounds and cover with another slice of bread.

Serve aesthetically on a plate with a little baby cress
as garnish.

✦ ✦

PRAWN SALAD
WITH GREEN MANGO AND PAWPAW

SERVES 12

36 medium tiger prawns, cooked and shelled
2 chillies, seeded and cut into a fine julienne
200 gm (7 oz) pawpaw, cut into fine strips
200 gm (7 oz) green mango, cut into fine strips
150 gm (5 oz) daikon radish, cut into fine julienne
½ bunch mint, picked
¼ bunch Thai basil, picked
½ bunch coriander, picked

LIME DRESSING
3 limes, juiced
175 ml (6 fl oz) peanut oil
60 ml (2 ¼ fl oz) fish sauce
1 clove garlic, finely chopped
1 tablespoon palm sugar

DRESSING PREPARATION Mix all the dressing ingredients together, refine the seasoning and allow to sit for 1 hour prior to serving.

SALAD PREPARATION Make sure that the prawns are cleaned well. Gently mix all the salad ingredients with the dressing except the coriander leaves which should be placed on top of the salad just prior to serving.

Prawns are a part of our Australian food culture and you won't go wrong serving them at a large gathering. They are quite robust and will withstand a strong dressing or sauce. If you like Asian flavours, you could easily double the basil, coriander and mint.

The lightly poached mushroom and zucchini
add a little texture to the dish..

Scallop Timbale

I think there is no better cut than the veal
rack and, when cooked on the bone and
rested for a good while, it is pure magic.
The racks can be cooked ahead of time and
gently reheated or cut when cool and then
grilled at a high heat.

Veal Rack with Porcini Sauce

✦ ✦

SCALLOP TIMBALE
WITH ZUCCHINI FLOWERS

SERVES 12

SCALLOP TIMBALE

550 gm (18 ½ oz) white scallops
6 egg whites
350 ml (12 fl oz) fresh cream
salt and white milled pepper

GARNISH

½ cup water
salt
10 ml (⅓ fl oz) white wine or Champagne vinegar
80 gm (2 ½ oz) diced button mushrooms, blanched
8 zucchini flowers, blanched in salted boiling water and refreshed in iced water
80 gm (2 ½ oz) diced tomato
small amount of chervil, picked and rinsed

CHAMPAGNE CREAM SAUCE

8 eschalots, chopped
1 clove garlic, chopped
60 ml (2 fl oz) olive oil
100 ml (3 ½ fl oz) white wine
200 ml (7 fl oz) fish stock
thyme, parsley and chervil stalks
10 black peppercorns, whole
400 ml (14 fl oz) cream
50 ml (1 ½ fl oz) Champagne
salt and white milled pepper

TIMBALE PREPARATION Purée the trimmed and cleaned scallops with the egg whites in a cold food processor until light and fluffy. Pulse in the cream and adjust the seasoning. Rest in the refrigerator for at least 20 minutes. Spray 12 dariole moulds with non-stick oil and fill with the scallop mixture using a piping bag. Wrap each mould with plastic wrap and place over boiling water in a steamer for 8–12 minutes until firm. Remove from the steamer and stand in a warm place for 10 minutes still covered. The timbales are best when served within an hour of being *cooked*. Have the dariole moulds filled with the scallop mousse, wrapped and ready to cook an hour prior to service for optimum freshness and flavour.

GARNISH PREPARATION In a small pot over moderate heat, place half a cup of water, and pinch of salt and the vinegar. Blanch the mushrooms, add the zucchini flowers and, lastly, the tomato to warm through. Remove from heat and drain just before serving.

CHAMPAGNE CREAM SAUCE PREPARATION Sweat the eschalots and garlic in olive oil without colouring. Add the white wine and reduce by half the volume. Add the fish stock and reduce by one-third of the volume. Add the herbs and peppercorns, then the cream and reduce by half. Add the Champagne, adjust the seasoning and ensure you have achieved a sauce-like consistency. Strain and reserve.

PRESENTATION Set the timbales in the centre of warm serving plates, spoon the garnish on and around the timbale, garnish with chervil and then spoon the hot sauce around.

VEAL RACK WITH PORCINI SAUCE,
ASPARAGUS AND WOOD MUSHROOMS

SERVES 10–12

VEAL
1 veal rack with 8 pins
100 gm (7 oz) cultured butter, diced

VEGETABLES AND SAUCE
12 King Brown mushrooms
100 gm (3 ½ oz) butter
2 cups chicken stock
salt and freshly milled black pepper
3 bunches green asparagus, trimmed and
    peeled 160 ml (5 ½ fl oz) Porcini Sauce
    (refer | Basics page 305)

ROAST POTATO
24 medium size désirée potatoes
1 tablespoon butter
1 tablespoon vegetable oil
salt and white milled pepper

VEAL RACK PREPARATION Trim the back of the veal rack removing the small fragment bones between the rib bones. Carefully scrape back the rib bones and then polish with a clean cloth. Tie between each cutlet with butchers twine and secure the twine onto the cutlet with a double knot. Leave the veal rack covered at room temperature until the chill of the refrigerator has disappeared. Preheat oven to 180°C (350°F). Heat a large pan and brush the rack with a little butter. Season liberally with salt and pepper and place over heat on the stove top. Sear the rack until a nice colour is achieved, place in a roasting tray, baste with butter and roast for 10 minutes then reduce the heat of the oven to 170°C (330°F). Continue to roast for 40–50 minutes or until cooked to medium. Rest the meat, covered in a warm place, for at least 20 minutes prior to carving. This gives you time to finish the sauté of the mushrooms and asparagus for serving.

VEGETABLE PREPARATION Cut the base off the stem of the King Browns and brush them with a dry towel to remove any dirt. Slice into two or three pieces each. Just prior to service, sauté the mushrooms in a heavy-based pan in 50 gm (1 ½ oz) butter. Bring the chicken stock to the boil in a saucepan and add 50 gm (1 ½ oz) butter, salt and pepper. When stock is boiling, add the asparagus. When cooked, drain, season and place in a warm dish.

ROAST POTATO PREPARATION Preheat oven to 180°C (350°F). Peel the potatoes and shape them into uniform sizes. Using a small knife, cut thin slices through one side of the potato and leave the other side attached. In a non-stick roasting tray, heat the butter and oil and add the potatoes with some salt. Cook for 15 minutes, mixing from time to time to achieve an even colour. Just before serving, season with salt and pepper and serve in a side bowl.

PRESENTATION Warm the Porcini Sauce and froth with a hand blender. Place mushrooms and asparagus under each sliced veal cutlet and pour the sauce at the table.

Wedding cake making is a specialised area of the pastry department but, with a good deal of determination, you should be able to put your own cake together. Purchase the marzipan and sugar paste and prepare the rest of the ingredients yourself. The best idea is to start with simple shaped cakes, either round or square.

Bathers' Wedding Cake

✦ ✦ ✦

BATHERS' WEDDING CAKE

SERVES APPROXIMATELY 60

CAKE (PREPARE A DAY AHEAD)
16 whole eggs
625 gm (21 oz) caster sugar
375 gm (12 oz) plain flour
100 gm (3 ½ oz) cocoa powder
125 gm (4 oz) corn flour
150 gm (5 oz) unsalted butter, melted

BUTTER CREAM FILLING
250 ml (8 fl oz) milk
1 vanilla bean
8 egg yolks
450 gm (15 oz) sugar
1 kg (2 lb) unsalted butter
250 gm (8 oz) dark chocolate, melted

EXTRAS
1.5 kg (3 lbs) marzipan, for coating
1.5 kg (3 lbs) sugar paste, for finishing
6 punnets raspberries
1 cup Grand Marnier
1 cup icing sugar, sieved, for dusting

CAKE PREPARATION Preheat oven to 200°C (400°F). Start preparing the cake the day before you finish and decorate it. Whisk the eggs with the sugar at room temperature until light and fluffy. Sprinkle in sieved flour, corn flour and cocoa powder. Mix gently by hand so that the sponge keeps its volume. Add the melted butter gently. Grease three heart-shaped medium-sized cake tins (about 30 cm–40 cm/12 in–16 in diameter). Fill the tins three-quarters full with the sponge mix. Bake for approx 30 minutes or until the cake springs back to the touch. You can also test with a wooden skewer that comes out clean when you pierce the cake and retrieve it. Cool for 5 minutes in the tin and turn out on a cooling rack. Once cool, wrap in plastic wrap and refrigerate until the next day to firm up.

CREAM FILLING PREPARATION Heat up the milk with the vanilla bean to just before boiling point. Mix the egg yolks with the sugar and add a touch of hot milk to dilute. Add the egg mix to the hot milk while whisking. Cook on a low heat until it is the consistency of light custard, strain and cool. Care must be taken when cooking the milk as it is very delicate and has a tendency to stick. Separately, beat the butter in an electric mixer until white and fluffy. Add the custard in small amounts until all used up and beat at medium speed until the mixture is white and creamy. Add the melted chocolate last and mix until a light chocolate butter cream is achieved. You will use this butter cream at room temperature.

ASSEMBLING THE CAKE If you do not have heart-shaped tins, cut sponge into a heart shape. Cut each cake into 2 layers and on each of the bases sprinkle the Grand Marnier, spread with butter cream and top with a scattering of raspberries. Top with the other sponge drizzled with Grand Marnier (save some for brushing the top) and press evenly to achieve a flat surface. Allow to set for 1 hour in the refrigerator.

recipe continues over

ASSEMBLING THE CAKE CONTINUED To assemble the cakes, cut the sides of two cakes to interlock them before you cover them with the marzipan. Set the cakes on a large presentation platter.

Sprinkle some icing sugar on a marble top and, using a rolling pin, roll out the marzipan to 2 mm (¹/8 in) thickness using the dusting of icing sugar to prevent sticking. Roll up onto the rolling pin and spread over the sponge making sure you cover the top and sides carefully. Trim away excess around the base with a knife, leaving about 2.5 mm (¹/8 in) around the cake. Smooth the surface with the palm of your hand to make sure you have a beautiful cake.

SUGAR PASTE FINISH PREPARATION Roll out the sugar paste on the marble top dusted with icing sugar to 2 mm (¹/8 in) thickness. Brush the marzipan with the remaining Grand Marnier to ensure you have a sticky surface and cover the cakes with the rolled out sugar paste. Smooth and polish the top and sides of the cakes with your hand to achieve a perfect surface. Using the excess sugar paste, roll two long strands to form a plait to finish the bottom edge of the cakes. Garnish with fresh flowers or marzipan leaves. Do not refrigerate, it will keep for a day or two in a cool place.

WINE NOTES

KRUG, Reims, Champagne, France The style of the House of Krug is very distinct, and their Champagnes, like all great wine, need time to evolve and reveal the greatness that they can achieve. Part of the distinct style of this house is that their base wines are barrel fermented in older French oak. With age they take on lovely biscuity flavours, their complexity and richness suiting food of equal standing. Krug is not a large production, and the 'Holy Grail' of their collection is from the Clos de Mesnil vineyard.

HARDY'S ARRAS, TAS, Australia This sparkling is a vintage style, and is a very good drink. It is considered one of the best styles produced in Australia, and certainly is complex and rich, gaining lovely creamy, biscuity flavours with age and maintains a fresh line of acidity.

YARRABANK CUVEE, VIC, Australia As a young wine it shows a lot of citrus character, with fine mousse and crisp acidity. Another of the best sparklings currently produced in Australia, showing an ability to age well and a style well suited to food.

⚜ ⚜
RASPBERRY VACHERIN

SERVES 12

MAIN INGREDIENTS
1 cup egg whites (approx 8 eggs)
400 gm (14 oz) caster sugar
6 cups raspberry sorbet (see recipe page 221)
2 punnets raspberries

PREPARATION Preheat oven to 110°C (220°F). Whisk the egg whites and all the sugar until firm peaks are reached. Place some baking paper on a tray and draw 24 circles of 8 cm (3 ¼ in) diameter. Turn the paper over so the markings don't come into contact with the meringue but they should still be visible through the paper. Using a piping bag with a plain 1 cm (½ in) nozzle, fill the circles with meringue by piping in a circular motion. Bake the meringues for about 2 hours until they are dry. Fill 12 egg rings with the sorbet and then firm up in the freezer.

PRESENTATION When ready to serve, sandwich the sorbet between two meringue circles and arrange on plates with a few raspberries to garnish.

What makes this dessert unique is the surprise of the crunchy vacherin. The best word to describe this dessert is 'pretty'. Once you have made the flat meringue the first time, you will want to use the recipe on many other occasions with different flavours – mango, guava, chocolate, coffee and kiwi fruit are many of the options as are coconut, lime and watermelon.

Raspberry Vacherin

Chapter Twelve

❧ RECIPES ❧
for celebrations

There is no direct translation for the French word 'hors-d'oeuvre'. Canapés, amuse-bouche, amuse-gueule, bouchées, friand, barquette, sandwich, tartine, croutes, canapés Danois, brioche garni and many more preparations fall under that banner. In essence, it can be anything but the main meal.

Canapés these days can include a little bowl of risotto, demitasse of soup, piroshki, mini quiche and may even finish with mignardises that are little tiny desserts. For many people, canapés offer a casual yet modern way of eating with less formality while still being able to sample many great dishes.

Celebrations, large and small, are an exciting part of any restaurant's life. The right canapés are an essential element of any successful function, pre-dinner drinks, intimate party or large dinner party. At Bathers' these events also present us with an opportunity to showcase new or unusual ingredients, and play with interesting combinations and presentations.

When planning your next special event, be a little adventurous and have some fun. Try new things or reinvent some old favourites. I hope you and your guests enjoy some of the recipes in this chapter at your next special celebration.

Oyster Shooters | Page 292

King fish Sushi
Cake | Page 287

Tandoori on Naan Bread | Page 287

Clockwise from top right: Garlic Snail Brioche (page 285), Marinated Ocean Trout Barquette (page 292) and Beef Tartare on Beetroot with Quail Egg (page 284).

At Bather's we catered for many funtions, large and small. This chapter contains some of our classic and our favourites.

BLINIS

Blinis are a sophisticated little pancake and have a great history in the world of canapés. They are of Russian origin and they could have been served on their own, or if one was part of the imperial court, with caviar. A trout tartare to me is a great alternative to the dwindling supply of caviar.

PÂTÉ DE FOIE EN GELÉE

This could be served with foie gras and you would end up with one of the best canapés ever, but that foie gras comes with a prohibitive cost. You could easily purchase a good alternative or with a bit of kitchen confidence you could produce your own pâté.

PITHIVIERS

Everyone loves a crispy pastry and pithiviers are in fact just a little pastry pie with an interesting filling. Pithiviers is a classic French dessert, named after the town, with a classic filling made of almond powder and egg. Savoury Pithiviers have existed since the time of Carème in the early 18th century.

TARTELETTES

Tartelettes or tartlets can easily be savoury or sweet. The most common would be fruit and berry tartlets. They can be baked raw with a filling like little quiche, almond frangipane or baked blind and filled afterward with a cod brandade, vegetable purée or cold seafood.

CRÊPES

Peking duck is a tasty and satisfying little course and perfect with crepes. The contrast of the freshness of the cucumber, the acidity and pungency of the spring onion, the sweetness of the hoisin sauce and the satisfying fattiness of the duck makes it a complete little meal.

FEUILLETÉE

This famous pastry that is created by layers of butter and flour dough has a contested birth, some refer to

Claude Lorrain as the inventor in the 17th century, others attribute it to a monsieur Feuillet, a pre-Carème pastry chef of great repute. Others think the credit goes back to the cooks of Florence; either way it is one of the most versatile doughs of French cuisine.

BARQUETTES

Barquettes are another form of tartlets normally with a pointy end but you are able to find many other forms. In Paris I always do a pilgrimage to E. Dehillerin one of the most historic and rustic kitchen shops, where it seems time stopped many centuries ago.

BRIOCHE

Brioche is a typical dough used in the making of canapés. It could be cooked in a bread mould then sliced and grilled or it could be used as raw dough to mould a filling. I find snails perfect to wrap with a touch of garlic butter as it produces an exotic and pleasant little bite.

TARTARE

There was an era not so long ago that every self-respecting French restaurant would have a steak tartare on its menu. These days there is still a fiery band of loyalists for this dish but less people are tempted by its unabashed celebration of rawness. At least they could count me as one of their supporters.

TANDOORI

The tandoori oven is one of the great inventions of the working kitchen but what people seem to remember is the taste of a tandoori. It is easy to replicate and the quail is a perfect substitute to turn this into a nice little canapé.

SUSHI

Japanese food has captured the imagination of the new generation of gourmets. Sushi is one reason for this popularity and for many valid reasons. Rice is a good substitute for bread and stunningly raw fish is unique in its delicacy. Combine them together with the saltiness of soy sauce and you have a recipe for success.

SHOOTERS

Who would not like these elegant and colourful little glasses of tasty food? There is no limitation to their composition and assemblage. A jelly is a good light way to separate your layers of ingredients as they appear to float on a cloud.

WINE NOTES

❊ **POL ROGER NV Champagne, France** With a history dating back to the mid 1800s, this champagne house remains family owned. Their non vintage style has equal parts pinot noir, chardonnay and pinot meunier. Lovely aperitif style, with citrus blossoms, white fruits and crisp acidity.

❊ **DELGADO ZULETA 'LA GOYA' Manzanilla, Spain** Aaaaah sherry. One of the often neglected, or even shunned great wines of the world. A perfect aperitif. Sip chilled with canapés, especially with ingredients such as oysters, olives, tomato, crab or sushi.

❊ **GEORG BREUER RÜDESHEIM ESTATE Riesling, Rheingau, Germany** German Rieslings are beautiful wines to drink — with their variety of fruit character they present a lingering fine acidity. The wines of Georg Breuer are dry in style, this wine having a range of citrus and stonefruit, with a hint of gun flint and refreshing acidity. Perfect for canapés with a hint of spice too.

❊ **KEITH TULLOCH SEMILLON, Hunter Valley, NSW** The Tulloch family is a well known name in the Hunter Valley. Keith started his own label when the family vineyard sold and makes an award winning semillon. A little different to the typical style of the region with part barrel fermentation of the wine. Makes for a great style with a little added texture in the middle palate.

❊ **DOMAIN MOREAU-NAUDET CHABLIS, Burgundy, France** Chablis is a white wine region in the Northernmost part of Burgundy and is made with chardonnay grapes. If big, buttery styles of chardonnay aren't for you, then try a chablis which typically are dry and steely as young wines. Perfect to start a meal, especially with seafood.

❊ **WILLOW CREEK SAIGNÉE ROSÉ Mornington Peninsula, VIC** This wine is made from pinot noir and in the style of the French rosés. Light in colour, it has vibrant red berry flavours with hints of violets and spice. Delicious with a variety of canapés and perfect on a summer day

BEEF TARTARE ON BEETROOT

MAKES 12

BEEF TARTARE

1 teaspoon Dijon mustard

1 egg yolk, very fresh, preferably organic

1 tablespoon sunflower seed oil

300 gm (10 oz) beef rump or fillet steak, minced just
  before use

6 baby cornichons

1 eschalot, peeled and very finely sliced

1 teaspoon baby capers, rinsed and chopped

1 anchovy, finely chopped

1 tablespoon roughly chopped flat leaf parsley

1 tablespoon Cognac

juice of ½ lemon

1 splash Tabasco sauce

salt and black milled pepper

12 pieces toasted brioche croutons (to fit under
  the beetroot circles), optional

12 quail egg yolks, very fresh, one for each serve

BEETROOTS

1 kg (2 lb) rock salt

300 gm (10 oz) fine salt

200 gm (7 oz) flour

3–4 egg whites, the quail egg whites can
  also be used

2 large beetroots, washed

1 tablespoon red wine vinegar

2 tablespoons olive oil

salt and white milled pepper

TARTARE PREPARATION Combine the mustard
with the single egg yolk and slowly add the sunflower
seed oil. Add the meat and the rest of the ingredients
(except the brioche and the quail yolks). Refine
the seasoning.

BEETROOT PREPARATION Preheat oven to
200°C (400°F). Mix the two salts and the flour
together, and then add the egg whites to form a soft
and pliable dough. Wrap the whole beetroots in this
dough ensuring that it will be airtight. Bake in the
oven for 1 ½–2 hours. Allow the beetroots to cool
down. Once cold, remove and discard the dough,
peel the beetroots and slice them 5 mm (¼ in) thick.
Then, use a round cutter 4 cm (1 ½ in) in diameter,
ensuring you cut them evenly. Marinate the beetroots
slices overnight in the red wine vinegar, olive oil and
seasoning.

PRESENTATION Place the small cutter you used to cut
the beetroot on top of a beetroot slice and fill the top
with the tartare. Repeat for all beetroot. Lastly, top
with the fresh yolk from the quail egg.

✤
GARLIC SNAIL BRIOCHE

MAKES 40

BRIOCHE

700 gm (23 oz) baker's flour, sifted
½ teaspoon salt
80 gm (2 ½ oz) sugar
5 eggs
175 ml (6 fl oz) milk
35 gm (1 ¼ oz) yeast
125 ml (4 fl oz) milk
250 gm (8 oz) butter, softened

GARLIC AND TARRAGON BUTTER

165 gm (5 ½ oz) butter, softened
1 clove garlic, peeled and finely grated
2 tablespoons chopped tarragon leaves
1 teaspoon Pernod
salt and white milled pepper

SNAILS

1 eschalot, peeled and finely chopped
1 carrot, peeled and diced
1 leek, trimmed and diced
1 stalk celery, trimmed and diced
1 cup white wine
2 cups chicken stock or water
40 snails, blanched, shelled and cleaned
2 heads of cos lettuce leaves trimmed from the
    centre and blanched in salted water

BRIOCHE PREPARATION The brioche dough needs to be rested overnight. Place all the ingredients, except the soft butter, in the bowl of an electric mixer and mix using the pastry hook until the dough is smooth. Slow the speed and 'machine knead' the soft butter into it until it becomes smooth again. Rest the dough overnight, allowing it to prove.

GARLIC AND TARRAGON BUTTER Make sure that the butter is soft. Place it in the bowl of an electric mixer, whisk for 1 minute until it is smooth then add all of the other ingredients. Refine the seasoning with salt and pepper. Pipe onto greaseproof paper in 2 cm (¾ in) diameter logs. Roll logs up in the paper and refrigerate (keeps well in the refrigerator for 1 week).

SNAILS PREPARATION Place all of the vegetable ingredients (except the cos), white wine and chicken stock in a pot and simmer for half an hour. Blanch the snails in salted water then remove them from their shells and trim. Place the snails in the stock and simmer them for approximately 2 hours. Once they are tender, discard the stock and strain the snails cooling them in the refrigerator as soon as possible. Place the blanched cos lettuce leaves on a cutting board, remove the hard middle of each leaf and cut them into small 5 cm (2 in) squares. You will need 40 squares. Place half a teaspoon of the garlic butter in the centre and put the snail over it, put another half a teaspoon of butter over the snail and wrap it up into a small parcel. Refrigerate.

MAIN PREPARATION AND PRESENTATION Lightly flour your hands and, while the dough is still cold, roll out the dough to sheets measuring 40 cm x 8 cm (16 in x 3 ¼ in) wide. Egg wash the surface and place the snail parcels 5 cm (2 in) apart (lengthways) and 3 cm away from the edge of the dough (you will fold the other half of the dough over it). Fold the pastry over and shape small square pillows, pushing the air out. Using a plain rolling cutter (same as a pizza cutter), cut even pillows. Allow the pillows to prove for an hour in the refrigerator. Preheat the oven to 180°C (350°F). Egg wash the exterior. Bake for approximately 15–20 minutes or until gold and puffy. Serve hot.

✤ ✤ KING FISH SUSHI CAKE

MAKES 60 PIECES

SASHIMI FISH

300 gm (10 oz) side Hiramasa king fish or tuna or salmon
2 sheets nori seaweed

RICE

250 gm (8 oz) sushi rice
2 tablespoons pickled ginger
2 knobs of ginger
1 stick lemongrass
¼ cup Japanese rice vinegar
1 tablespoon sugar
salt to taste

SALAD

1 packet seaweed vegetables of your choice

FISH PREPARATION Fish eaten raw needs to be kept over ice at all stages of preparation. Skin the king fish, remove a little of the blood line and pin-bone. Cut into 2 pieces lengthways, and reserve on ice. When ready to serve, slice the kingfish into 3 mm (⅛ in) thick slices like sashimi to top the rice cake.

RICE PREPARATION Rinse rice in cold water and place in a medium saucepan. Add ginger and lemongrass and fill the pot with three times the rice's volume in water. (Using soda or mineral water in a 50/50 ratio with tap water will give a much better result.) Place some baking paper with a hole in the centre touching the rice and foil on top of that. Simmer gently for 8 minutes, test to see if rice is almost cooked, minimal liquid will be left by now. Discard ginger and lemongrass and cool on a shallow tray. Bring the rice vinegar and the sugar to boil. Season with salt and cool. Add the rice vinegar seasoning to the rice using a fork or thin chopsticks to fold in the liquid. Re-cover and allow to cool to room temperature sitting in a warm place to the side of the stove.

CAKE PREPARATION Line the cake tin with plastic wrap or non-stick paper. Place a layer of rice in the bottom and gently press into the bottom of the tin. You need a thickness of 1 ½ cm (⅔ inch). Lay nori sheets to cover the rice and repeat with another layer of rice. Lay the thin slices of Hiramasa king fish on top of the last rice layer and cover with plastic wrap or non-stick paper. Press down with another cake tin the same size or the palm of your hand. Refrigerate for 20–30 minutes prior to serving.

PRESENTATION Slice the 'cake' into 3 cm (1 in) squares, garnish with the seaweed salad and serve with a light soy sauce.

TIP One square cake tin approximately 25 cm (11 in) is required for this recipe.

✤ ROAST CHINESE DUCK
WITH PLUM SAUCE IN A HERB CRÊPE

MAKES 16–20

1 Chinese roasted duck (available in Asian barbecue shops)
10 herb crêpes (see recipe page 192)
100 ml (3 ½ fl oz) hoisin sauce
1 cucumber, peeled, de-seeded and cut into sticks
16 pieces green onion same length as cucumber

PREPARATION AND PRESENTATION Separate the legs and the breasts from the duck removing any bones. Cut into bite-size pieces. Cut the crêpes in two and, in the middle of each crêpe, place a little of the hoisin sauce, cucumber, green onion and duck. Roll the crêpe up neatly and arrange on a platter.

TANDOORI ON NAAN BREAD

SERVES 12

TANDOORI QUAIL

12 whole quail

150 gm (5 oz) natural yoghurt

3 tablespoons tandoori paste

1 teaspoon ground cumin

1 teaspoon garam marsala

½ teaspoon powdered turmeric

½ teaspoon chilli powder

½ teaspoon garlic powder

½ teaspoon crushed coriander seed

NAAN BREAD

Makes 24 small pillows

250 gm (8 oz) plain flour

½ teaspoon baking powder

¼ teaspoon bicarbonate of soda

½ teaspoon salt

1 teaspoon sugar

1 teaspoons poppy seeds

1 egg, beaten

½ cup milk, or enough to form a soft dough

½ tablespoon melted ghee or clarified butter

GARNISH

½ cup fresh yoghurt

1 small English cucumber, peeled and diced very finely

1 tablespoon fresh mint, julienned

NAAN BREAD PREPARATION Mix all the ingredients, (except melted ghee) together until you form a smooth dough. Cover with a damp cloth and leave in a warm place for 2 hours. Preheat the oven to 200°C (400°F). Knead the dough on a well-floured surface for 3 minutes until smooth. Roll out into a long sausage shape then divide into 24 portions. Brush with water and place wet side down on a greased baking tray. Brush with melted ghee or butter and bake for 8–10 minutes or until golden brown.

TANDOORI QUAIL PREPARATION Bone the quail breast and remove the legs leaving leg bones intact. Mix the yoghurt, tandoori paste and spices together. Marinate the quail pieces for 30 minutes in the tandoori yoghurt. Preheat oven to 200°C (400°F). Sear the quail pieces in a cast iron pan to give them some colour then place in a baking tray and finish in the oven for 10 minutes.

PRESENTATION Place pieces of warm quail on pillows of warm naan. Top with the yoghurt, cucumber and fresh mint.

Roast Chinese Duck
with Plum Sauce in a Green
Herb Crêpe I Page 286

Marinated Ocean Trout
with Potato Blinis I Page 292

Chicken Liver Parfait
with Rosehip Jelly I Page 290

Foie Gras Mushrooms
with Pithivier I Page 290

Onion Vol au Vent
with Beaufort Cheese I Page 292

Salt Cod Tartlet
with Green Vegetable
Ratatouille I Page 293

✚ ✚

CHICKEN LIVER PARFAIT
WITH ROSEHIP TEA JELLY

MAKES 36

CHICKEN LIVER PARFAIT

6 eschalots, peeled and finely sliced

2 garlic cloves, peeled and finely chopped

300 gm (10 oz) butter, softened

500 gm (16 oz) chicken livers, trimmed

1 teaspoon of salt

white milled pepper, to taste

2 tablespoons brandy or Madeira

100 gm (3 ½ oz) foie gras (optional)

ROSEHIP TEA JELLY

600 ml (20 fl oz) rosehip tea, sweetened with
    4 tablespoons sugar, cold

4 gelatine leaves, soaked in cold water

1 tablespoon of cabernet sauvignon vinegar

PARFAIT PREPARATION In a non-stick pan at medium heat, cook the eschalots and garlic in a tablespoon of butter until they are translucent and have no colour. Increase the temperature in the pan and add the chicken livers and cook until medium rare. Season with salt and pepper and cool down. Blend in a food processor; add the brandy (and the foie gras to enrich your pâté if you have access to this), the salt and pepper and, lastly, the remaining butter. Pass the mixture through a fine sieve, taste to adjust the seasoning and transfer to a bottomless square or rectangular cake form (3 cm x 1.5 cm/1 ¼ in x ½ in). If you do not have a square tray then use a round spring-form cake tin but you will have some wastage. The pâté should be set to a maximum height of 1.5 cm. Smooth the top to ensure a flat surface. Cover with plastic wrap and refrigerate. Once cold, remove the plastic wrap and top with the jelly to cover and form a small coating.

ROSEHIP TEA JELLY PREPARATION Warm up a quarter of the tea and melt the soaked gelatine in this liquid.

ROSEHIP TEA JELLY PREP CONTINUED Remove from the heat; add the vinegar and strain. Cool until the jelly is near the setting point and pour on top of the cold parfait. You should prepare this jelly after the parfait is set and cold.

PRESENTATION Remove the form that held the parfait by running a small knife dipped in hot water around the edge. With a larger knife, again dipped in hot water, portion the parfait in fingers about 4 cm x 2 cm (1 ½ in x ¾ in). Set on toasted bread or brioche cut to the same or larger shape.

✚ ✚

OYSTER SHOOTER
WITH TOMATO JELLY

MAKES 20

TOMATO JELLY (*prepare the day before serving*)

550 gm (18 ½ oz) fresh ripe tomatoes, chopped

2 cloves garlic, peeled and finely chopped

½ celery stalk

¼ bunch basil, washed and picked

¼ bunch parsley, washed and picked

1 tablespoon chardonnay vinegar

500 ml (16 fl oz) tomato juice

1 cup vegetable stock

salt and milled black pepper

gelatine leaves, soaked in water (refer method)

SHOOTER

20 Sydney rock oysters, freshly shucked

3 tablespoons extra virgin olive oil

2 tablespoons red wine vinegar

salt and white milled pepper

½ cup fresh micro herbs (chervil, red and green basil)

TOMATO JELLY PREPARATION Combine all the ingredients (except the gelatine) in a blender and pulse. Leave this mixture to marinate overnight. The following day, strain through a sieve and then through cheesecloth.

PREPARATION CONTINUED Measure out the liquid and use four gelatine leaves per 4 cups of liquid. Soak the gelatine until soft, squeeze excess water and heat one cup of the liquid to melt the gelatine leaves. Strain and pour into the remaining liquid. Pour into the moulds or a tray and cool in the refrigerator.

OYSTER SHOOTER PRESENTATION To serve the oyster shooter, pour the tomato jelly in the shot glass, filling it about half full, place the freshly shucked oyster on top and garnish with the leaves. Season.

✦

FOIE GRAS PITHIVIER
WITH MUSHROOMS

MAKES ABOUT 24

MAIN INGREDIENTS

1 quantity of puff pastry (refer | Basics page 311)

2 tablespoons butter

4 eschalots, peeled and finely diced

1 clove garlic, peeled and finely diced

150 gm (5 oz) button mushrooms, firm and white, peeled and finely diced

150 gm (5 oz) Swiss brown mushrooms, finely diced

10 porcini mushrooms, soaked, trimmed and finely diced

1 teaspoon chopped flat leaf parsley

1 teaspoon finely chopped chives

salt and white milled pepper

100 gm (3 ½ oz) pâté de foie (duck liver pâté) optional

PREPARATION Place a pan on high heat. Melt the butter and sweat off the eschalots and the garlic. Add the finely diced mushrooms and cook them slowly until they are more or less dry. Incorporate the herbs, refine the seasoning and cool to room temperature. Preheat oven to 190°C (375°F). Roll out the puff pastry on a lightly floured bench to about 3 mm (¹/₈ in) thick. Cut 48 discs of approximately 6 cm (2 ½ in) in diameter. Egg wash half of them and place a teaspoon of the mushroom filling in the middle of these, then a piece of pâté if you are using this.

PREPARATION CONTINUED Sprinkle a little sea salt over and add another spoon of mushroom mixture to sandwich the liver. Place a plain pastry disc over the top, pushing the air out by shaping a round pillow, seal the pastry around the edges using a fork. Using a slightly smaller 'fluted' cutter, cut just inside the disc (trimming off the edge) to make it a perfect fluted round. Egg wash well, place in the refrigerator just to firm up, and egg wash again. Use the point of a small knife to draw some lines like a fan going all around the top — this marking is typical of pithivier.

PRESENTATION Bake the pithivier until the pastry is flaky and a beautiful golden brown colour. Remove from the oven, check that the dough is cooked underneath. Serve warm and crisp. You can also make larger versions of this recipe.

⚜

MARINATED OCEAN TROUT
WITH POTATO BLINIS

MAKES 36

MARINATED TROUT

100 gm (3 ½ oz) sea salt

600 gm (20 oz) ocean trout, de-boned, pin-boned, trimmed and skin on

50 gm (1 ½ oz) sugar

1 bunch picked and finely chopped dill

2 tablespoons yoghurt

1 cup celeriac, peeled and cut into brunoise (fine dice)

1 bunch finely chopped chives

POTATO BLINIS

½ teaspoon salt

1 teaspoon fresh yeast

1 pinch sugar

350 gm (12 oz) soft flour

50 gm (2 oz) buckwheat flour

120 gm (4 oz) potato, cooked and mashed

1 cup milk, tepid

4 egg whites, whipped until firm peaks form

1 tablespoon butter, for cooking

MARINATED TROUT PREP Sprinkle a third of the sea salt in a deep dish, place the trout over it, sprinkle the rest of the salt and the sugar over the top and sides. Cover with the dill. Allow the trout to marinate for 8–12 hours. Rinse the salt and dill off, pat trout dry. With a sharp knife remove the skin, cut the trout into very small dice.

BLINIS PREP AND PRESENTATION Mix salt, yeast, sugar, flours, potato mash and milk together. Allow this mixture to prove in a warm place for 40 minutes, covered. Fold in the whipped egg whites and shape small pancakes in a non-stick frying pan with a little fresh butter. Cook until coloured on both sides. Set the blinis on a warm tray, top with a small amount of diced marinated trout, then with some of the yoghurt. Lastly garnish with the celeriac and chives.

⚜ ⚜

ONION VOL-AU-VENT
WITH BEAUFORT CHEESE

MAKES 24

PASTRY

4 sheets (30 cm/12 in square) of good quality puff pastry (or refer | Basics page 311)

1 egg beaten with a tablespoon of water

FILLING

2 tablespoons olive oil

2 brown onions, peeled, halved and thinly sliced

1 Spanish onion, peeled, halved and thinly sliced

2 tablespoons caster sugar

100 gm (3 ½ oz) Beaufort or cheddar cheese, to serve

PASTRY PREPARATION Preheat oven to 180°C (350°F). Cut 24 circles of 5 cm (2 in) diameter from the sheets of puff pastry. Cut a further 24 the same size but with a smaller circle cut out of the centre (like a donut). Brush the 24 bases of pastry with the egg wash, top with the pastry with the hole in it and brush again with the egg wash. Place a sheet of baking paper over the top and bake for 10 minutes. Remove the paper and cook for a further 3–5 minutes until golden brown.

FILLING PREPARATION In a heavy pan, warm the olive oil. Add the onions and sugar and cook on a low heat until you have a caramelised onion compote. This might take 1 hour.

PRESENTATION Fill the vol-au-vents with the onion compote. Top with a small piece of cheese and warm up in the oven for a few minutes before serving.

SALT COD TARTLET
WITH GREEN VEGETABLE RATATOUILLE

MAKES 16

SALT COD

2 medium désirée potatoes, peeled and quartered

2 cloves garlic, peeled and left whole

75 ml (2 ¾ fl oz) cream, heated

400 gm (14 oz) salted cod, soaked overnight in
    milk or water

600 ml (20 fl oz) milk

1 garlic clove, peeled and crushed

2 sprigs thyme

sea salt and white milled pepper

50 ml (1 ½ fl oz) extra virgin olive oil

GREEN VEGETABLE RATATOUILLE

2 tablespoons extra virgin olive oil

2 eschalots, peeled and finely diced

4 small green zucchini, finely diced (discard the core)

sea salt and milled white pepper

½ cup bush or baby basil

TARTLET

250 gm (8 oz) plain flour

½ teaspoon salt

125 gm (4 oz) cold butter, cut into small cubes

½ egg, lightly beaten

100 ml (3 ½ fl oz) mineral water

TARTLET PREPARATION Sift the flour and the salt
together, add the cold butter and rub with your hands
until the mix reaches a light crumb consistency. Add
the whisked egg and the cold water together, knead
gently without overworking. Dust the dough with a
touch of flour and rest in the refrigerator for 2 hours
wrapped in plastic wrap. Preheat oven to 180°C
(350°F). Roll the dough to 3 mm (⅛ in) thick on a
floured surface. Spray 4–5 cm (1 ¾–2 in) diameter
tartlet moulds with non-stick spray, cut circles of pastry
to fit. Line the tartlet moulds with the pastry.

TARTLET PREPARATION CONTINUED Line the pastry
with baking paper and fill with baking weights or dried
beans and bake them in the oven until golden brown.
Remove the weights and cool the tartlets on a cooling
rack. If the bottoms of the tartlets are translucent and
still dough-like when the weights are removed, return
them to the oven without the weights and bake for a
further 2–5 minutes, and cool. You may have enough
pastry to make extra tarts — use them in another
recipe or make more cod tartlets.

FILLING PREPARATION Cover the potatoes and the
whole garlic cloves with salted water and simmer until
very soft. When ready, drain and dry in an oven (on
moderate temperature 160°C/300°F) for 15 minutes.
Put the potato and the garlic through a mouli and
slowly add hot cream to achieve a perfectly creamy and
firm mashed potato. Refine the seasoning and add the
extra virgin olive oil. Once the cod is soaked
thoroughly, poach it in the milk mixed with the
crushed garlic and the thyme sprigs. Poach until the
cod flakes off the bone and is tender. Pick the meat off
the bone carefully. Gently fold the flaked cod through
the warm potato. Refine the seasoning and keep warm.

RATATOUILLE PREPARATION Heat half the olive oil in
a non-stick pan on low heat and cook the eschalots.
When soft and translucent, add the zucchini and
season. Cook for a minute or two and remove the
pan from the heat. Immediately remove the zucchini
and eschalots to a small container to avoid
overcooking. Drizzle the rest of the oil on top and
add a touch of pepper.

PRESENTATION Spoon the hot cod mixture into the
tartlets, garnish with ratatouille and basil and serve
immediately.

OCEAN TROUT BARQUETTE

SERVES 8

MARINATED TROUT

600 gm (20 oz) ocean trout, cured or smoked
1 avocado, ripe, and diced
½ lemon, juiced
salt and white milled pepper
1 punnet baby cress
1 handful frisée lettuce

BARQUETTE

250 gm (8 oz) plain flour
½ teaspoon salt
125 gm (4 oz) cold butter, cut into small cubes
½ egg, lightly beaten
100 ml (3 ½ fl oz) mineral water

BARQUETTE PREPARATION Sift the flour and salt together, add the cold butter, rub with your hands until the mix reaches a light crumb consistency. Add the whisked egg and the cold water together, knead gently without overworking. Dust the dough with a touch of flour, rest in the refrigerator for 2 hours wrapped in plastic wrap. Preheat oven to 180°C (350°F). Roll the dough to 3 mm (⅛ in) thick on a floured surface. Spray the barquette moulds with non-stick spray and cut shapes of pastry to fit. Line the moulds with the pastry. Line the pastry with baking paper, fill with baking weights or dried beans and bake them in the oven until golden brown. Remove weights, cool on a cooling rack. If the bottoms of the barquettes are translucent and dough-like, return to the oven (without the weights) and bake for a further 2–5 minutes. Cool.

MARINATED TROUT PREP AND PRESENTATION Trim the ocean trout of any skin, sides and dried flesh. Cut long strips and then cut to form little cubes. Do the same for the avocado and gently toss together with the lemon juice and some seasoning. Fill the barquette and garnish with the cress and frisée.

Carrot Emulsion

Red Wine Sauce

Champagne Vinaigrette

Chunky Tomato

Mayonnaise

❧ Bathers' ❧
BASICS

In cooking, it is essential to master the
recipes included in this chapter as they form
the base for many larger recipe preparations.
In some instances, you may be able to
substitute with good quality commercially
available products. But the greatest sense
of satisfaction, and the best flavour,
will come from making your own stocks,
sauces or dressings.

Olive Oil EVO

Nam Jhim

Balsamic Vinaigrette

Basil Oil

Tapenade

Pesto

❧ Stocks and Jus ❧

✦ ✦
ASIAN MASTER STOCK

MAKES 2 LITRES (4 PINTS)

50 ml (1 ½ fl oz) canola oil
1 celery stalk, finely sliced
1 small carrot, peeled and finely sliced
1 large red chilli, de-seeded and finely sliced
2 cloves garlic, peeled and finely sliced
1 knob ginger, peeled and crushed in a mortar
1 knob galangal, peeled and crushed in a mortar
2 sticks lemongrass, crushed
5 lime leaves
5 star anise
1 cinnamon quill
1 pinch dried liquorice powder (optional)
2 strips orange peel, bruised with a mortar and pestle
50 gm (1 ½ oz) palm sugar
200 ml (7 fl oz) shao hsing wine
150 ml (5 fl oz) soy sauce
4 cups chicken stock
4 cups veal stock
1 small bunch mint, picked
1 small bunch basil, picked
½ bunch of coriander roots, cleaned of excess dirt
2 tablespoons oyster sauce
1 tablespoon kecap manis
1 tablespoon fish sauce

In a large pot, heat a small amount of canola oil on medium heat, lightly sweat the vegetables chilli, garlic, ginger, spices, liquorice powder and the orange peel. Add the palm sugar and lightly caramelise. Deglaze with the shao hsing wine and soy sauce. Add the chicken and veal stock and bring to the simmer for 20 minutes and remove from the heat. Using a mortar and pestle slightly bruise the mint, coriander root and basil, add to the hot stock and allow to infuse for 1 hour.

Strain through a fine sieve lined with muslin cloth. Adjust the seasoning with a little oyster sauce, kecap manis and fish sauce. Once cooled, refrigerate for up to 4 days.

❦
BEETROOT JUS SAUCE

MAKES 8 PORTIONS

6 eschalots, peeled and finely diced
2 whole beetroots, juiced
100 ml (3 ½ fl oz) red wine
200 ml (7 fl oz) chicken stock
200 ml (7 fl oz) fish or vegetable stock
50 gm (1 ½ oz) cold butter, diced

BEETROOT JUS PREPARATION To prepare the beetroot jus, sweat off the eschalots in a saucepan, add the beetroot juice with the red wine and reduce by half. Add the chicken and fish stock and reduce to a sauce consistency. Add the diced butter and whisk until melted and the sauce is thicker. Reserve for plating.

BORSCHT STOCK

MAKES 8 PORTIONS

(needs 5 days preparation time)

1 kg (2 lb) fresh beetroots, peeled
1 litre (2 pints) water
500 gm (1 lb) rye bread crusts
2 bay leaves
1 sprig rosemary
1 cinnamon quill
1 star anise
salt
200 ml (7 fl oz) cabernet vinegar
muslin cloth

Dice the beetroot into small cubes. Place in a large sterilised jar. Add the water, bread crusts, herbs, spices and the vinegar. Make sure the beetroot is covered in the liquid, otherwise add water to cover. Cover the jar with a lid made from the muslin cloth. Allow this mixture to ferment 4–5 days at room temperature. The development of the beetroot flavour will become full on the palate like the roundness of wine but without the complexity and alcohol of course.

When ready, pass the mixture through a fine sieve into a large pot and discard the beetroot.
Bring to the boil, while skimming the surface of impurities constantly. Strain through muslin cloth, refine the seasoning and reserve. When ready to serve, simply reheat; you will need about ½ cup per serving.

ASIAN MASTER STOCK

This is one of the best and most versatile stocks in my repertoire. I use it to cook chicken, quail, pork, seafood and even use it as a dressing or a bouillon with many dishes. The Master Stock can replace many heavier sauces. Once used, boil it again, skim and refrigerate until the next use and it will only gain flavour for many more uses.

CHICKEN STOCK

MAKES 4–6 CUPS

1 whole chicken or 1 kg (2 lbs) chicken bones
1 carrot, peeled
2 celery stalks
1 leek, washed and cut in two
1 large white onion, peeled and chopped
8 cups water
2 bay leaves
handful flat leaf parsley
1 sprig thyme
1 garlic clove, peeled and crushed
½ teaspoon black peppercorns
fine salt

Wash the chicken under cold water and put in a narrow but
tall pot. Chop all vegetables into small pieces. Place them
with the chicken in the pot; add the water, herbs, garlic,
peppercorns and a little salt. Bring to the boil and simmer
gently for 30 minutes. Remove the whole chicken to use for
another recipe and cook the stock for another hour. Cool.
Strain before use and discard the sediments. Store in
refrigerator until needed (up to 5 days) or in the freezer.

VEGETABLE STOCK

MAKES 4–6 CUPS

2 carrots, peeled
¼ bunch celery
2 leeks, washed
1 large white onion, peeled
8 cups water
handful flat leaf parsley
2 sprigs thyme
2 garlic cloves, peeled and crushed
½ teaspoon black peppercorns
fine salt

Chop all vegetables into small pieces. Place into medium-
sized pot, add the water, herbs, garlic, peppercorns and a
little salt. Bring to the boil and simmer for 30 minutes.
Cool, strain and discard the sediments before storing in
refrigerator until needed (up to 5 days) or in the freezer.

FISH STOCK

MAKES 4–6 CUPS

head and bones of 2 snapper or other white fish
1 medium carrot, peeled and chopped
1 celery stalk, chopped
1 small leek, washed and chopped
1 medium onion, peeled and chopped
1 bay leaf
handful flat leaf parsley
150 ml (5 fl oz) white wine
8 cups water

Place all ingredients in stockpot, bring to the boil and then simmer for 20 minutes, skimming frequently. Strain through damp muslin cloth that is sitting over a large bowl. Allow stock to cool. Pour in a storage container and discard the sediment at the bottom of the pot. Store in refrigerator until needed (up to 2 days) or in the freezer.

VEAL STOCK

MAKES 4–6 CUPS

1.5 kg (3 lb) veal bones
8 cups water
1 medium carrot, peeled and chopped
1 celery stalk, chopped
1 small leek, washed and chopped
1 medium onion, peeled and chopped
handful parsley stalks
½ teaspoon whole black peppercorns
1 teaspoon salt
1 bay leaf

Place the veal bones in cold water in a large pot (the pot should be taller rather than wider). Bring to the boil for 5 minutes, then drain, discarding water. Wash bones under cold water then return them to the pot with 8 cups fresh water or enough to cover the bones and add all the remaining ingredients. Simmer slowly for 4 hours without any heavy bubbling, skimming regularly. Strain, cool, then store in refrigerator until needed (up to 3 days) or in the freezer.

VEAL JUS

MAKES ABOUT 4 CUPS

2 kg (4 lb) veal bones
100 ml (3 ½ fl oz) olive oil
2 small carrots, diced
1 leek, diced
2 cloves garlic, peeled and diced
1 celery stalk, diced
1 medium onion, peeled and diced
1 bouquet garni (thyme, bay leaf, peppercorn, rosemary)
3 cups deep red wine (shiraz is good)
4 cups chicken stock or water, to cover
1 cup verjuice
1 sprig each thyme, tarragon, parsley stalk and rosemary
fine salt
½ teaspoon whole black peppercorns

Preheat oven to 220°C (425°F). In a roasting pan add the veal bones, a little olive oil, carrots, leek, garlic, celery, onion and bouquet garni. Roast for 20 minutes until the bones have some colour. Stir and cook for 10 minutes more. Deglaze with half the red wine and cook on the stove over moderate heat until the ingredients have nearly dried, approximately 15 minutes. Transfer to a large pot, cover with stock and simmer for 4 hours skimming the surface when scum forms. Strain stock when ready.

In a clean pot add the rest of the wine, verjuice, pepper and reduce to one-third of the volume. Add the stock and reduce slowly, skimming regularly, until you have a perfect jus. Strain through a wet muslin cloth into a clean pot and adjust the seasoning. Add the fresh herbs and cover the bowl with plastic wrap to infuse the herbs in the warm sauce for 10 minutes. Strain again and salt to achieve a balanced taste. This sauce is ready to use or perfect to add other flavourings to if you wish to make a pepper or shallot sauce. If you reduce this further, you could produce a glace de viande, which is useful to add punch to other sauces or to make a cream sauce.

❧ Vinaigrettes ❧

BASIC VINAIGRETTE

MAKES OVER 1 CUP

1 cup vegetable or grape seed oil
⅓ cup white or red wine vinegar
fine salt and white milled pepper

I use this vinaigrette just to moisten greens that are topping another dish or for leaves that need a very light coating like watercress or micro leaves. Olive oil is often too heavy for these.

VARIATION replace the red wine vinegar with champagne.

FRENCH VINAIGRETTE

MAKES 2 CUPS

1 cup grape seed oil or vegetable oil
½ cup walnut or hazelnut oil
¼ cup red wine vinegar
¼ cup Champagne or tarragon vinegar
1 small onion, grated
1 tablespoon honey
1 teaspoon Dijon mustard
1 tablespoon parsley, washed, dried and chopped
1 tablespoon chives, washed, dried and chopped
sea salt and black milled pepper

I use this vinaigrette for heavy leaf salads like cos, iceberg and oak leaf. It does have a great punch and a real authentic French taste.

CHAMPAGNE VINAIGRETTE

MAKES APPROX 3 CUPS

1 tablespoon Dijon mustard
1 teaspoon of sugar
1 small onion, grated
1 cup Champagne vinegar
1 cup peanut oil
1 cup olive oil
½ cup Champagne
salt and pepper

Blend mustard, sugar, onion and vinegar. Add peanut and olive oil. Finally, whisk in champagne. Correct the seasoning and serve.

BALSAMIC VINAIGRETTE

MAKES 1 ½ CUPS

1 cup virgin olive oil
½ cup balsamic vinegar
1 garlic clove, peeled, crushed or chopped finely
fine salt, black milled pepper

I use this vinaigrette for tomato salad or on bocconcini cheese or for any grilled Italian style vegetables like red and green capsicum and zucchini. Balsamic vinegars vary a great deal in quality — the price is often a good indication of quality. A basic principle is the more aged, the better quality and also the better sweetness. Another guide is the bottle size — the smaller bottle of traditional balsamic vinegar will be more prized so you will need less but will appreciate its special flavours and complexity.

❧ Flavoured Oils ❧

BASIL OIL

MAKES 1 CUP

1 bunch of basil, picked
1 cup extra virgin olive oil

Lightly blanch basil leaves for 2 seconds in rapidly boiling water. Refresh in iced water. Drain the water and pat the leaves dry with paper towel. Place leaves in a food processor and blend, slowly adding the olive oil. Strain through a fine strainer lined with muslin cloth. Serve immediately or store chilled.

SHELLFISH OIL

MAKES ABOUT 2 CUPS

500 gm (1 lb) shells of various raw shellfish like lobster,
    crab and prawn
1 cup grape seed oil
1 cup olive oil
3 tablespoons tomato paste
2 tablespoons ginger, chopped
2 tablespoons galangal, chopped
1 stick lemongrass, 2 star anise and 3 cardamom pods
1 tomato, chopped
6 eschalots, peeled and chopped
1 stick celery, chopped
2 garlic cloves, crushed
1 carrot, chopped
pinch saffron (optional)
¼ cup brandy
¼ cup Pernod

Crush the shellfish shells in a large pot using a mallet or another smaller heavy pot. Sauté all the ingredients, including the shells (but not the alcohol), in a heavy-bottomed pot with half the oil. Do this until the vegetables start caramelising or have some colour. Deglaze with the alcohol and burn it by lighting a match. Add the remaining oil and cook at low heat for 1 hour. Remove from the heat and let the ingredients infuse the oil for another hour. Strain through a fine sauce sieve. Decant to a sterilised bottle and discard the sediments.

❧ Dressings ❧

MAYONNAISE

MAKES 2 CUPS

2 egg yolks
1 teaspoon Dijon mustard
2 tablespoons white wine vinegar
1 ½ cup canola or vegetable oil
1 lemon, juice only
salt and white milled pepper
½ cup crème fraîche (optional, replacing ½ cup
    of the oil)

Place the egg yolks and mustards in a bowl and while mixing slowly add half the oil until the mix is fairly thick. Add the vinegar in stages to thin the mayonnaise and continue adding the oil and finish with the lemon juice. Season with the salt and the white milled pepper.

PESTO

MAKES 2 CUPS

4 cups basil leaves washed
2 pinch sea salt
1 cup olive oil
1 cup pine nuts, toasted and cool
2 garlic cloves, roasted and peeled
fresh milled white pepper
1 cup grated Parmesan cheese

Dry the basil leaves in a salad spinner and add to a food processor. Blend with the salt and half the olive oil until you have a rough texture. Add the pine nuts and garlic and blend until you have a fine texture and lastly add the pepper and Parmesan and blend for another 30 seconds. If the pesto is too dry add the balance of the oil. This pesto will keep in the refrigerator for up to a week.

❧ Spicy Jam and Tapenade ❧

❧

BLACK OLIVE TAPENADE

MAKES ABOUT 1 CUP

300 gm (10 oz) kalamata olives, pitted
1 tablespoon extra virgin olive oil
1 eschalot, peeled and chopped
2 anchovy fillets, chopped
2 cloves garlic, peeled and chopped
1 tablespoon baby capers, washed
black milled pepper
2 teaspoons continental parsley, chopped

Roughly chop the olives. Heat a small saucepan and add the olive oil, lightly sweat off the eschalot and anchovies. Allow to cool. Using a food processor, purée the olives, anchovies, garlic and capers to create a smooth paste, if necessary add extra olive oil. Season with milled black pepper, add chopped parsley to taste before each use.

❧

CHILLI JAM

MAKES ABUT 2 CUPS

100 ml (3 ½ fl oz) olive oil
12 eschalots, peeled and sliced
4 garlic cloves, peeled and chopped
1 teaspoon ground paprika
4 large dried red chillies, de-seeded and finely chopped
4 large fresh red chillies, finely sliced
120 gm (4 oz) palm sugar
2 tablespoon Thai fish sauce
1 lemon, juiced
¼ cup tamarind water

In a frying pan, place olive oil, eschalots, garlic and paprika. Cook slowly until ingredients are soft. Add both types of chillies and cook until soft. Add the palm sugar, tamarind water and the fish sauce and cook until it reaches a jam texture. Remove from heat then add lemon juice. Cool and store for up to 1 week in the refrigerator.

❧ Confit ❧

❧ ❧

BASIC DUCK CONFIT

SERVES 6

1 whole duck or 6 duck legs
100 gm (3 ½ oz) rock or sea salt
6 eschalots, chopped
4 cloves garlic, peeled and sliced
6 sprigs each thyme, rosemary and marjoram
3 bay leaves
10 juniper berries
4 cups duck or goose fat or olive oil

If using a whole duck, cut into 6 pieces. Dry each piece of duck on a paper towel. Place on a tray and sprinkle with salt, eschalots, garlic and herbs. Cover and refrigerate for 24 hours. Discard all seasonings and brush any visible salt off the duck. In a pot that will fit the duck tightly, insert all the pieces of duck, keeping the skin on top. Cover with fat or oil. Heat gently and simmer very slowly for up to 3 hours. Test with a fork — the meat should fall off the bone easily. Allow to cool in the oil and refrigerate. If covered, the duck will keep, refrigerated, for 1 month.

❧

CONFIT VEGETABLES

MAKES 2 CUPS

2 cups any vegetables for confit
2 cups olive oil

Wash and scrub or peel the vegetables and dry carefully on a clean tea towel. Put the vegetables in a small pot, cover with olive oil and cook on a very low heat. Cool in the oil then drain. I cook all types of small vegetables in this manner and those that are most suited include eschalot, radish, small onion, baby turnip, beetroot, zucchini, fennel, garlic, parsnip, baby leek and salsify.

✿ Sauces and Dressings ✿

✦ ✦

HOLLANDAISE SAUCE

MAKES ABOUT 3 CUPS

50 ml (1 ½ fl oz) white wine vinegar
eschalots
tarragon
4 egg yolks
400 ml (14 fl oz) clarified butter, lukewarm
1 lemon, juiced
salt and white milled pepper

Heat the white wine vinegar, eschalots, tarragon and pepper and reduce by half its original volume. Remove from the heat, and cool.

Add the egg yolks to the vinegar reduction in a stainless steel bowl placed on top of a double boiler on low heat. Whisk this mixture for about 3 minutes or until it becomes creamy and white. It will thicken and you must be careful to avoid overcooking the eggs or they will scramble and the sauce might become lumpy.

Remove from the heat and slowly incorporate the clarified butter — at first a little at a time and then more as the volume of your sauce increases. If the sauce becomes too thick, add a splash of hot water or a squeeze of lemon to thin it down. When all the butter is used, refine the seasoning with salt, milled white pepper and the balance of the lemon juice. Place in a warm spot until ready to serve.

✦ ✦

PORCINI SAUCE

MAKES ABOUT 3 CUPS

1 onion, finely chopped
1 clove garlic, crushed
15 black and 15 white peppercorns, crushed
1 tablespoon canola oil
50 gm (1 ½ oz) porcini mushrooms
1 cup brandy
2 cups Madeira
2 cups veal stock, reduced by half in
    a saucepan over medium heat
2 cups cream
½ bunch chervil and tarragon (do not cut, wash only)
salt
1 tablespoon foie gras, optional

Sauté the onions, garlic and peppercorns in the oil until they caramelise. Add the porcini mushrooms and cook a further 5 minutes. Deglaze the pan with brandy then Madeira. Reduce this liquid by half. Add the stock. Reduce again, by one-third this time or until syrupy. Add the cream and reduce the heat to low. Bring the liquid slowly to the simmer; be careful not to boil. Keep it at a constant simmer with a slight bubble. Remove the scum on the surface, and further reduce by one-quarter of the volume. Taste the sauce as you make it and follow its flavour development. This allows you to be more precise when checking seasoning. Constantly skim the sauce until it reduces to sauce consistency. Add the herbs at this stage and infuse for 20 minutes. Do not cut the herbs or they will turn the sauce a grey colour. Strain and serve.

TIP If you use a hand blender you can make a nice froth with the sauce prior to pouring at the table. I also use foie gras to enrich the sauce.

✦

PONZU DRESSING

MAKES 1 CUP

1 x 5 cm (2 in) piece kombu seaweed
⅓ cup soy sauce
⅓ cup lime juice
50 ml (1 ½ fl oz) peanut oil
1 tablespoon rice vinegar
1 tablespoon mirin
1 teaspoon sesame oil
2 teaspoons sugar syrup

recipe continues over

PONZU DRESSING CONTINUED Soak the kombu seaweed in cold water for 10 minutes. Drain, pat down with paper towel and chop roughly. Combine all the ingredients including the kombu seaweed and leave for 24 hours to develop. Strain and serve, or use within 4 days. Keep refrigerated.

NAM JHIM

SERVES ABOUT 2 CUPS

1 knob of ginger, thinly sliced
3 garlic cloves, thinly sliced
3 scud chili (small, green birds eye chillies)
3 eschalots
1 knob of galangal
3 coriander roots (cleaned of excess dirt)
5 limes juiced
3 tablespoons fish sauce
3 tablespoons palm sugar (light)

Using a mortar and pestle pound all the roots and herbs until they form a paste. Gradually add the lime juice and fish sauce then the palm sugar. When combined, pass liquid through a fine strainer and check the balance of sweetness, saltiness and spice and adjust if necessary. This dressing is perfect for noodle salad or a prawn salad.

CARROT EMULSION

MAKES 2 CUPS

1 to 2 carrots, juice only
¼ cup vegetable stock
¼ cup orange juice
1 cup grape seed oil
1 pinch saffron powder
salt and white milled pepper

Heat up the vinegar and dissolve the saffron, remove from the heat and add the stock and then the carrot juice and lastly the oil. Blend with a hand blender just before you use this over a carrot salad, on lettuce leaves or to serve over thinly sliced fish to marinate.

RED WINE SAUCE

MAKES ABOUT 4 CUPS

4 eschalots, peeled and finely chopped
1 onion, peeled and finely chopped
2 tablespoons olive oil
2 cloves garlic, finely chopped
1 teaspoon white and black peppercorns, crushed
1 field mushroom, diced
2 cups red wine
2 cups veal jus (see recipe this chapter)
2 sprigs thyme
2 sprigs rosemary

In a large pot, sauté and caramelise the eschalot and onion in the oil. Add peppercorns and mushroom and garlic last. Deglaze with half the red wine. Once the bottom of the pan is nearly dry add the rest of the wine. Reduce by three-quarters and add the veal jus. Bring this liquid to the boil, skim and simmer for a further 20 minutes only. Strain through a fine strainer into a smaller pot and bring to a simmer. Make sure you skim as much of the surface scum off as you possibly can, this will ensure that your sauce will be clear and shiny. Simmer for about 10 minutes.

To finish, add the herbs and infuse off the heat, covered with plastic wrap, for 10 minutes. Do not cook the herbs on the stove as they will make the sauce bitter. Pass through a fine strainer, to remove the herbs, and keep warm to serve.

SALMON MATELOTE SAUCE

MAKES ABOUT 3 CUPS

1 kg (2 lb) salmon bones, no skin, fat or head
1 onion, peeled and diced
1 leek, washed and diced
½ fennel bulb, trimmed, washed and diced
2 garlic cloves, peeled and chopped
olive oil
200 ml (7 fl oz) red wine
100 gm (3 ½ oz) peeled tomatoes
2 cups veal jus (see recipe this chapter)
1 cup fish stock (see recipe this chapter)
1 tablespoon red wine vinegar
1 teaspoon sugar

Preheat oven to 165°C (325°F). Place the salmon bones in a tray and roast until they are a light gold colour.

Sweat the mirepoix (onion, leek, fennel and garlic) in a large pot with a little oil until aromatic. Add the salmon bones at this stage. Deglaze the pot with the red wine and reduce slightly. Add the tomatoes, fish stock and the veal jus and simmer. Skim the surface continuously for 30 minutes. Adjust the sauce flavour with red wine vinegar and a little sugar then refine the seasoning to achieve a balanced flavour. Pass through a fine sieve lined with cheesecloth. Serve as per your recipe.

❧ Pommes/Potatoes ❧

POMME PURÉE

MAKES ABOUT 4 GENEROUS PORTIONS

500 gm (1 lb) about 10 large désirée potatoes
300 ml (10 fl oz) cream reduced by one-third over gentle heat in a saucepan
150 gm (5 oz) diced butter, at room temperature
sea salt

Preheat the oven to 190°C (375°F). Roast potatoes with the skin on for 1 ½ hours. Have the hot reduced cream and the diced butter ready. Using a large spoon, scoop the flesh of the potato into a warm mouli (grater) sitting on a warm pot, discard skins or dry them for a snack. Purée the potato adding a little butter from time to time to help its motion. Place the puréed potato in the pot on the stove, slowly add the hot cream and the remaining butter beating it so it remains smooth. Add the liquids until the desired consistency is achieved. Season with salt, keep warm for use.

TIP If you are making the potato for the Parmentier, you will only need the butter (no cream) so you have a firm texture.

POMMES FONDANTES

MAKES 8 PORTIONS

8 large désirée potatoes
60 ml (2 fl oz) clarified butter
4 cups chicken stock
150 gm (5 oz) butter

Preheat oven to 180°C (350°F). You will need a round stainless steel cutter 5 cm (2 in) diameter and 2 large stainless steel pots.
Slice the potatoes into slices about 2 cm (¾ in) thick. Using the round cutter, cut circles out from potatoes and trim the edges with a peeler. Sauté both sides of the potatoes until golden brown in the clarified butter. In a separate pot, heat up stock and butter and when hot add to just cover the potatoes. Place in oven for 30 minutes. Test with a sharp knife and, when cooked but still firm, take out and let cool. Remove the potatoes from the liquid and place on a tray with baking paper. For use, warm in the oven and plate as needed.

POTATO RÖSTI

SERVES 4

4 large pontiac or désirée potatoes
salt and pepper
100 gm (3 ½ oz) butter, melted
1 tablespoon vegetable oil

Peel and wash potatoes. Shred finely with a mandoline or grater and mix with salt and pepper and a little of the melted butter. Form this mixture into 4 medium-sized cakes using an egg ring or by hand, and then sauté each in a non-stick frying pan with the remaining butter and oil until cooked and golden. Depending on their thickness, you might have to finish cooking them in an oven set at 180°C (350°F) for 5 minutes or until cooked.

❧ Tomato Preparation ❧

I use Italian tomatoes to make sauces and vine ripened to make dice or a tomato garnish.

PEELED TOMATO

MAKES 24 HALVES

12 tomatoes, table or vine ripened
2 litres (4 pints) boiling water

Cut the eyes of the tomato out and, with a small knife, cut a cross at the round head of the tomato to score the flesh. Plunge tomatoes in boiling water for 30 seconds or longer if the tomatoes are not perfectly ripe. Remove and plunge in iced water or run under cold water for a couple of minutes. Using a small knife, peel the tomatoes and cut them in two. Squeeze or scoop the seed and juice out then cut them in your desired shape.

OVEN ROASTED TOMATO

MAKES 24 HALVES

12 tomatoes, Italian or Roma type
1 tablespoon olive oil
2 branches and leaves green basil
2 cloves garlic, peeled and sliced

Preheat oven to 220°C (425°F). Cut the tomato in half, squeeze to remove the excess seeds and juice and toss them in a bowl with the olive oil, basil leaves and garlic. Place the basil stalks on a baking tray basted with the olive oil from the bowl. Set the tomato halves on the tray skin-side up. Distribute the garlic slices over the tomato and roast for 5 minutes in oven or until the skin blisters. Remove from the oven, peel the tomatoes and discard the basil and garlic. This is an ideal base from which to prepare a tomato sauce. If you wish to have oven-dried tomatoes, return them to the oven on a clean tray cut side up. Reduce oven temperature to 100°C (210°F). Bake them for 1–2 hours depending on the degree of roasting/drying you desire.

CHUNKY TOMATO SAUCE

MAKES APPROXIMATELY 4 CUPS

2 medium white onions, peeled and finely diced
1 ½ cups water
1 ½ cup white wine vinegar
1 cups sugar
3 cloves garlic, peeled and crushed
8 medium tomatoes, peeled, de-seeded and diced
Salt and pepper

Simmer the diced onions in the water, white wine vinegar and sugar until soft. Add the crushed garlic and diced tomatoes until they are cooked through and soft, blend with an electric hand-held blender or in a blender, adjust the seasoning and cool prior to serving.

❧ Batters ❧

TEMPURA BATTER

MAKES 2 CUPS

2 egg yolks
275 ml (9 fl oz) iced water
200 gm (7 oz) corn flour, sifted
4 cups peanut oil for frying

Place the egg yolks in a bowl and mix the water in gradually. Add all the corn flour and stir briefly (preferably with a pair of chopsticks). Be sure not to mix the batter to a smooth paste, as it should contain small lumps of dry flour.

BATHERS' HOMEMADE BUTTER

MAKES APPROXIMATELY 500 gm

1 litre cream (35% fat)
10 gm fine salt

Pour 1 litre of fresh cream into mixer and whisk on medium speed until the butterfat separates from the whey. This takes approximately 20–30 minutes. Put butter onto strainer and refrigerate. Squeeze out any excess water whilst wearing rubber gloves and place butter onto scale. Add 1% salt (or 10 gm) and knead it into the butter using a dough hook on low speed. Mould into your desired shape and refrigerate again.

❧ Vegetable Preparations ❧

CHLOROPHYLL

MAKES 1 TABLESPOON

2 bunches English spinach, washed and spun dry

Put spinach through a juicer and then pass juice through a fine sieve. Place in a pan on the stove and start heating up over a low heat. The most important thing is to know when to remove this from the heat — basically, as soon as you see the solids start floating then it is ready to be removed. Speed is essential as the water should never pass the tepid stage. Remove immediately from the stove and pour the liquid into a sieve double-lined with wet cheesecloth. Place the sieve over a bowl and leave it overnight to drain the excess water. Scrape off the chlorophyll — this should give you about 1 tablespoon. Store in a covered bowl. This paste is a natural colouring for cold sauces, pasta and dressing and, because of its strength, you will not require much. This could also be used in a hot sauce but added only at the last moment and the sauce should be served immediately.

MUSHROOM DUXELLE WITH PORCINI

MAKES ABOUT 2 CUPS

2 tablespoons olive oil
4 eschalots finely chopped
3 cloves garlic, chopped finely
100 gm (3 ½ oz) diced butter
12 field mushrooms peeled, stems removed and finely
    chopped in a food processor
1 tablespoon dried porcini mushrooms, soaked and
    chopped finely
salt and pepper

Heat olive oil in a medium-sized pan and sweat the eschalot. When soft, add the garlic and cook for 1 minute or until the garlic is soft. Add the butter, increase the heat and add the field mushrooms. Cook until the mushrooms are soft and most of the moisture has evaporated. Add the porcini, season with salt and pepper and reserve.

ROCKET AND SPINACH PURÉE

SERVES 8

1 tablespoon butter
4 cups English spinach, picked and washed
2 cups rocket leaves, picked and washed
1 cup cream
1 garlic clove, peeled and finely chopped
6 eschalots, peeled and finely chopped
nutmeg
salt and white milled pepper

In a wide-bottomed pan on moderate heat, melt the butter and quickly wilt the spinach and rocket. Drain and cool down straight away on a tray in the refrigerator. Once cold, place the spinach and rocket in a food processor and process to achieve a smooth purée. You may have to adjust the speed to keep the spinach moving in the processor to achieve a smooth purée. When ready to serve, in a wide-bottomed pan place the cream with the chopped garlic, eschalots and a grating of nutmeg and reduce by three-quarters over gentle heat. Strain and add the purée to the reduced cream, season well, and serve hot.

❧ Sweet Things ❧

SUGAR SYRUP

MAKES 800 ML (28 FL OZ)

2 cups water
600 gm (20 oz) sugar

Put the sugar and the water in a high-sided saucepan and bring to the boil while stirring. Boil for a minute or two. Cool and refrigerate. This syrup is best used within a few days.

CHOCOLATE SPONGE CAKE

MAKES 1 TO 2 CAKES

7 eggs
250 gm (8 oz) caster sugar
50 gm (1 ½ oz) cocoa powder
175 gm (6 oz) plain flour

Preheat oven to 180°C (350°F). Whisk the eggs and sugar until they are light and fluffy. Sift the cocoa powder and plain flour together and fold this through the egg mixture. Spread onto a greased baking tray (30 cm x 20 cm/12 in x 8 in) and bake for 12 minutes. Sprinkle sugar onto a piece of greaseproof paper and turn sponge onto this. Allow to cool before use.

VANILLA CUSTARD

MAKES 4 CUPS

625 ml (21 fl oz) milk
625 ml (21 fl oz) cream
1 vanilla bean, split in half
270 gm (9 oz) caster sugar
90 gm (3 oz) corn flour
5 egg yolks

Bring the milk, cream, vanilla bean and caster sugar to the boil. Meanwhile mix the corn flour and egg yolks together and then add a small ladle of the milk mixture to dilute the egg mix. Add the egg mix to the large milk pot and mix constantly until you have a thick custard. Remove from heat. Cover with plastic wrap when cooler and refrigerate until needed. Custard can be gently reheated for use.

VANILLA SAUCE ANGLAISE

MAKES 3 CUPS

350 ml (12 fl oz) milk
300 ml (10 fl oz) cream
100 gm (3 ½ oz) caster sugar
8 egg yolks
1 vanilla bean, split in two

Mix all the ingredients in a glass bowl with a whisk including the split vanilla bean. Set the bowl over a pot of gently boiling water and stir with a wooden spatula cooking until it thickens. Chill over ice and keep cold until ready to use. If you like the vanilla seeds in the Anglaise, scrape the inside of the bean with a small knife and mix the seeds into the sauce. Wash and dry the bean and store in an air tight container with sugar to make vanilla sugar.

✤ Breads ✤

DATE, FIG AND WALNUT BREAD

MAKES ONE LOAF

200 gm (7 oz) walnuts
625 ml (21 fl oz) warm water
25 gm (1 oz) fresh yeast
½ cup honey
500 gm (1 lb) strong bread flour
500 gm (1 lb) plain flour
2 teaspoons sugar
1 tablespoon salt
100 gm (3 ½ oz) dates, pitted and chopped
150 gm (5 oz) dried figs, cut in half
3 tablespoons olive oil

TO SERVE
Milawa washed rind cheese

PREPARATION Preheat oven to 150°C (300°F). Roast the walnuts for 10 minutes in the oven. Mix water, yeast and honey in mixing bowl. Add all dry ingredients, except walnuts. Mix for a few minutes and add the olive oil. Mix well using dough hook in an electric mixer on slow speed for 1 minute, then increase to medium speed for approximately 5 minutes. Check for correct consistency, it should be slightly sticky. Add the roasted walnuts and blend them into the smooth dough until evenly distributed. Remove from bowl and knead on a floured board until rubbery. Place in a floured bowl, cover with a clean cloth and allow to prove in a warm place until doubled in size. Knock the dough back down then mould into a loaf and place on lightly greased baking sheet. Prove again, until doubled in size.

Preheat oven to 230°C (450°F). Lightly dust loaf with plain flour then bake for 20 minutes or until the bread sounds firm and cooked. Cut the loaf in slices. Cut the cheese in even wedges and serve on the warm or toasted bread.

❧ Pastry ❧

PUFF PASTRY

MAKES ABOUT 1 ½ KG (3 lb)

500 gm (1 lb) plain flour, sifted
60 gm (2 oz) butter, diced and soft
1 ½ teaspoons salt
300 ml (10 fl oz) tepid water
500 gm (1 lb) butter, softened
2 egg yolks, mixed with a teaspoon of water and a
    pinch of sugar, for the egg wash

Mix the flour with the 60 gm (2 oz) of butter until fully combined. Make a well in the centre of the mixture, add the salt into the water and pour the liquid into the well. Mix and knead until the dough is smooth and elastic. Form a ball and leave to stand for half an hour.

When rolling the dough, use a heavy rolling pin for the best results. Roll out the dough into a thick square 30 cm (12 in). Roll out the 500 gm (1 lb) butter between sheets of greaseproof paper to form a 20 cm (8 in) square. Firm up the butter and the dough in the refrigerator for 20 minutes so they are the same firmness and temperature. On a lightly floured bench, place the dough and put the butter in the centre of the dough. Fold the left and right ends of the dough over the butter to enclose it completely. Leave to stand in the refrigerator until rested and firm, about 30 minutes.

The following stage for the puff pastry is called the turning operation. Roll the dough out with a rolling pin on a lightly floured bench to obtain a rectangle measuring about 60 cm (24 in) long and 25 cm (10 in) wide. Fold the top and bottom ends of the pastry towards the middle and fold over again on each other, rest for 30 minutes in the refrigerator. Take out of the refrigerator, move the dough a quarter turn on the bench so the longer side is facing away from you, and repeat the rolling and turning sequence a further 4 times allowing the dough to rest in the refrigerator each time for 30 minutes to allow the butter to solidify. Give the dough a final two hours rest before you use it.

When ready, cut a piece for use, top with a small amount of flour and roll to 3 mm (1/8 in) thickness. Cut in the desired shape and brush with the egg wash. Rest again for 30 minutes before you bake the dough. The best temperature to bake puff pastry is 220°C (450°F) for 20–25 minutes or until golden brown.

SWEET PASTRY
FOR GIN AND LIME MERINGUE TART

MAKES ABOUT 1 ½ KG (3 lbs)

160g (5 oz) unsalted butter
100 gm (3 ½ oz) caster sugar
1 egg, beaten
250 gm (8 oz) plain flour
pinch of salt

Cream the butter and sugar then add the egg. Mix in the flour and salt to smooth dough. Cover and leave to rest in a cool place for 1 hour. Roll the pastry on a lightly floured surface and line your small tartlet tins. Chill in the refrigerator for 20 minutes. Preheat the oven to 180°C (350°F) and bake for 10 minutes.

PASTRY FOR LEMON TARTLET

MAKES 500 gm

100 gm (3 ½ oz) unsalted butter
100 gm (3 ½ oz) caster sugar
eggs
1 tablespoon vanilla essence
220 gm (7 ½ oz) plain flour
¼ cup icing sugar, for dusting

Using a food processor, blend butter and sugar until white and fluffy. Slowly add eggs one by one and the vanilla essence. Sift the flour and add to the mixture. Blend until combined. Wrap pastry in plastic wrap and refrigerate for 1 hour. Preheat oven to 180°C (350°F). Lightly flour your bench top, roll out pastry to 3 mm (1/8 in) thick. Using a 4 cm (1 ½ in) plain round cutter, cut 50–60 disks and place them on trays lined with baking paper. Remove a centre circle from half of them with a 2 cm (½ in) plain round cutter. Bake for 8–10 minutes and cool.

❧ Index ❧

Page numbers in bold denote illustrations

❧ A ❧

Almond and star anise tuiles **253**, **260**

Anchovy custard with focaccia grissini
44, **46**

Anchovy pillows and paillettes aux
anchois **15**, **19**

Apple gâteaux with Calvados chantilly
cream 231, **235**

Apricot frangipane with lime sabayon
232, **233**

Apricot pâté de fruit **253**, **259**

Arctic char with pork and prawn
dumpling **151**, 152

Asian master stock 298

Assiette de lapin – rack of rabbit with its
loin, shoulder and liver **165**, 166–167

❧ B ❧

Baked jewfish 'En Croûte' with zucchini,
carrot and basil, with mousseline
sauce 22, **26**, 27

Balsamic vinaigrette 302

Barbecue prawns with lime butter **128**, 129

Barbecue trout bundles with prosciutto
and button mushrooms 123, **126–127**

Barramundi with pancetta and shimeji
mushroom **143**, 153

Basil oil 303

Beef carpaccio with oxtail jelly and
porcini pannacotta **47**, **56–57**

Beef tartare on beetroot with quail egg
282, 284

Beef tenderloin with wild mushrooms
179, **182–183**

Beetroot jus 298

Berry financier **258**, **261**

Black olive tapenade 304

Blood orange compote with strawberries
and rhubarb 33

Blue cheese tortellini with cauliflower
and broccoli jus 43, **47**

Blue eye trevalla with parsnip crust,
spinach dumpling, and beetroot jus
154, 159

Blueberry vanilla tart 134, **135**

Bocconcini with tomato quenelle 37, **47**

Bombe Alaska 28–29

Borscht stock 298, 300

Brioche with mushroom duxelle 38, **46**

Butter, homemade 308

Butterscotch caramel log **239**, 243

❧ C ❧

CAKES

Apple gâteaux with Calvados
chantilly cream 231, **235**

Chocolate gâteau 31, 32

Chocolate hérisson cake **244**, 249

Chocolate mille feuille with hazelnut
mousse **244**, 248

Chocolate sponge 310

Quince cake with maple syrup ice
cream **245**, 246–247

Raspberry sponge **254**, 258

Wedding cake **276**, 277–278

Candied orange friand 257

Caramelised pineapple and ginger tart
226–227, **235**

Caramelised tomato, eschalot and fetta
tart 69, **74**

Carrot emulsion **296**, **306**

Casserole of seafood with turmeric and
chilli **91**, 94–95

Caviar brioche **47**, 51

Caviar on potato rösti **197**, 198

Champagne vinaigrette 302

Chestnut soup with lentils, garlic and
eschalots 78, **79**

Chicken liver parfait with rosehip tea
jelly **289**, 290

Chicken stock 300

Chilli jam 304

Chlorophyll 309

Chocolate gâteau 31, **32**

Chocolate hérisson cake **244**, 249

Chocolate log 257, **261**

Chocolate mille feuille with hazelnut
mousse **244**, 248

Chocolate pudding with two sauces **239**,
242

Chocolate sponge 310

Cigarettes with orange cream **253**, 256

Coconut and pineapple terrine **230**, 235

CONFIT

Confit vegetables 304

Duck confit (basic) 304

Confit vegetable parmentier **75**, 76

Corn soup 270

Crab and picked mushroom salad with
Asian noodles 102, **103**

Crab sandwich **269**, 271

Crispy pork ears with abalone and jelly
fish **160**, **161**

Cured salmon with citrus **268**, 270

❧ D ❧

Date, fig and walnut bread 310

Dressings see Sauces and Dressings;
Vinaigrettes

Duck confit (basic) 304

Duck confit and potato terrine **130–131**,
132–133

Duck rillettes, pâté, cured breast and its
salad **168**, 170–172

Duck salad on betel leaf 18

❊ F ❊

Fennel risotto 23, **26**
Fish **see also** Shellfish
    Anchovy custard with focaccia
        grissini 44, **46**
    Anchovy pillows and paillettes aux
        anchois **15**, 19
    Arctic char with pork and prawn
        dumpling **151**, 152
    Baked jewfish 'En Croûte' with
        zucchini, carrot and basil, with
        mousseline sauce 22, **26**, 27
    Barbecue trout bundles with
        prosciutto and button
        mushrooms 124, **126**–127
    Barramundi with pancetta and
        shimeji mushroom **143**, 153
    Blue eye trevalla with parsnip crust,
        spinach dumpling, and beetroot
        jus **154**, 159
    Caviar brioche 47, **51**
    Caviar on potato rösti **197**, 198
    Cured salmon with citrus **268**, 270
    King fish sushi cake **281**, 286
    King fish with fennel, vongole, caper
        and rocket pesto **147**, 149
    Marinated ocean trout with potato
        blinis **288**, 292
    Murray cod fillet with riso and risotto
        rice **146**, 148
    Ocean trout barquette **282**, 294
    Ocean trout with seaweed and
        spinach **140**, 141
    Pan seared dory with boudin rose
        and borscht **142**, 144–145
    Pan seared rouget with squid ink
        lasagne **96**, 98–99
    Potato crusted groper with zucchini
        noodle **155**, 158
    Salmon carpaccio 37, **46**
    Salmon cooked in coconut roti dough
        154, 156–157
    Salmon rillette 140
    Salt cod tartlet with green vegetable
        ratatouille **289**, 293
    Steamed gold band snapper with rice
        noodles and prawn **137**, 138–139
    Steamed john dory on toast **46**, 50
    Tuna Niçoise on potato fondante
        47, 55
    Tuna sashimi with steamed scallop
        83, **84**–85
    Yellowfin tuna with sea urchin
        dressing **47**, 50
Fish stock 301
Foie gras pithivier with mushrooms
    289, 291
French vinaigrette 302
Fried basil ravioli **263**, 271

❊ G ❊

Garlic snail brioche **282**, 285
Gazpacho sorbet with basil oil **46**, 54
Gin and lime meringue tart **260**, 261
Glass noodle salad in Asian box **120**, 122
Glazed duck with scallops and salsify
    169, 173
Goat's cheese cappelletti with asparagus
    and thyme butter **59**, 60
Grilled scampi tail with frisée salad **47**, 51
Guinea fowl with potato chartreuse **178**,
    180–181

❊ H ❊

Hollandaise sauce 305

❊ J ❊

Jam, chilli 304

❊ K ❊

King fish sushi cake **281**, 286
King fish with fennel, vongole, caper and
    rocket pesto **147**, 149

❊ L ❊

Lamb rissoles with couscous and stone
    fruit salad **121**, 125
Leek tartlet **117**, 119
Lemon tartlet **254**, 261, 311
Lemonade, homemade 129
Lemongrass Thai style pork sticks **113**, 114
Lime Turkish delight 254
Lobster ravioli with tomato and shellfish
    consommé 87, **88**–89
Loin of lamb 'aux trois façons' **190**,
    192–193
Lychee and gooseberry soup with mint
    and basil ice cream **223**, 237

❊ M ❊

Macaroons **252**, 256
Mango and passionfruit 'Ile Flottante'
    with guava sorbet and sauternes
    anglaise **222**, 224–225
Mango bavarois with almond and star
    anise tuile **212**, 213
Marinated goat's cheese with summer
    vegetables **116**, 118
Marinated ocean trout with potato blinis
    288, 292
Marinated saffron chicken brochettes
    113, 115
Mayonnaise **296**, 303
MEAT SEE ALSO POULTRY
    Assiette de lapin – rack of rabbit with
        its loin, shoulder and liver **165**,
        166–167
    Beef carpaccio with oxtail jelly and
        porcini pannacotta **47**, 56–57
    Beef tartare on beetroot with quail
        egg **282**, 284
    Beef tenderloin with wild
        mushrooms **179**, 182–183
    Crispy pork ears with abalone and
        jelly fish **160**, 161
    Lamb rissoles with couscous and
        stone fruit salad **121**, 123
    Lemongrass Thai style pork sticks
        113, 114
    Loin of lamb 'aux trois façons' **190**,
        192–193
    Oxtail gow-gee with seared scallops,
        soy and ginger sauce **90**, 92–93
    Pork flank with blood pudding and
        apple tarte à tatin **169**, 176–177
    Pork fritters with cucumber salad 19
    Rabbit terrine with pickled onion
        salad **35**, 49
    Skirt steak with beef brisket flan and
        roast garlic **208**, 210–211
    Sweetbreads with caramelised
        onions, potato and mache **184**,
        186–187

Veal fillet with marron tail and
hollandaise **169**, 174–175
Veal rack with porcini sauce,
asparagus and wood mushrooms
273, 275
Ménage à trois des chocolats **244**,
250–251
Moreton Bay bug with caramelised pork
and Asian mushrooms **97**, 100–101
Murray cod fillet with riso and risotto
rice **146**, 148
Mushroom duxelle with porcini 309

N

Nam jhim **297**, 306

O

Ocean trout barquette **282**, 294
Ocean trout with seaweed and spinach
140, 141
OILS, FLAVOURED
Basil oil **297**, 303
Shellfish oil 303
Onion vol-au-vent with beaufort cheese
289, 292
Oxtail gow-gee with seared scallops, soy
and ginger sauce **90**, 92–93
Oyster shooter with tomato jelly **281**,
290–291
Oysters with cucumber shots 110, 111

P

Pan seared dory with boudin rose and
borscht **142**, 144–145
Pan seared rouget with squid ink lasagne
96, 98–99
PASTA
Blue cheese tortellini with cauliflower
and broccoli jus **43**, 47
Fried basil ravioli **263**, 271
Goat's cheese cappelletti with
asparagus and thyme butter **59**, 60
Lobster ravioli with tomato and
shellfish consommé **87**, 88–89

Pan seared rouget with squid ink
lasagne **96**, 98–99
Squid ink pasta stack with avocado,
crab and goat's curd **46**, 48
Sweet onion and spinach ravioli with
goat's curd cheese 45, **46**
PASTRY
Puff pastry 311
Sweet pastry 311
Pear and rocket salad with radicchio and
bleu de bresse **75**, 77
Pesto **297**, 303
Pistachio and nuts nougat **254**, 259
Poached figs in Beaume de Venise with
glass biscuits **234**, 236
Poached tail of West Australian marron
with parsnip brandade **199**, 200–201
Pomme purée 307
Pommes fondantes 307
Ponzu dressing 305–306
Porcini sauce 305
Veal rack with porcini sauce,
asparagus and wood mushrooms
273, 275
Pork flank with blood pudding and apple
tarte à tatin **169**, 176–177
Pork fritters with cucumber salad 19
Potato crusted groper with zucchini
noodle **155**, 158
POTATOES
Pomme purée 307
Pommes fondantes 307
Potato rösti 307
POULTRY *SEE ALSO* MEAT
Chicken liver parfait with rosehip tea
jelly **289**, 290
Duck confit and potato terrine 130–
131, 132–133
Duck rillettes, pâté, cured breast and
its salad **168**, 170–172
Duck salad on betel leaf 18
Foie gras pithivier with mushrooms
289, 291
Glazed duck with scallops and salsify
169, 173
Guinea fowl with potato chartreuse
178, 180–181
Marinated saffron chicken brochettes
113, 115

Poussin 'En Cocotte' 24, **25**, 26
Roast chinese duck with plum sauce
in a herb crêpe **286**, 288
Roast duck with beetroot and sautéed
spinach 206, **207**
Roast pheasant with chestnut purée
185, 188–189
Roast truffled guinea fowl with
artichokes and broad beans
202–203, 204–205
Tandoori quail on naan bread **281**, 287
Poussin 'En Cocotte' 24, **25**, 26
Prawn salad with green mango and
pawpaw 272
Prawn toast with sesame seeds **42**, 47
Provençale vegetable plate with
chabichou **62**, 64
Puff pastry 311

Q

Quince cake with maple syrup ice cream
245, 246–247

R

Rabbit terrine with pickled onion salad
35, 49
Raspberry chiboust tart **218**, 220–221
Raspberry sponge **254**, 258
Raspberry vacherin 279
Red wine sauce 306
Risotto, fennel 23, **26**
Roast chinese duck with plum sauce in a
herb crêpe **286**, 288
Roast duck with beetroot and sautéed
spinach 206, **207**
Roast pheasant with chestnut purée **185**,
188–189
Roast truffled guinea fowl with
artichokes and broad beans **202–203**,
204–205
Roasted vanilla peach with parfait,
nougatine and apricot compote **238**,
240–241
Rocket and spinach purée 309
Rosewater Turkish delight **253**, 257

❧ S ❧

Salmon carpaccio 37, **46**
Salmon cooked in coconut roti dough 154, 156–157
Salmon matelote sauce 306–307
Salmon rillette 140
Salt cod tartlet with green vegetable ratatouille **289**, 293
SAUCES AND DRESSINGS *SEE ALSO* **VINAIGRETTES**
  Carrot emulsion **296**, 306
  Chlorophyll 309
  Hollandaise sauce 305
  Nam jhim **296**, 306
  Ponzu dressing 305–306
  Porcini sauce 305
  Red wine sauce **296**, 306
  Salmon matelote sauce 306–307
  Tomato sauce, chunky **296**, 308
  Vanilla sauce anglaise 310
Sautéed beans with beetroot **67**, 72–73
Scallop terrine with saffron cream sauce **20**, 21
Scallop timbale with zucchini flowers **273**, 274
Scallops with pickled daikon 36, **46**
SHELLFISH *SEE ALSO* **FISH**
  Barbecue prawns with lime butter **128**, 129
  Casserole of seafood with turmeric and chilli **91**, 94–95
  Crab and picked mushroom salad with Asian noodles 102, **103**
  Crab sandwich **269**, 271
  Crispy pork ears with abalone and jelly fish 160, **161**
  Glazed duck with scallops and salsify **169**, 173
  Grilled scampi tail salad with frisée salad **47**, 51
  Lobster ravioli with tomato and shellfish consommé **87**, 88–89
  Moreton Bay bug with caramelised pork and Asian mushrooms **97**, 100–101
  Oxtail gow-gee with seared scallops, soy and ginger sauce **90**, 92–93
  Oyster shooter with tomato jelly **281**, 290–291

Oysters with cucumber shots 110, **111**
Poached tail of West Australian marron with parsnip brandade **199**, 200–201
Prawn salad with green mango and pawpaw 272
Prawn toast with sesame seeds 42, **47**
Scallop terrine with saffron cream sauce **20**, 21
Scallop timbale with zucchini flowers **273**, 274
Scallops with pickled daikon 36, **46**
Squid ink pasta stack with avocado, crab and goat's curd **46**, 48
Tuna sashimi with steamed scallop **83**, 84–85
Veal fillet with marron tail and hollandaise **169**, 174–175
Yabby tail with squid ink cannelloni **39**, **47**
Shellfish oil 303
Silky spring pea soup **66**, 68
Silky tofu with shiitake and enokitake mushrooms 36, **47**
Skirt steak with beef brisket flan and roast garlic **208**, 210–211
SOUP
  Chestnut soup with lentils, garlic and eschalots **78**, 79
  Corn soup 270
  Lychee and gooseberry soup with mint and basil ice cream **223**, 237
  Silky spring pea soup **66**, 68
Squid ink pasta stack with avocado, crab and goat's curd **46**, 48
Star anise blancmange with poached cherries **215**, 216
Steamed gold band snapper with rice noodles and prawn **137**, 138–139
Steamed john dory on toast **46**, 50
STOCKS AND JUS
  Asian master stock 299
  Borscht stock **298**, 300
  Chicken stock 300
  Fish stock 301
  Veal stock 301
  Vegetable stock 300
Sugar syrup 309

Summer berries with citrus sablé, fromage blanc ice cream **217**, 219
Sweet onion and spinach ravioli with goat's curd cheese 45, **46**
Sweet pastry 311
Sweetbreads with caramelised onions, potato and mache **184**, 186–187

❧ T ❧

Tandoori quail on naan bread **281**, 287
Tapenade, black olive **297**, 304
TARTS
  Apple tarte à tatin **169**, 176–177
  Blueberry vanilla tart 134, **135**
  Caramelised pineapple and ginger tart 226–227
  Caramelised tomato, eschalot and fetta tart **69**, 74
  Gin and lime meringue tart 260, **261**
  Leek tartlet 117, **119**
  Lemon tartlet **254**, 261
  Raspberry chiboust tart **218**, 220–221
  Salt cod tartlet with green vegetable ratatouille **289**, 293
Tempura batter 308
TERRINES
  Coconut and pineapple terrine 230
  Duck confit and potato terrine 130–131, 132–133
  Rabbit terrine with pickled onion salad **35**, 49
  Scallop terrine with saffron cream sauce **20**, 21
  Tomato and basil terrine with yellow capsicum salad and basil oil **67**, 70–71
Tomato and basil terrine with yellow capsicum salad and basil oil **67**, 70–71
Tomato aspic with radish salad **80**, 81
Tomato sauce, chunky **297**, 308
TOMATOES
  Oven roast tomato 308
  Peeled tomato 308
Truffle and eschalot flan with mâche **63**, 65
Tuna Niçoise on potato fondante **47**, 55
Tuna sashimi with steamed scallop **83**, 84–85

Vanilla custard 310

Vanilla sauce anglaise 310

Veal fillet with marron tail and
    hollandaise **169**, 174–175

Veal jus 301

Veal rack with porcini sauce, asparagus
    and wood mushrooms **273**, 275

Veal stock 301

VEGETABLE

    Blue cheese tortellini with cauliflower
        and broccoli jus **43**, **47**

    Bocconcini with tomato quenelle
        37, **47**

    Brioche with mushroom duxelle
        38, 46

    Caramelised tomato, eschalot and
        fetta tart 69, **74**

    Chestnut soup with lentils, garlic and
        eschalots **78**, 79

    Confit vegetable parmentier **75**, 76

    Corn soup 270

    Fried basil ravioli **263**, 271

Goat's cheese cappelletti with
    asparagus and thyme butter **59**, 60

Pear and rocket salad with radicchio
    and bleu de bresse **75**, 77

Pomme purée 307

Pommes fondantes 307

Potato rösti 307

Provençale vegetable plate with
    chabichou **62**, 64

Rocket and spinach purée 309

Sautéed beans with beetroot **67**,
    72–73

Silky spring pea soup **66**, 68

Silky tofu with shiitake and enokitake
    mushrooms **36**, **47**

Sweet onion and spinach ravioli with
    goat's curd cheese **45**, **46**

Tomato and basil terrine with yellow
    capsicum salad and pesto oil **67**,
    70–71

Tomato aspic with radish salad 80, 81

Truffle and eschalot flan with mâche
    63, 65

Vegetable confit 304

Vegetable stock 300

VINAIGRETTES SEE ALSO SAUCES AND
    DRESSINGS

    Balsamic vinaigrette **297**, 302

    Basic vinaigrette 302

    Champagne vinaigrette **297**, 302

    French vinaigrette 302

Wedding cake **276**, 277–278

White chocolate fudge 261

Yabby tail with squid ink cannelloni
    39, **47**

Yellowfin tuna with sea urchin
    dressing **46**, **47**

❧ Wine Notes ❧

1770 Sauternes 213
1834 Roriz 209
1847 Duke of Wellington's Sherry 197
1887 Marcobrunner 199
1900 Château Haut-Bailly 202
1900 Muscatel 209
1911 Perrier Jouet 197
1917 Château d'Yquem 213
1918 Château Lafite 202
1918 Château Latour 202
1919 Château Graud-Larose en Magnum 202
1919 Château Rayne-Vigneau 213
1921 Niersteiner 199
1924 Château Pavie 202
1928 Château Cos d'Estournel 208
1928 Château Haut Brion 208
1928 Château Phélan-Ségur 208
1929 Bollinger 197
1929 Château Carbonnieux 207
1929 Château La Lagune 207
1929 Château Margaux 207
1929 Château Rouget 207
1929 Forster Kirchenstück 199
1929 Pommery and Greno Natur 197
1930 K.W.V. Muscatel 209
Albino Armani Val Adige Pinot Grigio 151
All Saints Rutherglen Muscat 248
Antinori Campogrande Orvieto Classico 62
Ata Rangi Pinot Noir 142
Balnaves Cabernet Sauvignon 190
Bannockburn Saignée 99
Beaurenard Côtes du Rhône Villages 30
Bernard Métrat Fleurie 'La Roilette' Vieilles
    Vignes 75
Bethany Grenache 109
Billecart-Salmon Rosé NV Champagne 85, 268
Bindi Pinot Noir 172
Boroli Madonna di Como Dolcetto d'Alba 63
Boroli Moscato d'Asti 109
Brokenwood Graveyard Shiraz 179
Brokenwood Semillon 71
By Farr Chardonnay 175
By Farr Pinot Noir 154
Campagnola le Bine Soave Classico 71
Campbells Classic Rutherglen Tokay 239
Cascabel Tempranillo, Graciano 73
Cave de Turckheim Réserve Pinot Gris 95
Château Dereszla '5 Puttonyas' Tokaji 238
Château Doisy-Daëne 248
Château du Pavilion 218
Château Jolys Jurançon 235
Château Margaux 190
Château Rieussec 247
Château Thieuley Bordeaux Blanc 87
Christa Rolf Shiraz Grenache 178
Clonakilla Shiraz Viognier 151
Clos des Paulilles Banyuls Rimage 249
Clos des Paulilles Collioure Rosé 101

Cullen Semillon Sauvignon Blanc 143
De Iuliis Verdelho 103
Delatite Dead Man's Hill Gewürztraminer 139
Delgado Zuleta 'La Goya' 283
Diamond Valley Blue Label Pinot Noir 109
Dom Pérignon 268
Domain de Durban Muscat 30
Domain Moreau-Naudet Chablis 283
Domaine Courbis St Joseph 95
Domaine de Durban Muscat Beaumes-de-
    Venise 234
Domaine Fenouillet Côtes du Ventoux 154
Domaine Pichot Vouvray Moelleux 235
Domaines Ott Rosé 187
Fermoy Estate Sauvignon 68
Frankland Estate Isolation Ridge Riesling 85
Freycinet Riesling 62
Frogmore Creek Riesling 75
Gembrook Hill Sauvignon Blanc 62
Georg Breuer Rüdesheim Estate 283
Giaconda Shiraz 169
Grande Maison Cuvée du Château
    Monbazillac 239
Grosset Polish Hill Riesling 139
Hardy's Arras 278
Hautes Cances CairanneTradition 179
Henri Bourgeois les Baronnes Sancerre 71
Hidalgo la Gitana Manzanilla 85
Hiedler Grüner Veltliner Maximum 143
Hirsch Zöbing Riesling 139
Howard Park Scotsdale Shiraz 157
Huet le Mont Vouvrey Demi Sec 157
Huia Gewürztraminer 103
Inniskillin Cabernet Franc Ice Wine 215
J.L. Chave Hermitage 169
Jacquesson Cuvée NV 109
Josmeyer 'Les Folastries' Gewürztraminer 101
Kaesler Old Wine Semillon 109
Keith Tulloch Semillon 283
Kellerei Kaltern Söll Pinot Grigio 30, 75
Kooyong Estate Clonale 143
Kracher Beerenauslese 247
Krug 278
La Querce Sorrettole Chianti Classico 74
Leo Buring Leonary Riesling 187
Lillypilly Botrytis Sauvignon Blanc 238
Lost Valley Cortese 73
Louis Roederer Brut Premier NV 268
Lucien Albrecht Pinot Gris 61
Maculan Dindarello Veneto 219
Marenco Brachetto d'Acqui Pineto 215
Margan Botrytis Semillon 225
Mas Carlot Rosé 99
Mas de Bressades Cuvée Tradition 93
McWilliams Mount Pleasant Semillon 87
Meera Park Alexander Munroe Semillon 146
Monte Antico Sangiovese 190

Mount Horrocks Semillon 147
Mount Langi Ghiran Shiraz 75
Mt Horrocks Cordon Cut Riesling 218
Müller-Catoir Haardter Burger Garten Riesling
    Kabinett Trocken 68
Nebbiolo Pizzini 30
Nepenthe Charleston Pinot Noir 142
Ninth Island Sparkling NV 30
Orlando Steingarten Riesling 175
Pala Crabilis Vermentino 99
Paringa Estate Pinot Noir 178
Pasanau Germans Ceps Nous Grenache,
    Merlot, Mazuelo 178
Pegasus Bay Sauvignon Blanc, Semillon 155
Pellegrino Moscato di Pantelleria 234
Peter Lehmann Semillon 146
Petaluma Viognier 87
Phillip Shaw No 11 Chardonnay 30
Pieropan la Rocca Soave 146
Pizzini Nebbiolo 30
Pol Roger NV Champagne 103, 283
Primo Estate Joseph d'Elena Pinot Grigio 61
Roaring Forties Pinot Noir 172
Sarocco Moscato d'Asti 225
Sauveroy Coteaux du Layon Cuvée Nectar 235
Scorpo Pinot Gris 95
Scorpo Rosé 151
Serge Daganeau Pouilly Fumé 147
Shaw & Smith M3 Chardonnay 61
Spring Vale Pinot Meunier 101
Stoneleigh Pinot Noir 73
Symphonia Pinot Grigio 74
T'Gallant Pinot Gris 187
Tahbilk Marsanne 155
Tamar Ridge Pinot Noir 63
Telmo Rodriguez Basa Verdejo 68
Telmo Rodriguez MR Moscatel 239
Teruzzi e Puthod Vernaccia 147
Torbreck Woodcutters Shiraz 179
Torres Viña Esmeralda Muscat
    Gewürztraminer 75
Trimbach Cuvée Frédéric Emile Riesling 74
Tyrell's Vat 1 Semillon 155
Veuve Cliquot Ponsardin Demi-Sec 219
Vieux Télégraphe Châteauneuf-du-Pape 172
Villa Maria Reserve Noble Riesling 251
Wellington Iced Riesling 235
Wellington Pinot Grigio 109
Wellington Pinot Noir 154
Westend Estate 3 Bridges 'Golden Mist'
    Botrytis Semillon 239
Willow Creek Saignée Rosé 283
Yalumba Eden Valley Viognier 157
Yarrabank Cuvée 278
Yering Station Rosé 142
Yves Cuilleron Condrieu 175

✦ Acknowledgements ✦

This is the place where I can recognise the people who have helped me put this book together. I will start with my kitchen team in the restaurant. Firstly, Simon, my Chef de Cuisine, who helped me develop many of the recipes and was an integral part of the process of cooking the food. Simon's team support his work every day – people like Sam, Anthony, Michael, Nick, Casper, Stefan, Henry, Alan, Evan and so many others who have worked with us over the years and are so crucial to our success.

Many thanks go to Birk, my first pastry chef, as we developed many of the classic desserts of Bathers' together. Thanks also to others who have made an impact over the years – super talented Lucy and productive Nichan. Much gratitude also goes to the person who prepared all the desserts for me and helped me refine those recipes, my present pastry chef – who left his executive role at The Savoy Hotel in London to join Bathers' – Nigel.

In other support roles, I have to thank Sally Harper, my sommelier, for such disciplined work over the years. Sally develops the wine lists of Bathers' and suggested the various wines to accompany recipes in this book. Sal is an essential constant of Bathers' and I value her role and her work. I cannot forget Jeremy, my restaurant manager, and his team as well as Garth and every other key manager. Thanks go to Jenn and Xavier for making sense of my old recipes and, in many instances, for suggesting additions to our repertoire. Their roles were not easy but were crucial in speeding up what could have been an exhausting project.

Keeping me on line and on target, I can always count on Kristy my able assistant – her help, advice and support are an essential part of Bathers' success – many thanks Kristy. The Bathers' team is a surprisingly large team and all contribute to our success – all my appreciation goes to them for their hard work and dedication.

The idea of a book cannot be realised without the skills of specialised team and what a team it was! William, your eyes and touch on the camera left me full of admiration – you are a gem to work with. Gayna, when talent was distributed you obviously got a double serving – this book is as much yours as mine. Your design, gentle guidance, concept and art direction produced a unique book full of polish, generosity and superb pages. Thanks also to Michaela Le Compte for the beautiful food styling. My full appreciation goes to Alison Moodie, my recipe editor, she has made poetry out of my often brutal explanation. Putting this team together and taking care of every large and small detail, was Helen. My deep appreciation and respect goes to Helen, she is a person of many talents who fosters the best in people. That Helen was also the editor of my first book has been a huge bonus as, again with this new book, her vision has proven so right.

Thank you to Yvette, my wife, for again putting up with my ritual of late nights writing when have I arrived home after work – I've been home but not really been there at the same time. Yvette's support and guidance is always treasured.

Lastly, I would like to thank someone who helped me set up Bathers' and has kept faith in me and my team. Robin is an unsung supporter and a key person in the life of Bathers' Pavilion. Without him, I would not own my dream restaurant. I hope I bring him enough joy for his trouble.

The publishers and author would like to thank the following Sydney suppliers
for props used in the photographs: Accoutrement, All Handmade, Camargue,
Foodservice Equipment International, Ici et la, Lucienne Linen, Lotus Britanica, Major and Tom,
Papaya, Seaforth Flowers and The Bay Tree.

Published by ABC Books for the
AUSTRALIAN BROADCASTING CORPORATION
GPO Box 9994 Sydney NSW 2001

ISBN 978 0 7333 1818 4

Cover and text designed by Greendot Design
Art direction by Gayna Murphy
Layout and typesetting by Kate O'Hara and Katy Wright
Food styling by Michaela Le Compte
Author photography by Liana Mawston
Typeset in Vendetta by Emigre, Aged by T26 Digital Type Foundry and Avenir by Linotype Library
Colour reproduction by Graphic Print Group, Adelaide
Printed and bound in Singapore by Tien Wah Press

5 4 3 2 1